I0524118

Armed Forces of the Republic of Vietnam

A Heroic Army Unjustly Abandoned and Left for Dead

Vĩnh-The Lam

Armed Forces of the Republic of Vietnam

A Heroic Army Unjustly Abandoned and Left for Dead

NHÂN ẢNH
2022

Armed Forces of the Republic of Vietnam
A Heroic Army Unjustly Abandoned and Left for Dead
Vinh-The Lam

Page Lay Out: **Nguyễn Thành**
Cover Design: **Uyên Nguyên Trần Triết**
Nhân Ảnh published 2022
ISBN: 9781088015803

Contents

Acknowledgments

This book is the compilation of a number of translated-into-English articles written by the author about the Republic of Vietnam and its Armed Forces, which have been posted on Vietnamese-language websites in the United States and Canada for the past several years. It was Dr. Tuong Vu, Head, Political Science Department, University of Oregon, who elicited the original idea for the book.

In spite of his very busy schedule of teaching, doing research, and managing his Department, Dr. Vu still spared his time to write the Foreword for the Vietnamese-language version of this book, and for this English version as well. My special and utmost thanks are reserved for Dr. Vu's nice consideration and valuable contributions.

I also would like to record here my heartfelt thanks to Mr. Nguyễn Khắc Phụng, who has spent time to proofread, correcting spelling mistakes and typos as well as sharing his excellent ideas on the contents of the book.

Last but not least, I feel very much indebted to the technical contributions by Nhân Ảnh Publishing House's staff:

- Mr. Lê Hân for his general management of the production of the book
- Mr. Nguyễn Thành for his page layout
- Mr. Uyên Nguyên Trần Triết for his cover design

List of Abbreviations

AFVN	Air Force of the Republic of Vietnam
ARVN	Army of the Republic of Vietnam
CIA	Central Intelligence Agency
CINCPAC	Commander-In-Chief, Pacific
CORDS	Civil Operations and Revolutionary Development Support
COSVN	Central Office for South Vietnam
DMZ	**D**e**M**ilitarized **Z**one
GAO	Groupe aérien d'observation et d'accompagnement au combat
JCS	Joint Chiefs of Staff (U.S.)
MACV	Military Assistance Command – Vietnam
NLF	National Liberation Front
NVA	North Vietnamese Army
PRG	Provisional Revolutionary Government of South Vietnam
RVN	Republic of Vietnam
TRAC	Third Regional Assistance Command
USSAG / 7AF	United States Support Activities Group / Seventh Air Force
VC	Viet Cong
VCI	Viet Cong Infrastructure

List of Illustrations

Chapter Two:

Chapter Three:

Chapter Four:

Chapters Five, Six, and Seven:

No illustrations

Chapter Eight:

Chapter Nine:

No Illustrations

Foreword

We are delighted to introduce to you this well-researched book by author Vinh-The Lam about the Armed Forces of the Republic of Vietnam (ARVN). As former Head, Library Science Department, Vạn Hạnh University in Saigon, South Vietnam, before 1975, and Head, Technical Services Division, University of Saskatchewan Library in Canada at his retirement, author Vinh-The Lam has conducted research and published two books on the Republic of Vietnam. Both the Vietnamese version, titled ***"Việt Nam Cộng Hòa, 1963-1967: Những Năm Xáo Trộn"*** and the English version, titled ***"Republic of Vietnam, 1963-1967: Years of Political Chaos"*** were published by Hoài Việt Publishing House in Hamilton, Ontario, Canada in 2008. The second edition of the English version, under the new title "***History of South Vietnam: the Quest for Legitimacy and Stability, 1963-1967"***, was published by the British publisher Routledge in 2021. His book by Routledge is currently the only study on this very special period in the history of the Republic of Vietnam (RVN).

The book you have in hand is a compilation of the author's several earlier-published articles on different aspects of the ARVN and the Vietnam War. In this book, based on numerous American and Vietnamese documents, Vinh-The Lam tries to find the answer to some of the most puzzling questions about the history of the Vietnam War. Why was the RVN defeated if the ARVN were not coward and incompetent as portrayed by the U.S. media and argued by authors in the "orthodox" camp in the debate on the Vietnam War? And why the ARVN, who had won important battles like An Lộc, Quảng Trị, and Xuân Lộc, completely disintegrated in less than two months after the loss of Ban Mê Thuột? As the sub-title of the book encapsulates, the answer is: the ARVN was a heroic army but was abandoned by the U.S., its ally, leading to its unexpected death.

For the "ARVN as a heroic army" theme, the book provides several interesting details on the Air Divisions of the South Vietnamese Air Force, on four distinguished generals, and on the two famous battles the ARVN was engaged in. For the second theme of "the ARVN abandoned," the book shows that the changes in U.S. policy have led to the signing of the 1973 Paris Accords, which were deeply disadvantageous for the Saigon government, and to the U.S. Congress' decision to drastically reduce military aid for the RVN. The author also presents many persuasive arguments to rebut "orthodox" authors' judgment that the Vietnam War was "an unwinnable war." Finally, the author analyzes President Nguyễn Văn Thiệu's wrong decision to abandoning the highlands and the ill-prepared troop withdrawal from II Corps by General Phạm Văn Phú. He reaches the conclusion that these two actions were the main reasons for the rapid collapse of the ARVN in less than two months (March-April 1975).

The conclusion of the book elicits larger questions on the role of the armed forces in the life of the RVN as a nation. In a nation having just escaped from colonialism and threatened by a new war, the ARVN became an important organization with a mandate of achieving stability and fighting the enemy. The larger the war became, the more militarized the Vietnamese society grew. Volunteered or drafted, millions of young men went to the army. The budget appropriated for the army was the largest part of the government budget. Even before they made the coup overthrowing the civilian government of President Ngô Đình Diệm, the military had already been involved in local administration at different levels. After the coup, the generals took turn to lead the central government.

The politicization of the military had begun under the First Republic when Mr. Ngô Đình Nhu tried to develop his Cần Lao Party in the army and the government. Although from the appearance this policy was not different from the Communist method of organizing and controlling their army, the Cần Lao Party did not have a robust structure and instead only relied on factors such as personal relationships and personal loyalties to the leader, and, thus, hindered the development of a professional army.

The struggle for political power among the RVN generals through quite a few military coups happened not only in South Vietnam but also in neighboring countries, such as Indonesia, Burma, Thailand, Pakistan and South Korea during that time. Unlike the armies of those countries, the military governments in the RVN were weaker and also less dictatorial, permitting the growth of a civil society and a freer press. Under the Second Republic, the government of General Nguyễn Văn Thiệu also implemented many promising programs to develop and stabilize the economy similar to those in South Korea and Thailand at the time.

On the one hand, the political involvement of the military strengthened the power of the army in society. On the other hand, it also brought significant negative publicity on the army's involvement in corruption, and on cases in which military personnel abused power and displayed dictatorial tendencies, despite the fact that the bad generals were not the majority. More important, the involvement of military officers in politics was detrimental to the professional organization of the army as political relationships and calculations unduly affected professional standards, weakened discipline, and generated uneven leadership capability. Unlike the military regimes in neighboring countries, the Second Republic of the RVN was in a war and, therefore, this weakness was a fatal one.

Another special characteristic of the ARVN was its enormous size (almost one million soldiers at its peak for a population of 14 million), its high specialization (including all services, and also special units such as Paratroopers and Marines) and its reliance on sophisticated arms (fighter jets, helicopters, tanks).

This special characteristic was born out of history and necessity but led to its heavy reliance on American military aid, especially for weapons, fuels, and the strategic air force. For example, for the Air Divisions of the VNAF, not only the aircrafts but also parts and fuels were totally dependent on American supplies. In terms of the strategic air force, the carpet bombings by B-52 flying fortresses played a significant role in the ARVN's victories in An Lộc and Quảng Trị.

Although generally speaking, people, not weapons, determined the outcomes of battles, in modern warfare both factors have the same level of importance. Communist propaganda claimed revolutionary heroism as the deciding factor in their victory, but, in reality, we have witnessed the tragic failure of that revolutionary heroism in the 1968 Tet Offensive (within the first month, Communist forces suffered a casualty of 40,000 dead or wounded soldiers, and were pushed out of most of the cities and towns of South Vietnam). The 1975 victory of the North Vietnamese army was brought about by modern weapons, including tanks, big guns, and the world's most sophisticated air defense system (SAM) supplied by the Soviet Union.

Modern weapons helped the ARVN win the great battles of An Lộc and Quảng Trị. But the military expenses of the RVN exceeded the country's economic and technical capabilities. Communist North Vietnam also relied heavily on its allies for weapons, fuels, and even for dried foods and clothing for its soldiers. The difference was the Soviet Union's and China's assistance to North Vietnam were steady and discreet, in sharp contrast with the American assistance to South Vietnam, which was highly volatile and almost always in the open. The difference between the two methods of intervention reflected the characteristics of the political regimes of the U.S. and the Communist countries and their strategic intentions. The end results of this difference became obvious after the signing of the Paris Accords, with clear advantages for North Vietnam.

Although the ARVN no longer exists, we need to know more about it in order to more clearly understand the history of Vietnam. Scholars of the Vietnam War are indebted to the valuable contributions by Vinh-The Lam. The image of the ARVN he provides in this book is completely different from what we commonly read in books on this subject by American authors (except for a few such as George Veith and Andrew Wiest). We hope that this book will get the attention of readers and inspire new research in the future on this important subject.

Dr. Tuong Vu
US-Vietnam Research Center
Political Science Department
University of Oregon

Author's Biographical Sketch

Vinh-The Lam, M.L.S.
Librarian Emeritus
University of Saskatchewan, CANADA
Email: Hoaivietnhan1981@gmail.com

Graduating from the Department of History and Geography, Faculty of Pedagogy, University of Saigon in 1963, Vinh-The Lam taught high schools for several years before receiving a scholarship to go to the U.S. for librarianship training. In 1973, after his successful completion of the Master of Library Science program at Syracuse University, he came back to Vietnam and served as Head of the Library Science Department, Van Hanh University, until the fall of Saigon. In September 1981, with his family, he emigrated to Canada. From 1982 on, he worked in the libraries and/or information centres and archives of several Canadian federal / provincial government agencies. In September 1997, he joined the University of Saskatchewan, serving first as Head of the Cataloguing Department (1997–2000) and then as Head of the Technical Services Division (2000–2003). He has authored a number of library science textbooks and a few dozens of research articles published in Vietnamese and English library science journals. He took retirement from the University of Saskatchewan in July 2006 with the rank of Librarian Emeritus.

Beside his activities in the library science field, Vinh-The Lam has also done a lot of research on the Vietnam War, especially for the period of the greatest political crisis of the Republic of Vietnam (1963–1967), which led to the U.S. Government's decision to send combat troops to Vietnam in 1965. His research work in this area has culminated in the publication of his scholarly work ***Republic of Vietnam, 1963-1967: Years***

of Political Chaos, published by Hoai Viet in 2010. The second, revised and enlarged edition of this book was published by Routledge (U.K.) in 2020 under title ***The History of South Vietnam: the Quest for Legitimacy and Stability, 1963-1967***.

He is the translator of ***The Price of Freedom: Exodus and Diaspora of Vietnamese People***, 2nd edition, published by Nguoi Viet Books in 2017, from the Vietnamese-language original book titled *Giá Tự Do* (translation: *Price of Freedom*) by Lâm Vĩnh Bình. He is also the translator and editor of ***Vietnam, Territoriality, and the South China Sea: Paracel and Spratly Islands***, published by Routledge (U.K.) in 2019, from the original Vietnamese book, *Những Bằng Chứng về Chủ Quyền của Việt Nam Đối Với Hai Quần Đảo Hoàng Sa Trường Sa* (translation: *Evidence of Vietnam's Sovereignty over the Paracel and Spratly Archipelagos*) by Hãn Nguyên Nguyễn Nhã.

The most recent work by Vinh-The Lam was: ***Full Circle: Memoir of a Vietnamese-Canadian Librarian***, published by Austin Macauley (U.K.) in 2022

A number of his selected works are now accessible from his bi-lingual (Vietnamese and English) personal Webpage called ***Tuyển Tập Vĩnh Nhơn Lâm Vĩnh Thế*** (translation: *Selected Works by Vĩnh Nhơn Lâm Vĩnh Thế*), at this URL: https://tuyentap-vinh-nhon-lam-vinh-the.blogspot.com/2016/06/trang-chu.html

Introduction

Around noon of April 30, 1975, after the surrender ordered by General Dương Văn Minh, the last President of the Republic of Vietnam (RVN) officially installed just a few days before by a vote of the National Assembly at its special emergency bi-cameral session in the evening of April 27, 1975, the Armed Forces of the Republic of Vietnam (ARVN – Army of the Republic of Vietnam), a heroic army with innumerable celebrated victories was painfully abandoned to death.

The finest battle-tested units of the ARVN have heroically fought back the invasion, defeating all general offensives by the North Vietnamese Army (NVA) for the past 20 years. And yet, it was also these same finest battle-tested units that were unable to maintain their frontlines and had to dramatically retreat from II Corps and then from I Corps, and, finally, within a short period of time, only 50 days (from March 10 to April 30, 1975) had to surrender in III and IV corps. Why? What happened? Several factors, political and military, subjective and objective, were combined to cause the rapid and painful defeat of the ARVN. Very clearly, that heroic army was unjustly abandoned and left for dead.

The war that was waged in the territory of the RVN was, under any examination angle, a defensive war against the invasion carried out by the armed forces coming from another country. In its fighting against that invasion, the RVN has been assisted by a number of allies, among which the most important was the United States (U.S.), which provided the RVN with necessary means to fight. Unfortunately, the internal political instability of the U.S., created by the popular anti-war tendency and actions caused by biased media networks, as well as by blinded partisan politics, has led to the decrease and ultimately to the total cut-off of all military aids to the RVN. The ARVN no longer had the means to fight, had to retreat from half of the RVN's territory, leading to the collapse of the fighting spirit and the disintegration of its finest battle-tested units. Its defeat and unconditional surrender were the inevitable results of the painful truth that the RVN did not have a totally reliable ally, who completely lacked the necessary patience to go to the end of this very difficult war. The RVN only had the just cause, which was totally meaningless before the gun barrels of the fanatic enemy, who had a high determination to win the war, and, at the same time, was assisted by their patient and ready-to-go-to-the-final-victory Communist allies.

This book is an effort to put together a number of significant articles written by the author about the ARVN and the Vietnam War, which have been published and/or posted in journals and/or websites in the United States and Canada for the past 20 years.

The book includes two parts:

Part One: A Heroic Army, with 5 Chapters:

• Chapter One: The development and coming of age of the ARVN, illustrated by the growth of the Air Force of the Republic of Vietnam (AFVN), the air force ranked no. 4 in the world.

• Chapter Two: The competent and virtuous commanding officers highly respected by the South Vietnamese people, illustrated by the four "clean" Generals: "1st ranked Thắng, 2nd ranked Chinh, 3rd ranked Thanh, 4th ranked Trưởng."

• Chapters Three and Four: The competence, heroism, and the spirit of accepting sacrifice for the country of the ARVN, illustrated by its defeating the Communist Summer 1972 general offensive: The Heroic Defense of An Lộc, and The Recapture of Quảng Trị.

• Chapter Five: American historians and authors of the Vietnam War belonging to the "revisionist" school, through their most recent serious research studies, have definitely vindicated and honoured the ARVN as a heroic army.

Part Two: A Heroic Army Unjustly Abandoned and Left for Dead, with 4 Chapters:

• Chapter Six: American historians and authors of the Vietnam War belonging to the "orthodox" school, have all believed that ***"The Vietnam War Was An Unwinnable War."*** This Chapter will analyze and determine if that assumption is right or wrong.

• Chapter Seven: The Paris Peace Accords, signed on January 27, 1973, was the starting point of the collapse of the RVN. This Chapter presents in details President Nguyễn Văn Thiệu's policy, role, attitude, and handling of his relations with the two U.S. Presidents Lyndon B. Johnson and Richard M. Nixon, as well as with U.S. National Security Advisor Henry Kissinger throughout the whole period of the Paris peace talks.

• Chapter Eight: The retreat from II Corps started the process of and led to the collapse of the ARVN was analyzed in details in this Chapter.

• Chapter Nine: The changes of U.S. policy on the Vietnam War leading to the decision to abandon the RVN were presented in details, showing clearly who was to blame.

PART ONE
A HEROIC ARMY

CHAPTER ONE

The Air Divisions of the ARVN

The Air Force of the Republic of Vietnam (AFVN) was the service of the ARVN that developed the most rapidly and the most spectacularly throughout the Vietnam War. From a small unit of the Army of the State of Vietnam (ASVN) totally dependent on the Air Force of the French Expeditionary Forces (1951-1955), the AFVN had developed really fast to be ranked as the No. 4 air force in the world in terms of the number of aircraft (after the U.S., the Soviet Union, and the People's Republic of China). Its history can bc divided into 5 periods, as follows: [1]

- Creation period: 1951-1955
- Development period: 1956-1964
- Modernization period: 1965-1968
- Expansion period: 1969-1972
- Post-Paris Peace Accords period: 1973-1975

At the end of 1974, the AFVN already had a human force of 61,147 people, and 65 squadrons with a total number of 2,071 aircraft, and was organized in 6 air divisions located all over the 4 military tactical regions of the RVN, as follows:

• Air Division 1: headquartered in Đà Nẵng, commanded by Brigadier-General Nguyễn Đức Khánh, responsible for providing support to operations carried out by I Corps, and including 3 Tactical Air Wings 41, 51, and 61.

• Air Division 2: headquartered in Nha Trang, commanded by Brigadier-General Nguyễn Văn Lượng, responsible for providing support to operations carried out by II Corps, and including 2 Tactical Air Wings 62 and 92.

• Air Division 3: headquartered in Biên Hòa, commanded by Brigadier-General Huỳnh Bá Tính, responsible for providing support to operations carried out by III Corps, and including 3 Tactical Air Wings 23, 43, and 63.

• Air Division 4: headquartered in Cần Thơ, commanded by Brigadier-General Nguyễn Hữu Tần, and including 3 Tactical Air Wings 64, 74, and 84.

• Air Division 5: an air transport division, directly under jurisdiction of the Air Command at Tân Sơn Nhứt Airbase, commanded by Brigadier-General Phan Phụng Tiên, and including 2 Tactical Air Wings 33 and 53.

• Air Division 6: originally headquartered in Pleiku, relocated to Phan Rang after April 16, 1975, commanded by Brigadier-General Phạm Ngọc Sang, responsible for providing support to operations carried out by II Corps (Highlands), and including 2 Tactical Air Wings 72, and 82.

Air Division 1

Figure 1.1. Insignia of the Air Division 1

The Air Division 1 was officially created in September 1970 at the Đà Nẵng Air Base under the command of colonel Nguyễn Đức Khánh, who was later promoted to Brigadier-General on April 1, 1974.

Figure 1.2. Brigadier-General Nguyễn Đức Khánh

Unlike most of the generals of the AFVN, who had been drafted in 1951, had graduated from the Nam Dịnh or Thủ Đức Reserve Officer School, and then later were transferred to the newly-created Vietnamese Air Force, Brigadier-General Nguyễn Đức Khánh volunteered to the Air Force in 1954, passed the examination, was sent to France to attend the famous Air Academy Salon-de-Provence, and graduated as a fighter pilot officer with the rank of Second-Lieutenant.[,2,3] General Khánh, while still a Lieutenant-Colonel, during the period of 1967-1970, was Commander of the Tactical Air Wing 41 in Đà Nẵng, the core tactical air wing of the Air Division 1.

The Air Division 1 was comprised of 3 Tactical Air Wings 41, 51, and 61.

Tactical Air Wing 41

Figure 1.3. Insignia of Tactical Air Wing 41

Tactical Air Wing 41 was created at the beginning of 1964 with Lieutenant-Colonel Phạm Long Sửu as its first commanding officer. [4,5,6] After 1972, Wing Commander was Colonel Thái Bá Đệ and Lieutenant-Colonel Nguyễn Văn Vượng as his Deputy. Tactical Air Wing 41 included 3 squadrons: 110, 120, and 427.

Before trying to learn more about these squadrons, we need to know that from around the beginning of the 1960s, the AFVN began to use a registration numbering system for all squadrons with the following characteristics:

- Each squadron registration number always consisted of 3 digits
- The first digit was used to indicate the branch in the AFVN:
  - o Number 1: for observation squadrons
  - o Number 2: for helicopter squadrons
  - o Number 3: for special-mission squadrons
  - o Number 4: for transport squadrons
  - o Number 5: for fighter and jet fighter squadrons
  - o Number 6: unused
  - o Number 7: for ELINT (Electronic Intelligence) squadrons

o Number 8: for gunship squadrons
o Number 9: for training squadrons

(**Note**: Originally, Number 6 was at first reserved for seaplanes but inapplicable, then was used for bomber squadrons but this practice did not last long; only one bomber flight, the Special Flight 615, was created equipped with B-57 Canberra bombers under the command of Major Nguyễn Ngọc Biên; this Special Flight 615 was disbanded in April 1966 because the B-57 Canberra bombers were not really fit to the battle needs in Vietnam and a quite sizable number of them were lost during combat operations)

The registration numbering system worked like this:

- The first digit (the hundred column): for the Branch in the AFVN
- The second digit (the dozen column): the first number to be used is Number 1
- The third digit (the unit column):
  - o The second digit minus 1
  - o For example, for an observation squadron 1 – 1 = 0
  - o Therefore, for the first observation squadron its registration number will be 110

- For every consecutive squadron, the registration number will increase by two

- Thus, all AFVN squadrons will bear registration numbers as follows: [7]

  - o Observation squadrons: 110, 112, 114, etc.
  - o Helicopter squadrons: 211, 213, 215, etc.
  - o Special-mission squadrons: 312, 314, etc.
  - o Transport squadrons: 413, 415, 417, etc.
  - o Fighter squadrons: 514, 516, 518, etc.
  - o Bomber squadron: 615
  - o ELINT squadrons: 716, 718

o Gunship squadrons: 817, 819, 821
o Training squadrons: 918, 920

According to the registration numbering system of the AFVN just mentioned, the two squadrons 110 and 120 both were observation squadrons.

Squadron 110, when Vietnam was still under French administration, called 1er GAOAC (Group aérien d'observation et d'accompagnement au combat, GAO in abbreviation), was created on October 1, 1952 in Nha Trang, relocated in Saigon (at Tân Sơn Nhứt –TSN-- Airbase) in 1953, moved to Huế in 1954, moved back to TSN in 1955, relocated in Đà Nẵng in November 1956, and officially became Observation Squadron 110 in January 1963. The squadron was also known under different names: Observation Squadron 1, First Observation Squadron, and Thiên Phong (Devine Wind) Squadron. The Squadron Commanders successively were: Nguyễn Ngọc Oánh, Trần Phước, Nguyễn Trọng Đệ, Ngô Tấn Diêu, Phan Văn Mạnh, Võ Trung Nhơn, Lê Sĩ Thắng, Nguyễn Tài Hiệp (Acting).[8]

Squadron 120 was created in May 1971 in Đà Nẵng with Lieutenant-Colonel Lê Công Thịnh as Commander.

Both squadrons, 110 and 120, were equipped with the most advanced observation aircraft of the 1970s supplied by the U.S.:

- O-1 Bird Dog observation aircraft:

Figure 1.4. O-1 Bird Dog Observation Aircraft

The O-1 Bird Dog observation aircraft, manufactured by Cessna Company, was re-designed from the L-19 observation aircraft employed by the AFVN from the mid-1950s. The O-1 Bird Dog had the following specifications: [9]

- Length: 7.88 m
- Wingspan: 10.97 m
- Height: 2.24 m
- Empty weight: 732 kg
- Engine: 1 Continental O-470-11 air-cooled flat-six propeller engine, 213 hp (159 kW)
- Cruise speed: 167 km/h, at 1,500 m
- Range: 850 km
- Maximum speed: 185 km/h
- Take-off distance to 15 m: 170 m
- Landing distance from 15 m: 180 m

- U-17 A/B Skywagon observation aircraft:

Figure 1.5. U-17 A/B Skywagon Observation Aircraft

The U-17 A/B Skywagon, also manufactured by Cessna Company, had the following specifications: [10]

- Length: 7.85 m
- Wingspan: 10.92 m
- Height: 2.36 m

- Weight: 783 kg
- Engine: Type A: 1 Continental IO-470 propeller engine, 260 hp; Type B: 1 Continental engine IO-520 propeller engine, 300 hp
- Speed: cruise 210 km/h; maximum 330 km/h
- Range: 4 h 30 mn
- Transport capacity: 6 persons including pilot

The transport squadron 427, officially called Thần Long (Sacred Dragon), was created in February 1972 at Airbase Phù Cát, province of Bình Định, II Corps, with the following commanding staff: [11]

- Commander: Lieutenant-Colonel Phạm Văn Cẩn
- Deputy Commander: Major Nguyễn Bá Đạm
- Chief of Operations: Major Trần Văn Minh
- Chief of Training: Major Hà Văn Hòa
- Chief of Flight Security: Major Nguyễn Văn Kim

Squadron 427 was the first transport squadron of the AFVN equipped with C-7 Caribou aircraft manufactured by De Havilland Company (Canada):

Figure 1.6. C-7A Caribou Transport Aircraft

The C-7 Caribou transport aircraft, belonging to the aircraft group called STOL (short takeoff and landing), did not need long runway (300 m would be enough), and had the following specifications: [12]

- Length: 22.12 m
- Wingspan: 29.13 m
- Height: 9.65 m
- Weight: 8,283 kg
- Engines: 2 Pratt & Whitney R-2000-7M2 propeller engines, 14-cylinder, 1,450 hp each
- Speed: 348 km/h
- Range: 2,103 km
- Ceiling: 7,559 m
- Air crew: 3
- Transport capacity: can carry a whole platoon of soldiers, or 2 Jeeps or 2 small-sized military trucks

Thanks to the special performance of the C-7 Caribou, which could land on any kind of runway, of dirt or grass, no need of concrete, and just around 300 m of length, Squadron 427 was able, on a daily basis, to carry out very dangerous missions of supplying and evacuating for the border-defensing Rangers Battalions or any other outposts located in isolated positions in the jungle within the area of responsibility of I Corps.

Here is the Summary of information for the squadrons belonging to Tactical Wing 41:

Units	Commanders	Names	Insignia
Squadron 110	First: Captain Nguyễn Ngọc Oánh Last (Acting): Lieutenant-Colonel Nguyễn Tài Hiệp	Thiên Phong (Devine Wind)	110

Squadron 120	Lieutenant-Colonel Lê Công Thịnh	Bạch Yến (White Canary)	
Squadron 427	Lieutenant-Colonel Phạm Văn Cần	Thần Long (Sacred Dragon)	

Tactical Air Wing 51

Figure 1.7. Insignia of Tactical Air Wing 51

Headquartered in Đà Nẵng, Tactical Air Wing 51, with Colonel Nguyễn Văn Vượng as its last Commander, included 6 helicopter squadrons: 213, 233, 239, 247, 253, and 257.

Compared to the other branches, e.g., transport, fighter, the helicopter branch was born late but was also the most rapidly developed branch and strongest branch of the AFVN. [13]

Generally, each UH-1 helicopter squadron includes 4 flights, 3 flights of lightly equipped helicopters (Slick), and 1 flight of heavily armed helicopters (Gun), each flight having 8 aircraft, totaling 32 UH-1 helicopters. Some squadrons may have up to 38 UH-1 helicopters. The CH-47 Chinook squadrons all had 16 aircraft. Just before April 30, 1975, the AFVN has acquired from the U.S. a total of around 800 UH-1 helicopters and 100 CH-47 Chinook helicopters. These UH-1 helicopters were used by the AFVN in a wide variety of operations: troop transports, medical evacuations, bringing supplies to outposts, search and rescue missions to save downed pilots, etc.

Squadron 213 was the oldest squadron of Tactical Air Wing 51. It was created on October 1, 1861 with 20 H-34 helicopters and with a commanding staff as follows:

- Commander: Captain Nguyễn Xuân Trường
- Deputy Commander: Captain Nguyễn Hữu Hậu
- Chief of Technical Services: First-Lieutenant Ngô Khắc Thuật
- Chief of Operations: Second-Lieutenant Nguyễn Văn Trang

H-34 helicopters had the following specifications: [14]

Figure 1.8. H-34 Helicopter

- Length: 17.28 m
- Height: 4.85 m
- Weight: 3,583 kg
- Engine: 1 Wright R-1820-84 radial engine rotor, with

diameter of 17.07 m, 1,525 hp
- Speed: maximum 278 km/h
- Range: 293 km
- Ceiling: 1,495 m
- Air crew: 2, 1 pilot and 1 co-pilot
- Transport capacity: from 12 (Type A) to 18 (Type B) soldiers; or 8 stretchers

Compared to H-19 helicopters left over by the French, the H-34 helicopters were already stronger, faster and having a longer range of action. From 1965, after U.S. troops had already been brought in South Vietnam, and helicopters were widely used in almost any type of operations, the H-34 helicopters were gradually replaced by UH-1 helicopters having wider range of action and being fully armed.

The remaining helicopter squadrons of the Tactical Air Wing 51 were all created after 1970. All of them (except for Squadron 247) together with Squadron 213 were using UH-1 helicopters. Squadron 247 was the only squadron of the Tactical Air Wing 51 using CH-47 Chinook helicopters.

The CH-47 Chinook was a big helicopter with very important transport and supply capacity.

Figure 1.9. CH-47 Chinook Helicopter

The CH-47 Chinook helicopter had the following specifications: [15]

- Length: 30.1 m
- Height: 5.7 m
- Weight: 10,185 kg
- Engines: 2 Lycoming T55-GA-714A turboshaft rotors, 4,733 hp each
- Speed: cruise 240 km/h, maximum 315 km/h
- Range: 741 km
- Ceiling: 5,640 m
- Air crew: 3, 1 pilot, 1 co-pilot, and 1 flight engineer
- Transport capacity: from 33 to 55 soldiers; or 12,700 kg goods
- Armament: 3 M24/FN MAG machine guns (7.62 mm), 1 on loading ramp and 2 at shoulder windows

The UH-1 helicopter, nicknamed "Huey," was a multi-use helicopter, and later became a symbol of the Vietnam War. It is quite safe to say that when talking about the Vietnam War, the first thing everyone, including Vietnamese and American, has in mind is the Huey chopper. In reality, what makes the big difference between the French military and the U.S. military is the great troop mobility of the US Army. And that was caused by the great use of helicopters by the U.S. Army in all of its operations. The ARVN, from 1965, has also acquired this high troop mobility, with all of these small and big helicopter-troop-transported operations all over the 4 Tactical Zones. The UH-1 Huey, however, was not only used in troop transport, but also in other types of operations, such as reconnaissance, tactical fire support, defoliation, medical evacuation, supplying, search and rescue missions, etc. That was why there were several different models of UH-1, such as 1A, 1B, 1D, 1H, etc., each model fitting to one type of operation [16,17]. Most of the UH-1 helicopters used by the AFVN were UH-1H.

Figure 1.10. UH-1 Huey Helicopter

The UH-1 Huey helicopter had the following specifications: [18]

- Length: 17.4 m
- Height: 4.39 m
- Weight: 2,365 kg
- Engine: 1 Lycoming T53-L-11 turboshaft rotor, 1,100 hp
- Speed: cruise 205 km/h, maximum 220 km/h
- Range: 510 km
- Ceiling: 5,910 m
- Air crew: 4, 1 pilot, 1 co-pilot, 1 flight engineer, and 1 gunner
- Transport capacity: 14 soldiers, or 6 stretchers, or 1,760 kg of goods
- Armament: up to 2 GAU-17/A machine guns (7.62 mm), and 2 rocket pods (70 mm)

Below is the Summary of information regarding the helicopter squadrons of Tactical Air Wing 51:

Units	Commanders	Names	Insignia
Squadron 213	First: Captain Nguyễn Xuân Trường Last: Lieutenant-Colonel Cao Quang Khôi	Song Chùy (Twin Mace)	

Squadron 233	First: Major Bùi Quang Chính Last: Lieutenant-Colonel Nguyễn Văn Thanh	Thiên Ưng (Devine Eagle)	
Squadron 239	First: Major Trần Duy Kỳ Last: Lieutenant-Colonel Nguyễn Anh Toàn	Hoàng Ưng (Golden Eagle)	
Squadron 247	Lieutenant-Colonel Nguyễn Văn Mai	Lôi Phong (Lightning Wind)	
Squadron 253	First: Major Phạm Đăng Luân Last: Major Hùynh Văn Phố	Sói Thần (Sacred Wolf)	
Squadron 257	Lieutenant-Colonel: Lê Ngọc Bình	Cứu Tinh (Savior)	

Tactical Air Wing 61

Figure 1.11. Insignia of Tactical Air Wing 61

Headquartered in Đà Nẵng, the Tactical Air Wing 61 had 4 fighter squadrons 516, 528, 538, and 550, all equipped with 2 types of jet fighters, the A-37B Dragonfly and the F5-A/B Freedom Fighter. Its first Commander was Lieutenant-Colonel Thái Bá Đệ.

Squadron 516 was the oldest squadron of Tactical Air Wing 61:

- First Commander was Captain Phạm Long Sửu.
- Called II Fighter Squadron, named Phi Hổ (Flying Tiger).
- Created in December 1961 in Nha Trang, and using T-28 fighters.
- Relocated in Đà Nẵng in 1964, and using A1-H Skyraider fighters.
- In 1968, all squadron members were sent to U.S. to receive training for A-37B Dragonfly jet fighters.

All remaining squadrons of Tactical Air Wing 61 were created after 1970:

- Squadron 528, named Hổ Cáp (Scorpius), created in 1970, with Major Cao Văn Khuyến as first Commander, and equipped with A-37B Dragonfly jet fighters.

- Squadron 538, named Hồng Tiễn (Red Arrow), created at the end of 1972, with Major Phạm Đình Anh was first Commander, and equipped with F-5A and F-5B jet fighters. In 1973, Squadron 538 was equipped with F-5E Tiger II jet fighters, much more modern and specially designed for dog fights. (**Important note:** Administratively, this squadron was under direct command of Tactical Air Wing 63 of Air Division 3 in Biên Hòa. This squadron was posted in Đà Nẵng on anticipation of potential air attacks by North Vietnamese MIG jet fighters).

- Squadron 550, named Nhện Đen (Black Spider), created at the end of 1972, with Major Lê Trai as first Commander, and equipped with A-37B Dragonfly jet fighters.

Figure 1.12. A-37B Dragonfly Jet Fighter

The A-37B Dragonfly jet fighter had the following specifications: [19]

- Length: 8.62 m
- Wingspan: 10.93 m
- Height: 2.70 m
- Weight: 2,817 kg
- Engines: 2 General Electric J85-GE-17A turbojet engines, with propulsion of 2,850 pounds each
- Speed: cruise 787 km/h, maximum 816 km/h

- Range: 1,480 km
- Ceiling: 12,730 m
- Air crew: 1 pilot
- Armament:

Guns:

1 × 7.62 mm (0.300 in) GAU-2B/A minigun in nose
Provision for SUU-11/A gun pods under wings
Hardpoints: 8 with a capacity of Inner four: 860 lb (390 kg), two intermediate: 600 lb (270 kg), two outer: 500 lb (230 kg),
Rockets: LAU-3/A rocket pods
Bombs:
250 lb (110 kg) Mark 81, 500 lb (230 kg) Mark 82 or 750 lb (340 kg) M117 bombs
BLU-32B or BLU-1C/B fire bombs
CBU-12, CBU-22 or CBU-24 cluster bombs

Figure 1.13. Armament of A-37B Dragonfly Jet Fighter

Figure 1.14. F-5A/B Freedom Fighter Jet Fighter

The F-5A/B Freedom Fighter jet fighter had the following specifications: [20]

- Length: 14.45 m
- Wingspan: 8.13 m
- Height: 4.08 m
- Weight: 4,349 kg
- Engines: 2 General Electric J85-GE-13 turbojet engines, with propulsion of 4,080 pounds each
- Speed: cruise 0.84 Mach (1.037 km/h), maximum 1,4 Mach (1.728 km/h)
- Range: 2,253 km
- Ceiling: 15,240 m
- Air crew: 1 pilot
- Armament: (2) 20-mm Cannons, (2) Sidewinder IR Missiles

Below is the Summary of information regarding the squadrons of Tactical Air Wing 61:

Units	Commanders	Names	Insignia
Squadron 516	First: Captain Phạm Long Sửu	Phi Hổ (Flying Tiger)	
Squadron 528	First: Major Tá Cao Văn Khuyên	Hổ Cáp (Scorpius)	
Squadron 538	First: Major Phạm Đình Anh	Hồng Tiễn (Red Arrow)	

Squadron 550	First: Major Lê Trai	Nhện Đen (Black Spider)	

Air Division 2

Figure 1.15. Insignia of Air Division 2

The Air Division 2 was officially created in July 1970 in Nha Trang under the Command of Colonel Nguyễn Văn Lượng, who was later promoted to Brigadier-General on November 1, 1972.

Figure 1.16. Brigadier-General Nguyễn Văn Lượng

Like most other generals of the AFVN, Brigadier-General Nguyễn Văn Lượng was crafted to the first class of the Nam Định Reserve Officer School, graduated in June 1952 with the rank of Second-Lieutenant. In December 1952, he passed the entrance examination to the Air Force, attended and graduated from Class No. 2 of the Observation Pilot Training Program at the Nha Trang Air Force Training Center in August 1953.[21]

The Air Division 2 had 2 Tactical Air Wings: 62 and 92.

Tactical Air Wing 62

Figure 1.17. Insignia of Tactical Air Wing 62

Tactical Air Wing 62 was created in March 1964 in Pleiku and then was relocated to Nha Trang in January 1965. Its first Commander was Lieutenant-Colonel Trần Văn Minh, who later became Lieutenant-General Commander of the AFVN.[22] The Deputy Commander was Major Nguyễn Hữu Tần, who later became Brigadier-General Commander of the Air Division 4 in Cần Thơ. Tactical Air Wing 62 had 4 squadrons and 1 special flight: Squadrons 114, 215, 219, 817, and Special Flight 259C.

Squadron 114 was an observation squadron, whose predecessor had been the 3rd Observation Squadron created in December 1962 in Đà Nẵng, renamed Squadron 114 in January 1963, relocated to Pleiku at the end of 1963, and finally relocated to Nha Trang in January 1965. Its first Commander was Captain Phan Quang Phúc. This squadron also employed 2 types of observation aircraft, i.e., O-1 and U-17 just like the previously mentioned Squadrons 110 and 120 of Air Division 1.

Squadron 215, the second one bearing this number, was a helicopter squadron. The first Squadron 215 was created at the beginning of 1963 at Tân Sơn Nhứt Airbase to take care of training. It failed and thus was disbanded in May 1964. In September 1964, a new helicopter squadron was created in Đà Nẵng, was given this number, and named Thần Tượng (Sacred Elephant), with the following commanding staff:

- Commander: Captain Trần Minh Thiện
- Deputy Commander: First-Lieutenant Đặng Trần Dưỡng
- Chief of Operations: Second-Lieutenant Nguyễn Văn Trang
- Assistant Chief of Operations: Second-Lieutenant Phạm Bính

Squadron 215, together with Squadron 213, both equipped with UH-1 helicopters, were responsible for training and operations until the beginning of 1965 when both of them were relocated to Nha Trang.

Squadron 219, named Long Mã (Dragon Horse), was created in Đà Nẵng at the beginning of 1966 by the fusion of two H-34 helicopter special flights, which had been specialized in dropping the Lôi Hổ (Lightning Tiger) teams of the Special Forces. At the beginning, Squadron 219 was under command of Special-Mission Squadron 83 headquartered at Tân Sơn Nhứt Airbase until Squadron 83 was disbanded in 1969, and was then transferred to the command of Tactical Air Wing 62. At its creation, Squadron 219 had its first commanding staff, as follows:

- Commander: Captain Hồ Bảo Định
- Deputy Commander: Captain Trần Văn Luân
- Chief of Operations: Captain Nguyễn Văn Nghĩa
- Assistant Chief of Operations: Captain Nguyễn Phi Hùng
- Chief of Training: First-Lieutenant Nguyễn Hữu Lộc

- Chief of Flight Safety: First-Lieutenant Đỗ Văn Hiếu

After its creation, Squadron 219, with its H-34 helicopters, continued to carry out the Lightning Tigers commando dropping missions. At the end of 1971, like other Squadrons 213 and 215, Squadron 219 switched to the use of UH-1 Huey helicopters.

Special Flight 259C was the special flight C of the Squadron 259, named Nhân Ái (Kindness), a helicopter squadron specializing in medical evacuations. Squadron 259 had a total of 8 special flights bearing an additional letter from A to H, and located at airbases as in the following listing:

- Special Flight 259A: Phù Cát (Province of Bình Định)
- Special Flight 259B: Pleiku
- Special Flight 259C: Nha Trang
- Special Flight 259D: Phan Rang
- Special Flight 259E: Biên Hòa
- Special Flight 259F: Cần Thơ
- Special Flight 259G: Tân Sơn Nhứt
- Special Flight 259H: Bình Thủy (Province of Phong Dinh)

Squadron 817 was a gunship squadron, and equipped with AC-47D aircraft:

Figure 1.18. AC-47D Spooky Gunship

In fact, the AC-47D Spooky was a DC-3 Dakota equipped with a very strong fire power to be used in missions of providing fire support to friendly units or isolated outposts surrounded by the enemy. This type of aircraft had the following specifications:[23]

- Length: 19 m

- Wingspan: 28.9 m

- Height: 5.2 m

- Weight: 8,201 kg

- Engines: 2 Pratt & Whitney R-1830-90C propeller engines, 1,200 hp each

- Speed: cruise 280 km/h; maximum 375 km/h

- Range: 3,500 km

- Ceiling: 7,450 m

- Air crew: 7, 1 pilot, 1 co-pilot, 1 navigator, 1 flight engineer, 1 loadmaster, and 2 gunners

- Armament:

    o Guns:

        ▪ 3 × 7.62 mm General Electric GAU-2/M134 miniguns, 2,000 rpm or

        ▪ 10 × .30 in Browning AN/M2 machine guns

    o 48 × Mk 24 flares

Below is the Summary of information regarding the squadrons of Tactical Air Wing 62:

Units	Commanders	Names	Insignia
Squadron 114	First: Captain Phan Quang Phúc Last (Acting): Lieutenant-Colonel Võ Văn Oanh	Sao Mai (Morning Star)	
Squadron 215	First: Major Trần Minh Thiện Last: Lieutenant-Colonel Khưu Văn Phát	Thần Tượng (Sacred Elephant)	
Squadron 219	First: Major Tá Hồ Bảo Định Last: Lieutenant-Colonel Phạm Đăng Luân	Long Mã (Dragon Horse)	
Special Flight 259C	Major Nguyễn Minh Lương	Nhân Ái (Kindness)	
Squadron 817	Lieutenant-Colonel Huỳnh Quang Tòng	Hỏa Long (Fire Dragon)	

In Operation Lam Sơn 719 carried out during February and March of 1971 by the ARVN with the objective of destroying Communist supply bases on the Ho Chi Minh Trail, AFVN helicopter squadrons have participated very actively, executing several dangerous missions of landing troops, bringing supplies, and medical evacuations, and, as a result, have suffered a lot of damages and casualties. Unfortunately, up to the present, there is still no final tally of the damages and losses of the helicopter branch of the ARVN in this extremely important operation. The article ***"Chuyến bay tử thần vào Đồi 31 Hạ Lào"*** (The Deadly flight into Hill 31 in Lower Laos) by author Bùi Tá Khánh, a former pilot of the Dragon Horse Helicopter Squadron 219, has recounted the tragic and heroic sacrifices of two air crews of Squadron 219, which the author had witnessed.[24] One detail in the article that should be noted is that, at that time (February 1971), Squadron 219 was still using H-34 helicopters and still under the command of Tactical Air Wing 51, Air Division 1 based in Đà Nẵng.

Tactical Air Wing 92

Figure 1.19. Insignia of Tactical Air Wing 92

Tactical Air Wing 92 was created in mid-1972 and located in Phan Rang, with Lieutenant-Colonel (later promoted to Full Colonel) Lê Văn Thảo as its first Commander, and included 3 squadrons 524, 534, and 548, all equipped with A-37 jet fighters, and 1 Special Flight 259D equipped with UH-1 helicopters for medical evacuations.

Squadron 524, named Thiên Lôi (Devine Lightning), whose predecessor had been a special flight of Squadron 516, was created on September 15, 1965 in Nha Trang, with Captain Nguyễn Quang Ninh as its first Commander, and Lieutenant-Colonel Sử

Ngọc Cả as its last Commander. Squadron 524 was the first squadron to receive A-37 jet fighters.

Squadron 534, named Kim Ngưu (Golden Buffalo), also an A-37 jet fighter squadron, was created in mid-1972 in Phan Rang, with Major (later promoted to Lieutenant-Colonel) Nguyễn Văn Thi as its first and only Commander until April 30, 1975.

Squadron 548, named Ó Đen (Black Hawk), also equipped with A-37 jet fighters, was created at the end of 1972 in Phan Rang, with Major Trần Mạnh Khôi (later promoted to Lieutenant-Colonel) as its first Commander.

In addition to these 3 jet fighter squadrons, Tactical Air Wing 92 also included the Special Flight 259D for medical evacuations with UH-1 helicopters.

Below is the Summary of information regarding the squadrons and the special flight of Tactical Air Wing 92:

Units	Commanders	Names	Insignia
Squadron 524	First: Captain Nguyễn Quang Ninh Last: Lieutenant-Colonel Sử Ngọc Cả	Thiên Lôi (Devine Lightning)	
Squadron 534	Lieutenant-Colonel Nguyễn Văn Thi	Kim Ngưu (Golden Buffalo)	
Squadron 548	Lieutenant-Colonel Trần Mạnh Khôi	Ó Đen (Black Hawk)	

Special Flight 259D	Major Tô Thành Nhân	Nhân Ái (Kindness)	

Air Division 3

Figure 1.20. Insignia of Air Division 3

Air Division 3 was created in May 1970 in Biên Hòa, with Colonel Huỳnh Bá Tính (later promoted to Brigadier-General on November 1, 1972) as its Commander. Brigadier-General Tính graduated from Class 1 (Class Lê Văn Duyệt) of Thủ Đức Reserve Officer School (June 1952) as a Second-Lieutenant. He passed the entrance examination to the Air Force, and graduated from the pilot training program in Marrakech, Morocco, North Africa, and became one of the first pilots of the AFVN. Before assuming the command of the Air Division 1, he was successively commanders of the 2 following units: Observation Squadron No. 2 in Nha Trang, and Tactical Air Wing 74 in Cần Thơ.[25]

Figure 1.21. Brigadier-General Huỳnh Bá Tính

Air Division 3 had 3 Tactical Air Wings 23, 43, and 63.

Tactical Air Wing 23

Figure 1.22. Insignia of Tactical Air Wing 23

Tactical Air Wing 23 was created in mid-1964 in Biên Hòa, with Lieutenant-Colonel Phạm Long Sửu as its first Commander, and with Major Phạm Phú Quốc as Deputy-Commander. Its last Commander was Colonel Hoàng Thanh Nhã.

Tactical Air Wing 23 had a total of 4 squadrons: 2 observation squadrons 112 and 124 equipped with O-1 Bird Dog and U-17 Skywagon observation aircraft, and 2 fighter squadrons 514 and 518 equipped with A-1 Skyraider fighter aircraft.

Squadron 112, whose predecessor had been Observation and Combat Support Squadron No. 2, was created in January 1952 in Nha Trang, moved to Tân Sơn Nhứt Airbase in October 1956, received number 112, and named Thanh Xà (Green Serpent) in January 1963, and finally relocated to Biên Hòa in June 1964. Its first Commander was Captain Võ Dinh, who later became Brigadier-General, Chief Staff of the AFVN. [26] Its last Commander was Lieutenant-Colonel Lý Thành Ba.

Squadron 124, the last observation squadron of the AFVN, named Thanh Điểu (Green Bird), was created at the end of 1971 in Biên Hòa, with Lieutenant-Colonel Võ Trung Nhơn as its Commander.

Squadron 514, named Phượng Hoàng (Phoenix), was the oldest fighter squadron of the AFVN. Its predecessor, the First Fighter and Reconnaissance Squadron, was created in 1956, equipped with F-8F Bearcat fighters, and its first Commander was Captain Huỳnh Hữu Hiền, who later was promoted to Colonel and assumed the Command of the AFVN for a short period of time, 1962-1963. In 1960 it was renamed Squadron 514, equipped with A-1H Skyraider fighters, with Captain Nguyễn Quang Tri as its new Commander. Captain Tri was one of the first fighter pilots of the AFVN. He graduated from the world-famous French Air Force Training School Salon-de-Provence, and later he has himself successfully trained many talented fighter pilots for the AFVN. One of these pilots was Mr. Lê Bá Định, who later became Major, Commander of the Fighter Squadron 530 (named Thái Dương (Supreme Sun), and then Lieutenant-Colonel, Commander of Tactical Air Wing 72, Air Division 6 in Pleiku. Captain Tri was later promoted to the rank of Full Colonel, Assistant to the Commander of the AFVN, responsible for Air Defense. After his arrival in the U.S. in the H.O. Program, Colonel Tri worked for several years as the Webmaster of the two Websites, ***Bạn Già Không Quân*** (Old Friends from the Air Force) and ***Cánh Chim Tự Do*** (Free Birds), very well-known among former members of the AFVN. The last Commander of Squadron 514 was Lieutenant-Colonel Nguyễn Văn Vượng.

Squadron 518, named Phi Long (Flying Dragon), was created at the beginning of 1964, equipped with A-1H Skyraider fighters, and with Major Phạm Phú Quốc as its first Commander (Quốc was one of the 2 fighter pilots who bombed the Independence Palace on February 27, 1962; on April 19, 1965, already promoted to Lieutenant-Colonel and Commander of Tactical Air Wing 23, he was shot down and killed when he was commanding a flight of A-1H Skyraider fighters in an attack mission in Hà Tĩnh, North Vietnam). The last Commander of Squadron 518 was Lieutenant-Colonel Lê Quốc Hùng.

The A1-H Skyraider fighters, employed by Squadrons 514 and 518, were the AD-6 fighter aircraft manufactured by Douglas Company, as illustrated by the following Figure:

Figure 1.23. A-1H Skyraider Fighter Aircraft

The A-1H Skyraider fighter aircraft had the following specifications: [27]

- Length: 11.84 m
- Wingspan: 15.24 m
- Height: 4.78 m
- Weight: 5,429 kg
- Engine: 1 Wright R-3350-26WA propeller engine, with propulsion of 2,700 hp

- Speed: cruise 319 km/h, maximum 518 km/h
- Range: 2,115 km
- Ceiling: 8,685 m
- Air crew: 1 pilot
- Armament:

Guns: 4x 20 mm AN/M3 cannon with 200 rounds per gun

Hardpoints: 15 external hardpoints with a capacity of 8,000 lb (3,600 kg), with provisions to carry combinations of:

Other: bombs, torpedoes, mine dispensers, unguided rockets, and gun pods.

Below is the Summary of information regarding the squadrons of Tactical Air Wing 23:

Units	Commanders	Names	Insignia
Squadron 112	First: Captain Võ Dinh Last: Lieutenant-Colonel Lý Thành Ba	Thanh Xà (Green Serpent)	
Squadron 124	Lieutenant-Colonel Võ Trung Nhơn	Thanh Điểu (Green Bird)	
Squadron 514	First: Captain Huỳnh Hữu Hiền Last: Lieutenant-Colonel Dương Bá Trát	Phượng Hoàng (Phoenix)	
Squadron 518	First: Major Phạm Phú Quốc Last: Lieutenant-Colonel Nguyễn Quan Vĩnh	Phi Long (Flying Dragon)	

Tactical Air Wing 43

Figure 1.24. Insignia of Tactical Air Wing 43

Tactical Air Wing 43, created in Biên Hòa, was a helicopter air wing, and had a total of 6 squadrons and 1 special flight:

- Squadron 237 equipped with CH-47 Chinook helicopters
- Squadrons 221, 223, 231, 245, and 251, all equipped with UH-1 Huey helicopters
- Special Flight 259E also equipped with UH-1 Huey helicopters for medical evacuations

Its last Commander was Colonel Vũ Quang Triệu.

Below is the Summary of information regarding the squadrons of Tactical Air Wing 43:

Units	Commanders	Names	Insignia
Squadron 221	First: Major Nguyễn Văn Ức Last: Lieutenant-Colonel Nguyễn Văn Trọng	Lôi Vũ (Lightning Rain)	221

Squadron 223	Lieutenant-Colonel Trần Văn Luân	Lôi Điểu (Lightning Bird)	
Squadron 231	Lieutenant-Colonel Nguyễn Hữu Lộc	Lôi Vân (Lightning Cloud)	
Squadron 237	First: Lieutenant-Colonel Tá Hồ Bảo Định Last: Lieutenant-Colonel Nguyễn Phú Chính	Lôi Thanh (Lightning Sound)	
Squadron 245	Lieutenant-Colonel Nguyễn Hữu Lai	Lôi Bằng (Lightning Eagle)	
Squadron 251	Lieutenant-Colonel Dương Quang Lễ	Lôi Thiên (Lightning Sky)	
Special Flight 259E	First: Major Đặng Kim Quy Last: Major Huỳnh Văn Du	Nhân Ái (Kindness)	

In Summer 1972, Major Nguyễn Văn Ức, Commander of Helicopter Squadron 221 (after January 1973, he was promoted to Lieutenant-Colonel, and became Deputy Commander of Tactical Air Wing 64, Air Division 4 in Cần Thơ), was designated to command all helicopter operations for landing troops, bringing supplies, and medical evacuations of Squadron 221 in the Battle of An Lộc.[28]

Tactical Air Wing 63

Figure 1.25. Insignia of Tactical Air Wing 63

This tactical air wing had only F-5 jet fighters. Tactical Air Wing 63 was, therefore, given the nickname of F-5 Tactical Air Wing. It had a total of 6 squadrons of F-5 jet fighters: Squadron 522, Squadron 536, Squadron 538 (specially on loan to Air Division 1 in Đà Nẵng, as mentioned earlier), Squadron 540, Squadron 542 and Squadron 544, with their commanders, names, and insignia listed in the following table:

Units	Commanders	Names	Insignia
Squadron 522	Captain Nguyễn Quốc Hưng	Thần Ưng (Sacred Eagle)	
Squadron 536	Major Đàm Thượng Vũ	Thiên Ưng (Divine Eagle)	
Squadron 538	Major Phạm Đình Anh	Hồng Tiễn (Red Arrow)	

Squadron 540	Major Nguyễn Tiến Thành	Hắc Ưng (Black Eagle)	
Squadron 542	Major Trịnh Bửu Quang	Kim Ưng (Golden Eagle)	
Squadron 544	Major Nguyễn Văn Tường	Hải Ưng (Sea Eagle)	

Air Division 4

Figure 1.26. Insignia of Air Division 4

Air Division 4 was created in March 1970 in Cần Thơ with Colonel Nguyễn Huy Ánh as its first Commander. Colonel Ánh was later promoted to Brigadier-General on November 1, 1971. As a civilian, he had passed the entrance examination to the Air Force, and was then sent to France to attend pilot training school and graduated top of his class in 1955 with the rank of Second-Lieutenant. He was also one of the first helicopter pilots trained in the U.S. Before becoming Commander of Air Division 4, General Ánh was Commander of Helicopter Squadrons 215 and 211, and Commander of Tactical Air Wings 74 and 62. He was killed on duty in a helicopter accident on April 27, 1972 and was promoted posthumously to the rank of Major-General.[29]

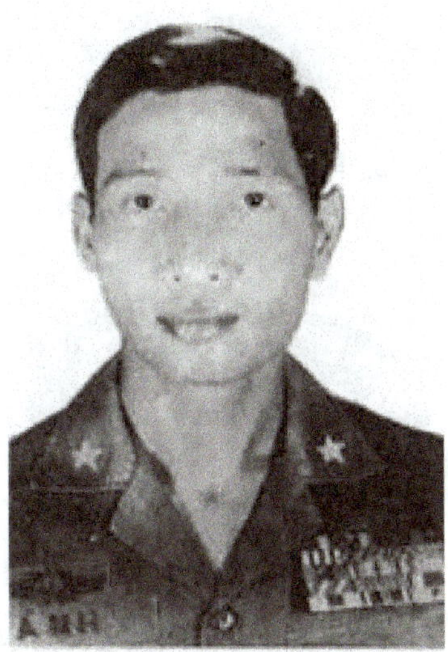

Figure 1.27. Brigadier-General Nguyễn Huy Ánh

Colonel Nguyễn Hữu Tần, Deputy Chief of Staff for Operations at VNAF Headquarters, was nominated to replace General Ánh as Commander of Air Division 4 at the end of April 1972. On April 1, 1974, Colonel Tần was promoted to Brigadier-General. General Tần graduated from Class 1 (Class of Lê Lợi), Nam Định Reserve Officer School in June 1952, as a Second-Lieutenant. He was then transferred to the Air Force, attended Nha Trang Air Force Training Center, and graduated top of his Class 5 of observation pilot in 1956. Before his nomination as Commander of Air Division 4, he was Commander of the First and Second Observation Squadrons, and Deputy- Commander of Tactical Air Wing 62 just created under the Command of Lieutenant-Colonel Trần Văn Minh, who would become Lieutenant-General, Commander of the AFVN. [30]

Figure 1.28. Brigadier-General Nguyễn Hữu Tần

Air Division 4 included 3 tactical air wings: 64, 74, and 84.

Tactical Air Wing 64

Figure 1.29. Insignia of Tactical Air Wing 64

Tactical Air Wing 64, headquartered in Cần Thơ, and under the command of Lieutenant-Colonel Trương Thành Tâm (a graduate of Class 16 of the Đà Lạt Military Academy, and former Commander of Helicopter Squadron 217), had a total of 3 squadrons and 1 special flight of helicopters: Squadrons 217 and 255 equipped with UH-1 helicopters, Squadron 249 with CH-47 Chinook helicopters, and Special Flight 259F also using UH-1 helicopters for medical evacuations.

Squadron 217, named Thần Điểu (Sacred Bird), was one of the first helicopter squadrons of the AFVN, which was switching its use of H-19 helicopters (of the Expeditionary French Forces) to H-34 helicopters. Headquartered in Đà Nẵng in April 1964, this squadron had its first commanding staff including the following officers: [31]

- Commander: Captain Ong Lợi Hồng (his last rank being Colonel, Deputy-Commander of Air Division 4)
- Deputy-Commander: First-Lieutenant Mai Văn Hải
- Chief of Operation: Second-Lieutenant Nguyễn Văn Phú Hiệp
- Chief of Flight Safety: Second-Lieutenant Hồng Văn Tý
- Chief of Technical Services: Warrant-Officer Trần Phước Hội

The squadron was relocated to Tân Sơn Nhứt Airbase for a short while and then located permanently at Trà Nóc Airbase in Cần Thơ. After a few years, Squadron 217 had a new commanding staff with Major Trương Thành Tâm (later promoted to Lieutenant-Colonel) as Commander and Captain Nguyễn Thanh Hải as Deputy-Commander (Captain Hải was later promoted to Lieutenant-Colonel and worked as an Inspector of Flight Safety at the AFVN Headquarters at Tân Sơn Nhứt Airbase). The last Commander of Squadron 217 was Lieutenant-Colonel Nguyễn Văn Vọng. A short time after its move to Trà Nóc Airbase, Squadron 217 was equipped with UH-1 helicopters.

Squadron 255, named Xà Vương (King Serpent), one of the last UH-1 helicopter squadrons, created at the beginning of 1973, was under the command of Lieutenant-Colonel Nguyễn Kim Huờn.

Squadron 249 was the last CH-47 Chinook helicopter squadron of the AFVN, created in December 1972, was placed under the Command of Major Tống Phước Hào (later promoted to Lieutenant-Colonel).

The last unit of Tactical Air Wing 64 was the Special Flight 259F, equipped with UH-1, responsible for medical evacuations, and commanded by Major Nguyễn Thành Quới.

Below is the table summarizing information relating to the units of Tactical Air Wing 64:

Units	Commanders	Names	Insignia
Squadron 217	First: Captain Ong Lợi Hồng Last: Lieutenant-Colonel Nguyễn Văn Vọng	Thần Điểu (Sacred Bird)	
Squadron 249	First: Major Tống Phước Hào Second: Major Phạm Văn Trung Last: Major Phạm Xuân Việt	Mãnh Long (Strong Dragon)	
Squadron 255	Lieutenant-Colonel Nguyễn Kim Hườn	Xà Vương (King Serpent)	
Special Flight 259F	Major Nguyễn Thành Quới	Nhân Ái (Kindness)	

Note: Major Phạm Văn Trung, from Class 63A of the AFVN, served in helicopter Squadrons 215, 219, 237, 241, assumed command of Squadron 249 on December 10, 1974, and killed in action on December 12, 1974 at the Battle of Mộc Hóa when his CH-47 Chinook was shot down by an infrared-homing surface-to-air SA7 missile. He was promoted posthumously to Lieutenant-Colonel.[32]

Tactical Air Wing 74

Figure 1.30. Insignia of Tactical Air Wing 74

Tactical Air Wing 74 was created in April 1964 in Cần Thơ with the following successive commanders:

- First: Lieutenant-Colonel Trần Văn Minh (later Lieutenant-General, Commander of the AFVN)
- Second: Lieutenant-Colonel Huỳnh Bá Tính (later Brigadier-General, Commander of Air Division 3)
- Third: Lieutenant-Colonel Nguyễn Huy Ánh (later Brigadier-General, Commander of Air Division 4)
- Last: Colonel Nguyễn Quang Ninh

Tactical Air Wing 74 had a total of 5 squadrons:

- 2 observation squadrons: Squadron 116 equipped with O-1 Bird Dog observation airplanes, and Squadron 122 equipped with U-17A/B Skywagon observation airplanes
- 3 fighter squadrons: Squadron 520, Squadron 526, and Squadron 546, all equipped with A-37B Dragonfly jet fighters

Squadron 116, named Sơn Ca (Lark; previously names Thần Ưng = Sacred Eagle), was created in June-1964 in Nha Trang, and later relocated in Cần Thơ in July-1964. Its last Acting-Commander was Lieutenant-Colonel Bùi Thanh Sử.

Squadron 122, named Họa Mi (Nightingale; previously named Thần Tiễn = Sacred Arrow), was created in August-1972, with Lieutenant-Colonel Trần Trọng Khương as Commander.

Squadron 520, named Thần Báo (Sacred Panther), was created in 1964 in Biên Hòa, with Captain Nguyễn Ngọc Biện as its first Commander, equipped with A-1H Skyraider fighters, relocated to Cần Thơ in mid-1965, and in 1968 switching to A-37 jet fighters.

Squadron 526, named Quỷ Vương (Satan), was created in 1971 in Cần Thơ, with Major Huỳnh Hữu Hải as its first Commander.

Squadron 546, named Thiên Sứ (Angel), was created at the end of 1972, with Major Lê Mộng Hoan as its first Commander.

Below is the table summarizing information relating to the squadrons of Tactical Air Wing 74:

Units	Commanders	Names	Insignia
Squadron 116	Lieutenant-Colonel Bùi Thanh Sử	Sơn Ca (Lark)	
Squadron 122	Lieutenant-Colonel Trần Trọng Khương	Họa Mi (Nightingale)	
Squadron 520	Captain Nguyễn Ngọc Biên	Thần Báo (Sacred Panther)	

Squadron 526	Major Huỳnh Hữu Hải	Quỷ Vương (Satan)	
Squadron 546	Major Tá Lê Mộng Hoan	Thiên Sứ (Angel)	

Tactical Air Wing 84

Figure 1.31. Insignia of Tactical Air Wing 84

Tactical Air Wing 84, Created in Sóc Trăng and later relocated to Cần Thơ, has 3 UH-1 helicopter squadrons: 211, 225 and 227, and 1 Special Flight 259H for medical evacuations.

Below is the summary of information relating to squadrons of Tactical Air Wing 84:

Units	Commanders	Names	Insignia
Squadron 211	First: Captain Nguyễn Đức Hớn Last: Lieutenant-Colonel Trần Quế Lâm	Thần Chùy (Sacred Mace)	

Squadron 225	Lieutenant-Colonel Lê Văn Châu	Ác Điểu (Ferocious Brid)	
Squadron 227	Lieutenant-Colonel Trần Châu Rết	Hải Âu (Sea Gull)	
Special Flight 259H	Major Nguyễn Trọng Thanh	Nhân Ái (Kind-ness)	

Air Division 5

Figure 1.32. Insignia of Air Division 5

Air Division 5 was created in January 1971 at Tân Sơn Nhứt Airbase under the command of Colonel Phan Phụng Tiên, who was later promoted to Brigadier-General on November 1, 1972. General Tiên graduated Class 1 (Class of Lê Lợi) from the Nam Định Reserve Officer School in June 1952 as a Second-Lieutenant. He was then transferred to the Air Force. He graduated Class 52F1 in Marrakech, Morocco, North Africa together with Messrs Huỳnh Hữu Hiền (later Colonel, Commander of the AFVN, 1962-1963), Phạm Ngọc Sang (later Brigadier-General, Commander of Air Division 6) and Huỳnh Bá Tính (later Brigadier-General, Commander of Air Division 3). He was promoted to Captain in 1954 and assumed command of the Number 1 Transport Squadron. He was the pilot of the C-47 transport plane, which carried Colonel Nguyễn Chánh Thi and other paratrooper officers to Phnom Penh, Cambodia seeking political asylum after their failed military coup of November 11, 1960. After the successful coup of November 1, 1963, he came back to Vietnam, and was promoted to the rank of Major. He became a Colonel in 1968 and was given the command of the Tân Sơn Nhứt Airbase after Colonel Lưu Kim Cương was killed in action during the Tet Offensive[33]

Figure 1.33. Brigadier-General Phan Phụng Tiên

Air Division 5 had 2 tactical air wings: Tactical Air Wing 33 and Tactical Air Wing 53.

Tactical Air Wing 33

Figure 1.34. Insignia of Tactical Air Wing 33

Tactical Air Wing 33, located at Tân Sơn Nhứt Airbase, was created in January 1964 with the following successive Commanders:

- Colonel Hà Xuân Vịnh
- Colonel Phạm Ngọc Sang
- Lieutenant-Colonel Lưu Kim Cương
- Colonel Dương Thiệu Hùng
- Colonel Phan Phụng Tiên
- Colonel Bùi Đức Mỹ

Tactical Air Wing 33 had a total of 5 squadrons and 1 Special Flight: Special-Mission Squadron 314, 2 Transport Squadrons 429 and 431, 2 Electronic Intelligence Squadrons 716 and 718, and Special Flight 259G for medical evacuations.

Special-Mission Squadron 314, named Thần Tiễn (Sacred Arrow), with Major Nguyễn Hữu Trí as its first Commander, was, in principle, a transport squadron employing a number of C-47, DC-6B transport airplanes, but, in reality, it was a squadron with assigned special missions of providing transportation for important political and military personalities of the Government of the Republic of Vietnam. Therefore, within the AFVN, it was given the nick name of VIP Squadron.[34]

Figure 1.35. C-47 airplane of Special-Mission Squadron 314

Figure 1.36. DC-6B airplane of Special-Mission Squadron 314

The two Squadrons 429 and 431, together with Squadron 427 (already above-mentioned in the section for Air Division 1) were all transport squadrons using C-7A Caribou airplanes. These 3 squadrons were all created at Phù Cát Airbase (Province of Bình Định) in the following order: first Squadron 427 (in February 1972), then Squadron 429 (in April 1972), and, finally, Squadron 431 (in June 1972). In June 1972, Squadron 427 was moved to Đà Nẵng Airbase, and placed under the direct command of Air Division 1.

Squadron 429, named Sơn Long (Mountain Dragon), had Lieutenant-Colonel Cung Thăng An as Commander and Lieutenant-Colonel Nguyễn Viết Xương as Deputy-Commander;

in April 1973, it was relocated to Tân Sơn Nhứt Airbase and placed under the direct command of Tactical Air Wing 33.

Squadron 431, named Phương Long (Phoenix Dragon), had the following commanding staff:

- Commander: Lieutenant-Colonel Nguyễn Viết Xương (transferred from Squadron 429)
- Deputy Commander: Major Huỳnh Ngọc Nghĩa
- Chief of Operations: Major Nguyễn Đình Thảo

In November, Squadron 431 was relocated to Tân Sơn Nhứt Airbase to join Tactical Air Wing 33.[35]

Squadron 716 and Squadron 718 were both electronic/signal intelligence squadrons. Administratively, they were units of Air Division 5, but, operatively, they were under the command of Bureau 17 of J-7 of the General Staff Headquarters (responsible for signal intelligence or SIGINT).[36]

Squadron 716 was equipped with U-6A Beaver airplane, which was a re-designed De Havilland Company's L-19 observation airplane, as pictured in the following photo:

Figure 1.37. U-6A Beaver Airplane

The U-6A Beaver had the following specifications:

- Length: 9.24 m
- Wingspan: 14.63 m

- Height: 2.74 m
- Weight: 1,293 kg
- Engine: 1 Pratt & Whitney propeller engine, R-985-AN type, 450 hp
- Speed: cruise 177 km/h, maximum 225 km/h
- Range: 1,239 km
- Air crew: 1 pilot
- Armament: none

Squadron 718 was officially created in 1973 at Tân Sơn Nhứt Airbase with the following commanding staff:[37]

- Commander: Lieutenant-Colonel Nguyễn Hữu Bách
- Deputy-Commander: Major Phan Văn Lộc
- Administrative Assistant: Major Nguyễn Văn Thắng

Squadron 718, performing signal intelligence flights (usually from 3 to 5 hours), was a squadron with a large force of more than 500 soldiers and 36 EC-47 transport airplanes equipped with an ALR-34 system. The air crew carried out their duties totally in secret. They never revealed what they were doing even to their family members. All of them had to take the Polygraph test, and followed very strict regulations, e.g., never revealing their secret missions, and never taking pictures of their airplanes, either inside or outside. Because of these regulations, photos of this squadron's activities were extremely rare.

Figure 1.38. EC-47D Dakota Airplane

The EC-47D Dakota was a military version, specially equipped with electronic machines used in signal intelligence, of the Douglas Company's DC-3 Dakota widely known as the most successfully designed airplane in the history of the world's air transportation industry (as the oldest commercial airplane – manufactured in 1936 -- the DC-3 is still in use in the world; in 2013, it was estimated that there was a total of around 2,000 of them still flying safely all over the world)

The EC-47D Dakota had the following specifications:[38]

- Length: 19.43 m
- Wingspan: 29.41 m
- Height: 5.18 m
- Weight: 8,226 kg
- Engines: 2 Pratt & Whitney propeller engines, R-1830-90C type, 1,200 hp each
- Speed: 380 km/h
- Range: 2,575 km
- Ceiling: 8,045 m
- Air crew: 3
- Armament: no gun, only 16 flares to counter infrared-homing SA7 missiles; inside the plane there were electronic equipment used to search and intercept communication messages of the enemy, especially to search and locate the enemy's ARDF (airborne radio direction finding), which was extremely important since these signal-emitting machines were always present right beside the commanders of the combat troops in the battlefields. Right after the diameter of the target area (about 300 m) was determined, bombers (occasionally B-52s) would be dispatched to liquidate the target.

The Special Flight 259G, like any other special flights of the Squadron 259, was equipped with UH-1 helicopters for medical evacuations.

Below is the summary of information relating to the squadrons of Tactical Air Wing 33:

Units	Commanders	Names	Insignia
Squadron 314	Lieutenant-Colonel Đặng Ngọc Hiển	Thần Tiễn (Sacred Arrow)	
Squadron 429	Lieutenant-Colonel Cung Thăng An	Sơn Long (Mountain Dragon)	
Squadron 431	Lieutenant-Colonel Nguyễn Viết Xương	Phương Long (Phoenix Dragon)	
Squadron 716	First: Major Nguyễn Anh Tuấn Last: Lieutenant-Colonel Huỳnh Minh Thoại	Hoàng Long (Royal Dragon)	
Squadron 718	Lieutenant-Colonel Nguyễn Hữu Bách	Thiên Long (Divine Dragon)	
Special Flight 259G	Major Trần Quang Võ	Nhân Ái (Kindness)	

Tactical Air Wing 53

Figure 1.39. Insignia of Tactical Air Wing 53

Tactical Air Wing 53, with Colonel Huỳnh Văn Hiến as its Commander, also located at Tân Sơn Nhứt Airbase, had a total of 8 squadrons:

- 6 transport squadrons:
  - Squadron 413 with C-119 Flying Boxcar;
  - Squadrons 421, 423, and 425 with C-123 Provider
  - Squadrons 435 and 437 with C-130 Hercules
- 2 gunship squadrons: Squadron 819 with AC-119G Shadow and Squadron 821 with AC-119K Stinger.

Squadron 413, named Xích Long (Red Dragon), received 16 AC-119G Shadow in 1968, operated for 3 years and was dissolved at the end of 1971. All staff were transferred to Squadron 821 that was equipped with AC-119K Stinger.

Squadron 421 was created in April 1971 with Major Nguyễn Quế Sơn as its Commander. Squadron 423 was created in July 1971 with Major Mạc Hữu Lộc as its Commander. Squadron 425 was created in December 1974 with Major Nguyễn Thế Thân as its Commander. Each squadron was equipped with 16 C-123K airplanes. After 2 years of operation, there was a total of 10 of these 48 C-123K Provider that crashed including 4 were shot down by enemy fire. These 3 squadrons were dissolved at the beginning of 1973 and all C-123K were returned to the U.S. Army.[39]

Both squadrons 435 and 437 were equipped with 16 C-130 Hercules each.

The C-119 Flying Boxcar was a transport airplane, manufactured by Fairchild Company, and having 2 propeller engines:

Figure 1.40. C-119 Flying Boxcar Transport Airplane

The C-119 Flying Boxcar had the following specifications:[40]

- Length: 26.37 m
- Wingspan: 33.3 m
- Height: 8.08 m
- Weight: 18,053 kg
- Engines: 2 Pratt & Whitney propeller engines, 28-cylinder R-4360-20W type, 3,500 hp each
- Speed: cruise 174 km/h, maximum 242 km/h
- Ceiling: 7,300 m
- Range: 2,849 km
- Air crew: 5 persons including 2 pilots, 1 navigator, 1 radio operator, and 1 crew chief

- Transportation capacity: 67 soldiers, or 35 stretchers, or 12,500 kg of goods

The C-123 Provider was also a transport airplane, manufactured by Fairchild Company, and having 2 propeller engines:

Figure 1.41. C-123 Provider Transport Airplane

The C-123 Provider had the following specifications:[41]

- Length: 23.25 m
- Wingspan: 33.53 m
- Height: 10.39 m
- Weight: 16,042 kg
- Engines: 2 Pratt & Whitney propeller engines, R-2800-99W type, 2,500 hp each; or 2 General Electric J85-GE-17 turbojet engines, 2,850 lbf each
- Speed: cruise 278 km/h, maximum 367 km/h
- Ceiling: 6,430 m
- Range: 1,666 km
- Air crew: 4 persons
- Transportation capacity: 60 soldiers, or 50 stretchers, or 11,000 kg of goods

The C-130 Hercules, the largest transport airplane, with 4 propeller engines, was transferred by the US Army to the AFVN through the Enhance Plus military aid program after the Paris Accord was signed at the beginning of 1973.

Figure 1.42. C-130A Hercules Transport Airplane

The C-130A had the following specifications:[42]

- Length: 29.7 m
- Wingspan: 40.4 m
- Height: 11.6 m
- Weight: 34,400 kg
- Engines: 4 Allison T56-A-15 turboprops, 4,590 hp each
- Speed: cruise 540 km/h, maximum 592 km/h
- Ceiling: 7,700 m
- Range: 3,800 km
- Aircrew: 5 persons including 2 pilots, 1 navigator, 1 mechanic, 1 loadmaster
- Transportation capacity: 92 passengers, or 64 paratroopers, or 74 stretchers with 5 medical staff; 2-3 Humvees, or 2 M-113 personnel carriers, or 1 155-mm Howitzer

Squadron 821, a gunship squadron, named Tinh Long (Elite Dragon), was created at the beginning of 1973 at Tân Sơn Nhứt Airbase, when the U.S. Air Force transferred all AC-119K to the AFVN according to the "Enhance Plus" aid program after the Paris Accord was signed. In addition to the special flights located at Tân Sơn Nhứt Airbase to provide support to the III and IV Corps, Squadron 821 also had 2 more special flights, one located in Đà Nẵng Airbase to provide support to I Corps, and one located at Phù Cát Airbase ro provide support to II Corps.

After the retreat from II Corps in mid-March 1975, the special flight located at Phù Cát Airbase had to be relocated at Phan Rang Airbase, and after a few days it was moved to Tân Sơn Nhứt Airbase. Squadron 821 had the following commanding staff: [43, 44]

- Commander: Lieutenant-Colonel Hoàng Nuôi
- Deputy-Commander: Major Nguyễn Minh Nhựt
- Chief of Operations: Major Nguyễn Hồng Sơn
- Chief of Training: Captain Nguyễn Văn Chẩn
- Chief of Flight Safety: Captain Nguyễn Trọng Quỳnh (replacing Captain Nguyễn Phúc Hải killed in a training flight accident)

Squadron 821 had a 300-member staff including pilots, co-pilots, operators, mechanics, flare specialists, and gunners. Its sorties were always carried out at nights to provide direct fire supports to distant and isolated outposts under communist overwhelming ground attacks.

Squadron 821 was equipped with AC-119K Stinger gunships having the following specifications: [45]

Figure 1.43. AC-119K Stinger Gunship

- Length: 26.35 m
- Wingspan: 33.30 m
- Height: 8.12 m
- Weight: 18,200 kg

- Engines: 2 R-3350s propeller engines, 2,500 hp each

- Speed: cruise 130 km/h, maximum 330 km/h

- Range: 3,110 km

- Ceiling: 7,100 m

- Air crew: 10 persons including 1 pilot, 1 co-pilot, 1 navigator, 1 night observation sight (NOS) operator, 1 radar specialist, 1 mechanic, 1 flare specialist, and 3 gunners

- Armament and equipment: 4 SUU-11A 7.62 mm guns with 21,500 rounds of ammunition; later replaced by MXU-470/A guns; 2 M61-A1 20 mm guns with 3,000 rounds of ammunition (both types of guns were computer-operated); 24 MK-24 flares with LAU-74/A launcher; 3 types of radar: APQ-136 forward looking radar, AAD-4 forward looking infrared radar, and AN/APQ-133 beacon tracking radar; 1 APR-25/26 ECM (electronic countermeasures warning device)

In April 1975, just like a number of units of Air Division 1 were relocated to Tân Sơn Nhứt Airbase, Squadron 821 was still fighting and was sacrificed on the last day of the war, as reported in the following article: [46]

"... Khoảng 7 giờ sáng ngày 29 tháng 4, Tinh Long 7, chiếc AC-119K cuối cùng, đang tiêu diệt VC ở vòng đai phi trường Tân Sơn Nhứt, bị trúng hỏa tiễn SA-7 bốc cháy và nổ tung trên bầu trời, phi hành đoàn hy sinh..."

(Translation:

"... Around 7 a.m. of April 29, Tinh Long no. 7, the last AC-119K, while destroying the VCs on the edge of Tân Sơn Nhứt Airbase, was hit by a SA-7 missile, engulfed in flame and exploded in the air; the aircrew was sacrificed...")

Below is the summary of information about the squadrons of Tactical Air Wing 53:

Units	Commanders	Names	Insignia
Squadron 413	Not Found Yet	Xích Long (Red Dragon)	
Squadron 421	Major Nguyễn Quế Sơn	Not Found Yet	
Squadron 423	Major Mạc Hữu Lộc	Not Found Yet	
Squadron 425	Major Nguyễn Thế Thân	Not Found Yet	
Squadron 435	Lieutenant-Colonel Lâm Văn Phiếu	Not Found Yet	
Squadron 437	Lieutenant-Colonel Mạc Mạnh Cầu	Not Found Yet	
Squadron 819	First: Major Đặng Văn Đức Last: Lieu-tenant-Colonel Nguyễn Văn Hồng	Hắc Long (Black Dragon)	

Squadron 821	Lieutenant-Colonel Hoàng Nuôi	Tinh Long (Elite Dragon)	

Air Division 6

Figure 1.44. Insignia of Air Division 6

Air Division 6 was created in June 1972 in Pleiku, and later, after Ban Mê Thuột was overrun and II Corps had to retreat from Pleiku in mid-March 1975, was relocated to Phan Rang. Its Commander was Colonel Phạm Ngọc Sang, who, later, was promoted to Brigadier-General on April 1, 1974. General Sang graduated from Class 1 (Class Lê Văn Duyệt) of the Thủ Đức Reserve Officer School in June 1952 as a Second-Lieutenant. In October 1952, he passed the entrance examination to the Air Force, and was sent to France and Morocco to attend transport airplane pilot classes and was promoted to First-Lieutenant during that time. He came back to Vietnam at the beginning of 1955, was promoted to Captain in October and made Commander of the Liaison Flight (predecessor of the Special-Mission Squadron 314). Before becoming Commander of Air Division 6, he was Commander of the Nha Trang Air Force Training Center, and Commander of Tactical Air Wing 33 at Tân Sơn Nhứt Airbase.[47]

Figure 1.45. Brigadier-General Phạm Ngọc Sang

Air Division 6 had two Tactical Air Wings: Tactical Air Wing 72 and Tactical Air Wing 82.

Tactical Air Wing 72

Figure 1.46. Insignia of Tactical Air Wing 72

Tactical Air Wing 72, headquartered in Pleiku, with Lieutenant-Colonel Lê Bá Định as its first Commander and Lieutenant-Colonel Lê Văn Bút as its last Commander (Lieutenant-Colonel Bút was Commander of Helicopter Squadron 229), had the following squadrons: Observation Squadron 118, two Helicopter Squadrons 229 and 235, Fighter Squadron 530, and Special Flight 259B for medical evacuations.

Below is the summary information about these squadrons:

Units	Commanders	Names	Insignia
Squadron 118	First: Major Võ Công Minh Second: Lieutenant-Colonel Võ Ý Last (Acting): Major Nguyễn Văn Được	Bắc Đẩu (North Star)	
Squadron 229	First: Lieutenant-Colonel Lê Văn Bút Last: Lieutenant-Colonel Đoàn Văn Quang	Lạc Long (Wonderful Dragon)	
Squadron 235	First: Major Vĩnh Quốc Last: Lieutenant-Colonel Huỳnh Hải Hồ	Sơn Dương (Mountain Goat)	
Squadron 530	First: Major Tá Lê Bá Định Second: Major Nguyễn Văn Mười Last: Major Bạch Diễn Sơn	Thái Dương (Brightest Sun)	
Special Flight 259B	Captain Trịnh Viết Hảo	Nhân Ái (Kindness)	

Tactical Air Wing 82

Figure 1.47. Insignia of Tactical Air Wing 82

Tactical Air Wing 82, headquartered at Phù Cát Airbase (Province of Bình Định), with Lieutenant-Colonel Nguyễn Văn Trương as its first Commander, had the following squadrons: Squadron 241 equipped with CH-47 Chinook helicopters, Squadron 243 equipped with UH-1 helicopters, Squadron 532 equipped with A-37 jet fighters, and Special Flights 259A equipped with UH-1 for medical evacuations.

Below is the summary of information about these squadrons:

Units	Commanders	Names	Insignia
Squadron 241	Lieutenant-Colonel Đỗ Văn Hiếu	Thiên Bằng (Divine Eagle)	
Squadron 243	First: Lieutenant-Colonel Nguyễn Văn Thân Last: Lieutenant-Colonel Huỳnh Văn Bông	Mãnh Sư (Strong Lion)	

Squadron 532	Major Tá Lê Trai	Gấu Đen (Black Bear)	
Special Flight 259A	Major Nguyễn Hữu Nghề	Nhân Ái (Kindness)	

Among the 6 generals of the AFVN, Brigadier-General Phạm Ngọc Sang was the only one who was captured as a prisoner of war by the enemy at the Battle of Phan Rang on April 16, 1975, as reported by himself in his article about that Battle of Phan Rang:

"... Lúc 9 giờ tối, dưới sự hướng dẫn của Đại tá Lương, đoàn người bắt đầu rời Thôn Mỹ Đức. Chưa đi được bao xa thì bị phục kích. Tr/Tướng Nghi, Ông Lewis và tôi cùng một số quân nhân bị địch bắt. Chúng dẫn 3 chúng tôi ngược về Nha Trang sáng hôm sau. Trên đường tôi thấy rất nhiều xe địch nằm la liệt dọc hai bên đường, và từng nhóm đồng bào ngơ ngác, thất thểu, lang thang đi ngược trở về. Tôi bỗng cảm nhận rất có tội đối với đồng bào, vì làm tướng mà không giữ được thành. Ở tại Đồn điền Yersin 2 ngày, chúng đưa chúng tôi ra Đà Nẵng bằng đường bộ. Tại đây, ngày 22.4.1975 chúng đem phi cơ chở chúng tôi ra Bắc, giam tại nhà giam Sơn Tây nơi từng giam giữ tù binh Mỹ. Chúng thả Ông Lewis vào tháng 8.1975, Tr/Tướng Nghi vào năm 1988 và tôi năm 1992...." [48]

(Translation:

"... At 9 pm, under the guidance of Colonel Lương, our group began leaving the Village of Mỹ Đức. Not having gone far enough, we were fallen into an ambush, Lt-General Nghi, Mr. Lewis, and I together with a number of soldiers were captured by the enemy. They brought the three of us back to Nha Trang the next morning. On the way, we saw many of their trucks left on both sides of the road, and groups by groups of

our people wandering about back to where they had left. Suddenly, I felt very much guilty toward our people because, as a general, I had failed them by letting the fort lost to the enemy. After a two-day stay in the Yersin plantation, they brought us to Đà Nẵng by truck. There, on April 22, 1975, they brought us to the North by airplane, and put us in the Sơn Tây prison where they had kept the American POWS. They released Mr. Lewis in August 1975, Lt-General Nghi in 1988, and me in 1992...")

Support Units

In addition to the above-mentioned Tactical Air Wings, each Air Division had a Headquarter with all needed departments (Planning, Flight Safety, Personnel, Finances, Political Warfare…) and a number of dependent Air Wings as follows:

• 1 Air Wing for Maintenance and Supply having following name:

- Air Division 1: Air Wing 10 for Maintenance and Supply, at Đà Nẵng Airbase, with Colonel Nguyễn Bình Trứ as its last Commander (missing in action (?) when Đà Nẵng was lost)

- Air Division 2: Air Wing 20 for Maintenance and Supply at Nha Trang Airbase

- Air Division 3: Air Wing 30 for Maintenance and Supply at Biên Hòa Airbase, with Colonel Hoành (last name unknown) as its Commander

- Air Division 4: Air Wing 40 for Maintenance and Supply at Bình Thủy Airbase (Cần Thơ)

- Air Division 5: Air Wing 50 for Maintenance and Supply at Tân Sơn Nhứt Airbase

- Air Division 6: Air Wing 60 for Maintenance and Supply at Cù Hanh Airbase (Pleiku), with Lieutenant-Colonel Đỗ Hữu Sung as its Commander

• 1 (or 2) Air Wing for Base Support, according to the number of airbases within the area of responsibility of the Air Division:

- Air Division 1: Đà Nẵng Air Wing for Base Support

- Air Division 2: Nha Trang Air Wing for Base Support, and Phan Rang Air Wing for Base Support with Colonel Trần Đình Giao as its last Commander

- Air Division 3: Biên Hòa Air Wing for Base Support with Colonel Phùng Văn Chiêu as its last Commander

- Air Division 4: Bình Thủy (Cần Thơ) Air Wing for Base Support, with Lieutenant-Colonel (later promoted to Colonel) Bùi Quan Khương as its Commander

- Air Division 5: Tân Sơn Nhứt Air Wing for Base Support, with Colonel Nguyễn Trung Sơn as its last Commander

- Air Division 6: Pleiku Air Wing for Base Support, with Lieutenant-Colonel Phạm Bá Mạo as its Commander (also captured by the enemy together with Brigadier-General Pham Ngọc Sang in Phan Rang) and Phù Cát Air Wing for Support, with Colonel Phạm Hữu Phương as its Commander

Each Air Wing for Maintenance and Supply would have a number of Brigades for Maintenance, Supply and Ammunition. Each Air Wing for Base Support would have a number of Brigades for Support and Defense.

The organizational chart of Air Division 3 presented below would illustrate the organizational structure of an Air Division of the AFVN:

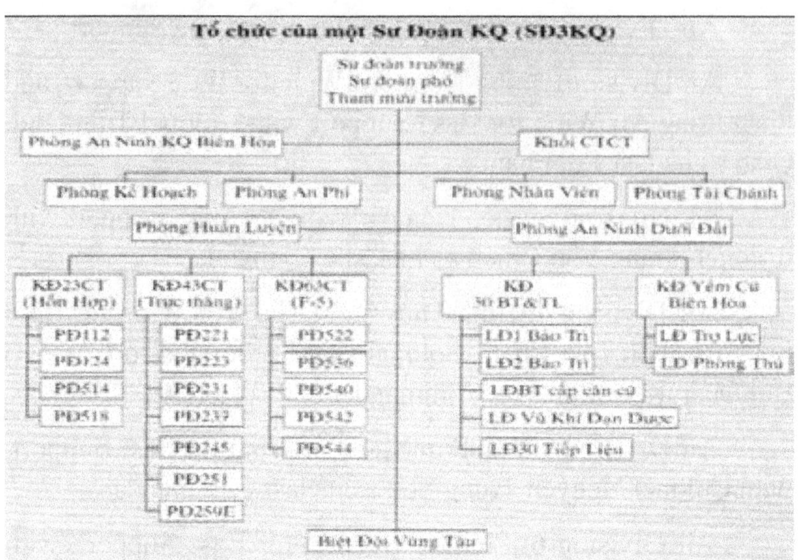

Organizational Chart of Air Division 3 of the AFVN

(Source: History of the Air Force of the Republic of Vietnam, p. 165)

Translation:

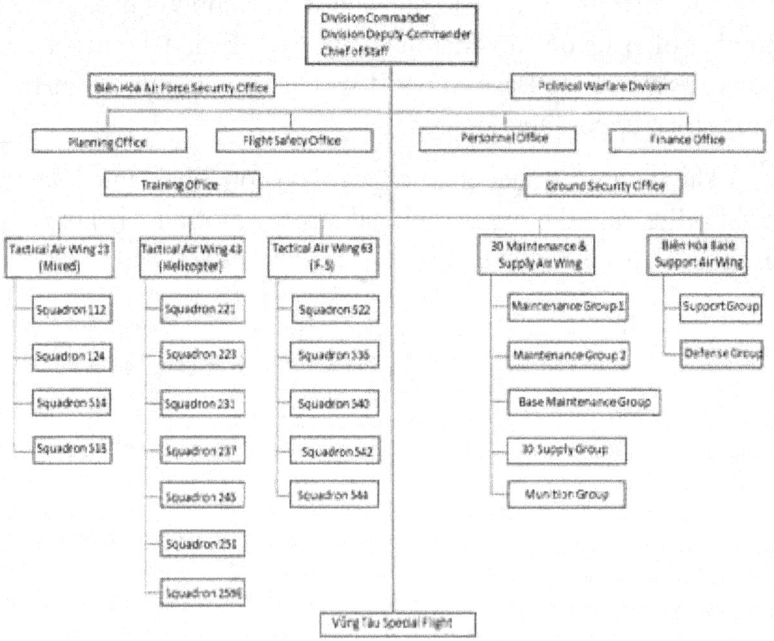

In addition to the 6 Air Divisions presented above, the AFVN also had 3 more big units equivalent to air divisions as follows:

- The Command of Technical and Supply Services, headquartered at Biên Hòa Airbase, and with Brigadier-General Từ Văn Bê as its Commander (from the beginning to the end).

- The Nha Trang Air Force Training Center at Nha Trang Airbase, with Brigadier-General Nguyễn Ngọc Oánh as its last Commander (General Oánh was also the first Commander of the Center when he was still a Captain when the French transferred it to the Armed Forces of the State of Vietnam on July 1, 1955)

- The Command of Air Force Operations, with Colonel Vũ Văn Ước as its last Commander.

Concluding Remarks

The AFVN was a very important service of the ARVN. It actively participated and made significant contribution in human lives in the fighting for the freedom of South Vietnam throughout the whole period of 20 years. Together with the other services of the ARVN, with the U.S. military aid, the AFVN had developed into a very strong air force, squarely compared with other air forces in the world. Regrettably, toward the end of the war, with serious cuts in aids from the U.S., the Air Divisions of the AFVN no longer had enough means to provide adequate support to the other services of the ARVN. The sacrifice in the last days of the war of the aircrew of an AC-119K gunship of Squadron 821 at Tân Sơn Nhứt Airbase on April 29, 1975, and the capture of Brigadier-General Phạm Ngọc Sang (while he had more than necessary means to escape), Commander of Air Division 6 in Phan Rang on April 16, 1975, were outstanding facts symbolizing the fighting spirit and the sharing of sacrifices with friendly forces by the soldiers of the AFVN.

CHAPTER TWO

The Four Incorruptible Generals of the ARVN: "First Thắng, Second Chinh, Third Thanh, Fourth Trưởng"

During the 1970s, in South Vietnam, there was a popular saying ***"Nhứt Thắng, Nhì Chinh, Tam Thanh, Tứ Trưởng = First Thắng, Second Chinh, Third Thanh, Fourth Trưởng,"*** which revealed the admiration of the people toward these four honest and incorruptible generals of the ARVN in a country where the corruption has become something commonplace among the political and military leaders.

First Thắng

The general who was first on the list was Lieutenant-General Nguyễn Đức Thắng (1930- 2020).

Figure 2.1. Lieutenant-General Nguyễn Đức Thắng

He was born in January 1930 in the Province of Cao Bằng, North Vietnam. He began attending Class I of the Nam Định Reserve Officer School on October 1, 1951 but after two weeks he was transferred to the Thủ Đức Reserve Officer School, and graduated on June 11, 1952 as a Second-Lieutenant in Artillery.

He moved up the ranks in the Army as follows:[1]

- First-Lieutenant in February 1953
- Captain in October 1954
- Major in 1955
- Lieutenant-Colonel in 1958
- Colonel in February 1961
- Brigadier-General on August 11, 1964
- Major-General on November 1, 1965
- Lieutenant-General on June 3, 1968

General Thắng was made Commander of a number of big units of the ARVN as follows:

- 1st Infantry Division: from January 1, 1961 to October 15, 1961
- 5th Infantry Division: from October 16, 1961 to December 19, 1962
- IV Corps: from February 29, 1968 to July 1, 1968

He was also a cabinet member of the two following successive governments:

- Nguyễn Cao Kỳ government: Commissioner for Rural Development from October 1, 1965 to November 8, 1967
- Nguyễn Văn Lộc government: Minister of Rural Development from November 9, 1967 to February 23, 1968

Within the South Vietnamese people, stories, anecdotes about his honesty and incorruptibility, about his love for the soldiers and for the people have been widely circulating for years, as follows:

"Có lần tướng Thắng đã cầm đầu một phái đoàn đi tham quan ngoại

quốc. Trên nguyên tắc, tùy thời hạn, mỗi sĩ quan trong phái đoàn đều được đổi mỗi người một ít ngoại tệ để tiêu xài và chánh phủ cho riêng một ít tiền túi. Còn ông tướng trưởng phái đoàn thì có thêm một ngân khoản gọi là "ngân sách tiếp tân." Khi ra nước ngoài, tướng Thắng đã không xử dụng số tiền tiếp tân của chánh phủ cấp phát. Lúc về nước, ông đã đem trả đủ số tiền không chi tiêu ấy vào ngân sách cho chánh phủ... Vốn là một sĩ quan to con, khỏe mạnh, hiếu động, tướng Thắng thích tự thân xông pha với các chiến sĩ của ông trong những cuộc hành quân bình định đại qui mô. Những dịp này, nếu có đồng bào hay thường dân từ trong những vùng quê xa xôi, hẻo lánh, mất an ninh, bồng bế, dắt díu nhau đi ra, tướng Thắng thường làm gương cho binh sĩ là đi bộ, nhường xe vận tải chở thường dân, nhất là đàn bà và trẻ thơ... Hôm ấy là dịp tướng Thắng, tư lệnh vùng, đi thị sát lãnh thổ trách nhiệm và hội họp bộ tham mưu tại tiểu khu Rạch Giá. Như thế, tất nhiên vị tiểu khu trưởng kiêm tỉnh trưởng địa phương, theo lệ thường, phải khoản đãi quan khách một bữa ăn thịnh soạn. Bữa ăn đó thường diễn ra trong tỉnh đường và do công quỹ đài thọ. Nhưng tướng Thắng đã không dự tiệc, mà lại ra ngồi ngoài xe Jeep, gân cổ lên "quạp" ổ bánh mì thịt to tổ nái."[2]

(Translation:

"Once he was head of a government delegation visiting a foreign country. In principle, based on the length of the visit, each officer was given some travel allowance as well as allowed to have some foreign currency for their own expenses. For the general head of the delegation, some special fund was provided for him to cover his own expenses for "public relations." During the visit, General Thắng did not spend this fund. After the trip, he gave back all the money to the Government's Treasury... Being himself an officer with a large body, very strong, and dynamic, he was always personally actively involved with his soldiers in those large pacification operations. During these times, if there were civilian people moving out with their children from those isolated and insecure areas, he always made examples for his soldiers by walking with them, never used his own Jeep, and ordered them to let the trucks transport the people, especially women and children... On that day, General Thắng, as Corps Commander, was making an inspection tour of

the area under his responsibility, and had a staff meeting at the sub-section of Rạch Giá. As usual, the sub- section chief / province chief, of course, had to provide a good and copious lunch. The meal was served in the administrative headquarter of the province, and paid for by the provincial budget. But General Thắng did not participate in the lunch. Instead, he went out to his Jeep and savored a big submarine sandwich he brought from his home.")

The Americans also heard of his reputation as a clean, honest, incorruptible, and serious, hard-working general. They respected and admired him. That was why both the military and civilian American personnel have actively supported him very much. An American author has observed:

"Thang had a reputation for honesty and hard work, which won him not only the respect of his American civilian and military advisors but also substantial American support for his revolutionary development campaign." [3]

The U.S. Central Intelligence Agency (CIA), in its numerous weekly reports on the Situation in South Vietnam, also had good remarks on his personality, behavior, and working method as well as on his thoughts regarding the rural development.

The CIA weekly report dated 24 October 1966, in Part II, Revolutionary Development (i.e., rural development) made the following remark:

"He was particularly critical of the "new life hamlet program" which was designed to provide security from Viet Cong incursions and to provide a "new life" to the peasant. Thang maintains that the latter goal of the program has not been successfully achieved and in his words, "has not provided a new life for the people in the hamlets." There has been no true social revolution, he asserted and "the Communists… have not been wiped out." Thang implied that government interference in the life of the peasants must be minimal and that hamlet residents should control their own programs. The Revolutionary Development Cadres, which he claims have

started to take hold in the provinces, should act mainly as an "emotional bridge" between the peasant and the government, according to Thang." [4]

Because of his honest, incorrupt nature, because of his straightforward and serious, hard- working behavior, in addition to his positive thoughts on rural development, and his strong support from the Americans, General Thắng, undoubtedly, was victim of other South Vietnamese generals' suspicion and jealousy, and he, therefore, has sometimes thought of resigning. One CIA weekly report has made the following remark:

"There is some indication that Minister of Revolutionary Development General Nguyen Duc Thang may be thinking of resigning his post because of criticism from other members of the Directorate... Part of the difficulty in Thang's relationship with other members of the Directorate may stem from the fact that he has received a great deal of support and praise from American advisers, which has probably generated envy and suspicion." [5]

At the beginning of 1968, he passed the Ministry of Rural Development over to Lieutenant-General Nguyễn Bảo Trị, and on February 29, 1968, he assumed the command of the IV Corps replacing Major-General Nguyễn Văn Mạnh. President Nguyễn Văn Thiệu, who did not like him since General Thắng, on behalf of other generals supporting Major-General Nguyễn Cao Kỳ, has tried to persuade him not to pursue his candidacy in the 1967 presidential election,[6] had been under great pressure from the American, and finally, reluctantly, accepted to appoint General Thắng, known for his incorruptibility to replace General Mạnh, notorious for his corruption. General Thắng, therefore, could not keep his command for long. He had to pass his command of IV Corps over to Major-General Nguyễn Viết Thanh on July 1st, 1968. He assumed the command of Artillery Service of the ARVN for a short time before being appointed Assistant for Planning for General Cao Văn Viên, Chief of General Staff, a powerless position. In 1973, he requested a non-salaried leave to go back to school, and was released from the Army at the end of the year. Toward the end of April 1975, he was recalled but was not appointed to any position in the Army yet when the Republic of Vietnam collapsed. After April 30th, 1975, he lived in the state of Connecticut, USA. He passed away in 2020 at the age of 90.

Second Chinh

The general listed no. 2 was Lieutenant-General Phan Trọng Chinh (1930-2014).

Figure 2.2. Lieutenant-General Phan Trọng Chinh

General Chinh was born on February 1, 1931 in the Province of Bắc Ninh, North Vietnam. He attended Class No. 5 of the Đà Lạt Inter-Arm Military Academy, and graduated on April 24, 1952 as a Second-Lieutenant.

He moved up the ranks of the Army as follows:[7]

- First-Lieutenant in January 1954
- Captain on September 29, 1954
- Major in September 1956

• Lieutenant-Colonel in December 1963
• Colonel on March 6, 1965
• Brigadier-General in 1966
• Major-General in 1968
• Lieutenant-General in 1973

During 1954-1956, he was the first Commander of the 3rd Airborne Battalion. At the end of November 1956, he was promoted to Major and held the position of Chief of Staff of the Airborne Brigade. On October 26, 1960, he left the Airborne Brigade and assumed the command of the Rangers. On November 11, 1960, he participated in the military coup under the leadership of Colonel Nguyễn Chánh Thi, Commander of the Airborne Brigade. The coup failed, he was arrested, tried by the Saigon Military Tribunal and sentenced to 18 years of labor work and sent to Côn Đảo Prison.

After the successful coup of November 1, 1963, overthrowing the Ngô Đình Diệm Government, he was freed by the Military Revolutionary Council. His sentence was abolished, he was promoted to Lieutenant-Colonel, and appointed Chief of the Province of Pleiku. On Machi 6, 1965, he was promoted to in-service Colonel when he was appointed Commander of the 25th Infantry Division.

It was during the period of time when he was Commander of the 25th Infantry Division that he left very clear marks of his great virtues: incorruptible, never abusing his power for personal or family gains, totally dedicated in his work and duty, loving his soldiers and sharing all dangers with them. Following are some anecdotes on these virtues of him, which have been circulating among South Vietnamese people:

"Trong suốt mấy năm liền đảm nhiệm trọng trách đó, tôi thấy tướng Chinh không mấy khi về Sài Gòn thăm gia đình vợ con và bạn bè. Ông bận lo thị sát chiến trường, thanh tra các địa phương. Một đặc điểm đáng nêu lên đây là tướng Chinh đi thanh sát toàn bằng xe, di chuyển trên

đường bộ, mặc dù vùng ông trấn đóng rất nguy hiểm. Bọn CS địa phương thường hay đặt mìn, bắn sẻ và phục kích từng toán lẻ tẻ. Thỉnh thoảng về thăm gia đình, vợ con, ông cũng dùng xe chớ không bao giờ dùng trực thăng như đa số các vị tướng lãnh khác. Đoàn xe của tướng Chinh di chuyển thường chỉ gồm có một chiếc Dodge 4x4 trí súng đại liên với mấy tay xạ thủ, một jeep ông ngồi cùng với tài xế và đại úy Đoàn, sĩ quan tùy viên của ông." [8]

(Translation:

"Throughout those successive years when he had that great responsibility, I rarely saw him go to Saigon to visit his family or his friends. He kept himself busy all the times making tours at the outposts of his troops, or inspecting different areas under his division's responsibility. It's really noteworthy that General Chinh made these trips always by cars, on the roads although the area under his responsibility was extremely dangerous. The local VC always laid mines, sniped, and ambushed small groups of ARVN. Occasionally when he went home to see his family, he also used cars and never used helicopter like the majority of other generals. His personal convoy usually consisted of a 4 x 4 Dodge equipped with machine guns and gunners, and his own Jeep with himself sitting in the front seat with the driver, and with Captain Đoàn, his orderly officer, siting in the back.")

"Khoảng năm 1966-67, đường Saigon – Đức Hòa còn là đường đất bụi. Hôm đó, tôi trên xe cứu thương, trương cờ Hồng Thập Tự mà chạy. Xe tôi đi sau một đoàn xe của quân đội, tôi bóp kèn, thì tất cả đều dạt vào trong. Nhưng đến xe đầu tiên thì tôi biết là xe của ông Tướng (vì có gắn ngôi sao), xe tôi không dám vượt qua. Nhưng tôi thấy Tướng Chinh vỗ vai người tài xế, và xe ông dạt vào trong cho xe tôi chạy. Đến tối, tôi xin gặp Trung Tướng và xin lỗi. Nhưng Tướng Chinh nói: "NGÔI SAO CỦA TÔI KHÔNG THỂ BẰNG SINH MẠNG CỦA MỘT THƯƠNG BINH". Câu nói đó đã chạm vào tim tôi, nước mắt tự rơi không kềm được. Một câu nói thật ngắn, gọn, nhưng sao hay trong văn chương, đẹp trong tình người đến như vậy." [9]

(Translation:

"Around 1966-67, the road between Saigon and Đức Hòa was still a dirt one. On that particular day, I was in the ambulance rushing with a Red Cross flag on it. We were behind a military convoy. We blew the horn and every truck of the convoy yielded the way for the ambulance. When we reached to the first vehicle of the convoy, I knew right away that it was the general's jeep (because of the star on the plate). We dared not pass it. But right at that moment I saw the general pat the driver's shoulder, and the jeep yielded the way for the ambulance too. In the evening, I came, asked to see the general and apologized to him. But General Chinh said: ***"MY STAR IS NOTHING COMPARED TO THE LIFE OF A WOUNDED SOLDIER."*** *I was deeply moved by his statement and the tears came down uncontrollably. A short statement but so eloquent, beautiful, and full of compassion."*)

With such straightforwardness, General Chinh just could not avoid having some confrontations with a number of U.S. advisors, who expressed contempt (or sometimes even insulted) toward the ARVN. Because of those unpleasant incidents, the Americans did not like him, and, thus, they did not give him good evaluations in their reports. Following is a distorted remark about General Chinh in a CIA report:

> ***"The controversial commander of the ARVN 25th Division, General Phan Trong Chinh has stepped-up the tempo of hamlet construction to one month, and consolidation phases to one and one-half months. Chinh's order has been issued in an apparent attempt to make the pacification effort in his area look good."*** [10]

Naturally, this kind of remark about General Chinh from the Americans, had certainly some influence on the GVN leadership. Following is a clear proof of President Nguyễn Văn Thiệu's decision not to appoint him Commander of II Corps in April 1972:

"MR 2 commander Gen. Ngo Dzu simply panicked and fled from Corps headquarters at Pleiku to coastal Nha Trang, leaving the de facto leadership of ARVN forces in the interior to MR 2 senior adviser John Paul Vann… Thieu was considering replacing him with a known incompetent named Phan Trong Chinh. Acting on an ostensibly spontaneous impulse, Bunker sent Thieu a list of candidates on which Chinh's name did not appear. Thieu picked one that did, that of Gen. Nguyen Van Toan." [11]

After he left the 25th Infantry Division, General Chinh was appointed to the following successive positions:

- Vice-Commander of III Corps, 1968
- Commander of the Directorate General of Military Instruction, 1969-1973
- Commander of the Command and Staff School, 1974-1975

After April 30, 1975, he lived in Rockville, Maryland, USA. He passed away on November 17, 2014 in Vienna, Virginia, USA, at the age of 85. His funeral was celebrated very solemnly with all the honors reserved for a general of the ARVN.

Third Thanh

The third general on the list was Major-General Nguyễn Viết Thanh (1931-1970).

Figure 2.3. Major-General Nguyễn Viết Thanh

General Thanh was born on March 31, 1931 in Tân An, Province of Long An. He attended Class 4 of the Đà Lạt Inter-Arm Military Academy, and graduated on December 1, 1951 as a Second-Lieutenant. He moved up the ranks of the Army as follows:[12]

- First-Lieutenant in December 1953
- Captain in 1955
- Major on October 26,1959
- Lieutenant-Colonel in 1964
- In-service Colonel on October 9, 1965
- Colonel in December 1965
- Brigadier-General on June 19, 1966
- Major-General June 19, 1968

He was made commander of the following combat units:

- Platoon 12, Company 51, Vietnamese 15th Battalion, in December 1951
- Company 51, 15th Battalion, end of 1952
- Local Battalion 707 in 1953
- Regiment 12, 7th Infantry Division in 1962
- 7th Infantry Division October 9, 1965
- IV Corps on July 1, 1968

Within the ARVN, he had the reputation of an exemplary, clean, incorruptible officer with many anecdotal stories, as reflected in the following passage:

"Vào giữa năm 1968, Thiếu Tướng Nguyễn Viết Thanh được bổ nhiệm làm Tư Lệnh Quân Đoàn IV, Quân Khu IV. Lúc đó tôi làm Tổng Thư Ký Hội Đồng Tái Thiết Phát Triển kiêm Trung Tâm Trưởng Trung Tâm Điều Hợp Tỉnh Kiên Giang. Hàng tháng tôi thường về họp tại Trung Tâm Điều Hợp Quân Khu do Đại Tá Phạm Văn Út làm Trung Tâm Trưởng và thỉnh thoảng có ghé qua thăm Thiếu Tướng Thanh. Nhân một buổi họp cuối năm, tôi có chở theo vài món đặc sản Rạch Giá như nước mắm nhĩ Phú Quốc, khô cá thiều và một ít bánh ú lá dừa biếu gia đình ông. Vì biết tôi có quà cho Tướng Thanh nên Trung Tá Tỉnh Trưởng Kiên Giang

cũng nhờ tôi chở theo một số quà biếu Tư Lệnh. Ông nghe tiếng Thiếu Tướng Thanh rất thanh liêm, không ưa vụ biếu xén quà cáp, nên ông không dám đích thân đi biếu mà nhờ tôi là chỗ thày trò cũ, may ra được nhận chăng? Hôm đó sau buổi họp ở văn phòng Đại Tá Út, tôi qua thăm Tư Lệnh. Thiếu Tướng Thanh niềm nở tiếp tôi, hỏi thăm chuyện vợ con, hỏi thăm Thiếu Tướng Khuyên, rồi ông nói: "Bây giờ cũng trưa rồi, Quý qua bên nhà ăn cơm với vợ chồng tôi nhé, ăn chay đó." Tôi thưa: "Cám ơn Thiếu Tướng, hôm nay đàn em không xin được trực thăng, phải đi đường bộ, về trễ sợ nguy hiểm, lần sau sẽ xin ghé tư dinh thăm chị luôn." Tôi tranh thủ trình bày vụ biếu quà, ông bảo: "Thôi được, món nào của anh thì tôi nhận, nhưng chỉ lần này thôi nhé. Còn của anh Tỉnh Trưởng thì anh đem về nói là tôi rất cám ơn, nên đem mấy món quà đó tặng cho anh em thương bệnh binh nhân dịp Tết cho họ mừng. Đó là điều mà cấp chỉ huy nên làm." Bất giác tôi chợt nhớ đến cái Tết 10 năm trước ở Vĩnh Bình. Sáng mồng một Tết, ông cùng Thiếu Tá Khuyên vào bệnh viện tỉnh thăm thương bệnh binh. Rồi suốt ngày mồng hai Tết, ông hết đứng lại ngồi đăm chiêu trước bản đồ hành quân để nghiên cứu địa hình và tình hình địch. Hình như ông nóng lòng trông cho mau đến ngày mồng 3, hết hạn hưu chiến để tổ chức hành quân Bình Định. Cuộc đời của ông chỉ biết phục vụ, phục vụ và phục vụ, chí công vô tư, xả thân vì nước." [13]

(Translation:

"In mid-1968, Major-General Nguyễn Viết Thanh was appointed Commander of IV Corps. At that time, I was Secretary-General of the Reconstruction Council and Head of the Coordination Center of the Province of Kiên Giang. I had monthly meetings at the Corps Coordination Center with the Head of the Center, Colonel Pham Văn Út, and, occasionally, I came to see Major-General Thanh. On the occasion of one year-end meeting, I brought some special products of Rạch Giá, such as Phú Quốc fish sauce, giant catfish dried fish, coconut leaf-wrapped pyramidal plain rice cakes for his family. Because he knew that I would bring something as a gift for General Thanh, the Lieutenant-Colonel Province Chief of Rạch Giá asked me to also bring something for the General. He had heard of General Thanh's incorruptibility, his dislike of subordinates' offering of gifts. He dared not to present his offerings himself, and thought

that maybe if his offerings were presented by me, General Thanh could accept them out of his teacher-student relationship with me. On that day, after my meeting with Colonel Út in his office, I went to see The Commander. General Thanh received me very warmly, asking me about my family, requesting me to convey his health wishes to Major-General Khuyên, and then said: "It's now almost noon, Quý, come to my home and have a vegetarian lunch with me and my wife." I answered him: "My General, thank you so much, but I can't. Today I can't get a helicopter lift back home, I will have to go back by road. I'm afraid that it will be a bit late and dangerous. Next time I will come to your home and see your wife too." I immediately presented the gifts to him, and General Thanh said: "All right! I accept what you've brought for my family, and this time only, there won't be a next time, OK? Now, for those things from the Province Chief, bring them back to him, tell him I thank him very much, but he should donate them to the wounded soldiers as Tết holiday gifts, they will be very happy. That is something a commander should be doing." Suddenly, memories of Tết 10 years ago in Vĩnh Bình flashed back. I remember that on the morning of the First Day of Tết, together with Major Khuyên, he came to the hospital to visit the wounded soldiers. And then he spent all day of the Second Day of Tết, sometimes sitting at his desk, sometimes standing facing and thinking deeply in front of the operational map, studying the area on the map and the enemy situation. It looked like he was wishing that the Third Day of Tết would pass quickly, the truce would be over so that he could begin his pacification operation. All his life the only thing he had in mind was to serve, to serve, and to serve, honestly, and being ready to sacrifice for the country.")

In addition to his integrity and incorruptibility, just like Generals Thắng and Chinh, General Thanh also had another reputation for his closeness and loving care of the people during the times he was the Province Chief of Long An (1961) and Gò Công (1963), resulting in the following unimaginable story recounted by an American, Major-General George S. Eckhardt, Senior IV Corps advisor:

"Gen. Thanh's senior IV Corps adviser in 1968 and 1969, Major General George S. Eckhardt, recounted another tale of Thanh's popularity. On one occasion the two generals flew to My Tho, Thanh's former divisional headquarters, in search of a quiet lunch. But when word of their arrival got out, townspeople crowded into the restaurant to welcome their former commander. For forty-five minutes Gen. Thanh bowed and shook hands with the stream of well-wishers; most South Vietnamese senior officers never fraternized with their peasant soldiers or with the rural population." [14]

Beside these above-mentioned virtues, General Thanh was also respected by the soldiers under his command for his almost legendary bravery in battles. He was one of only a few ARVN generals who was awarded the highly-honorable Silver Star as a Corps Commander as we can see in the following citation:

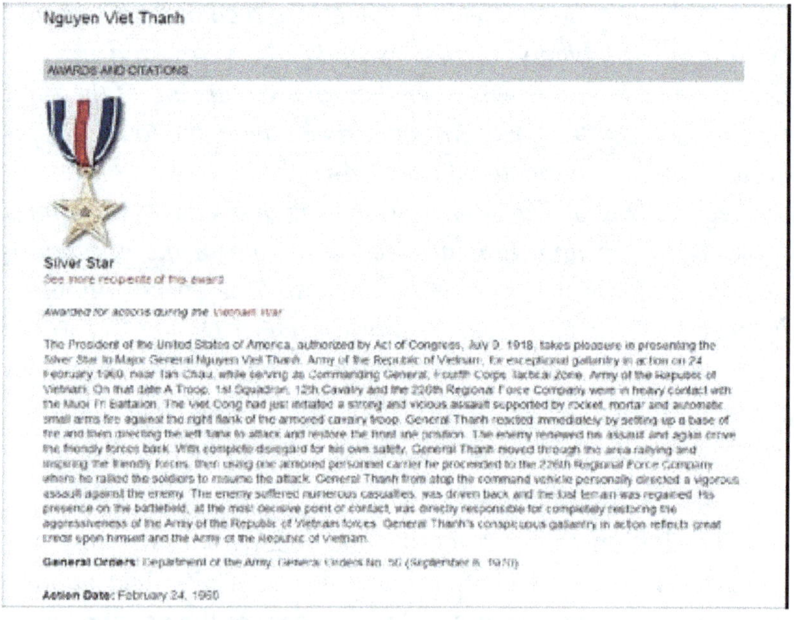

Nguyen Viet Thanh

AWARDS AND CITATIONS

Silver Star

See more recipients of this award

Awarded for actions during the Vietnam War

The President of the United States of America, authorized by Act of Congress, July 9, 1918, takes pleasure in presenting the Silver Star to Major General Nguyen Viet Thanh, Army of the Republic of Vietnam, for exceptional gallantry in action on 24 February 1969, near Tan Chau, while serving as Commanding General, Fourth Corps Tactical Zone, Army of the Republic of Vietnam. On that date A Troop, 1st Squadron, 12th Cavalry and the 220th Regional Force Company were in heavy contact with the Muoi Tri Battalion. The Viet Cong had just initiated a strong and vicious assault supported by rocket, mortar and automatic small arms fire against the right flank of the armored cavalry troop. General Thanh reacted immediately by setting up a base of fire and then directing the left flank to attack and restore the front line position. The enemy renewed his assault and again drove the friendly forces back. With complete disregard for his own safety, General Thanh moved through the area rallying and inspiring the friendly forces, then using one armored personnel carrier he proceeded to the 226th Regional Force Company where he rallied the soldiers to resume the attack. General Thanh from atop the command vehicle personally directed a vigorous assault against the enemy. The enemy suffered numerous casualties, was driven back and the lost terrain was regained. His presence on the battlefield, at the most decisive point of contact, was directly responsible for completely restoring the aggressiveness of the Army of the Republic of Vietnam forces. General Thanh's conspicuous gallantry in action reflects great credit upon himself and the Army of the Republic of Vietnam.

General Orders: Department of the Army, General Orders No. 50 (September 8, 1970)

Action Date: February 24, 1969

Citation presented at the same time with the Silver Star Medal awarded to Major-General Nguyễn Viết Thanh, Commander of IV Corps for his exceptionally brave action on February 24, 1969 in Tân Châu

On May 2, 1970, at 1:40 pm, while inspecting the battle front along Vietnam-Cambodia border, he was killed when his helicopter collided with a Cobra helicopter. He was promoted posthumously to Lieutenant-General and awarded the Second-Class Bảo Quốc Huân Chương (National Order Medal).

Fourth Trưởng

The general listed as Number 4 was Lieutenant-General Ngô Quang Trưởng (1929-2007).

Figure 2.4. Lieutenant-General Ngô Quang Trưởng

He was born on December 13, 1929 in the Province of Bến Tre (later, renamed Kiến Hòa). He attended Class 4 of the Thủ Đức Reserve Officer School, graduated on June 1, 1954 as a Second-Lieutenant, and volunteered to join the Airborne as a Platoon Commander of the 5th Airborne Battalion.

He moved up the ranks in the Army as follows:[15]

- First-Lieutenant on December 1, 1955
- Captain in 1961
- Major in 1964
- Lieutenant-Colonel in April 1965

• Colonel on June 19, 1966
• Brigadier-General on February 4, 1967
• Major-General on June 3, 1968
• Lieutenant-General on November 1, 1971

He was well-known as a general who was exemplary in military discipline, extremely dedicated to his duties, and always present at hot points within his area of responsibility, as presented in the following descriptive passage:

"Tư-Lệnh Quân-Đoàn I & Quân-Khu I Ngô Quang Trưởng được hầu hết mọi người khâm-phục. Ông đã dành nhiều tâm-trí, công-sức, và thì-giờ vào các cuộc hành-quân hơn là vào công việc văn-phòng. Ông thường-xuyên mặc chiến-phục, đội mũ sắt, mang áo giáp, bay đến tận từng đồn + chốt khắp Quân-Khu, để quan-sát, nghiên-cứu tình-hình tại chỗ, và kiểm-tra tác-phong, kỷ-luật của các cấp quân-nhân. Bản-thân ông ít thích truy-hoan, nên cấm sĩ-quan thuộc quyền đến khiêu-vũ ở các nhà hàng ca + vũ + nhạc, khiến các Tỉnh-Trưởng và Thị-trưởng cấm luôn cả các phòng trà ca-nhạc tổ chức khiêu-vũ cho bất cứ giới khách hàng nào." [16]

(Translation:

"General Ngô Quang Trưởng, Commander of I Corps & Region 1, was respected and admired by almost everyone. He reserved more of his time, his energy and his thoughts for military operations than for the paper work in his office. Always in combat fatigue, wearing a helmet and an anti-bullet vest, he flew to every outpost all over I Corps in order to be able to study the conditions and the situations on the spot, and to inspect behavior and discipline of his men. He himself did not like to spend time at bars and clubs, and, thus, he forbade his subordinates to come to dancing, bars and clubs. The province chiefs, therefore, also forbade clubs to organize dancing to even civilian clients.")

He also had the reputation of a clean, incorruptible general, who did not tolerate his subordinates to do bad things or to steal from the people, as illustrated in the following anecdote:

"Trong giữa năm 1974, Ông đã có một hành động rất ngoạn mục. Lính của một sư đoàn tại vùng I đã lùa một đàn bò của dân chúng, đem cất giấu tại thung lũng Quế Sơn. Khi nghe dân chúng tố cáo, ông đích thân bay đi tìm và đem trao trả cho khổ chủ. Số bò còn thiếu, ông trừ lương từ Trung Đoàn Trưởng đến binh sĩ, lấy tiền mua bò trả đủ số cho dân, không dung dưỡng bao che các việc làm mờ ám của thuộc cấp, như một số các vị chỉ huy khác." [17]

(Translation:

"In mid-1974, he had a very spectacular action. The soldiers of one division of I Corps had stolen a herd of cows, and hidden them in the valley of Quế Sơn. When he heard of the accusation by the people, he personally flew over the area and searched for the cows, retrieved and returned them to the owner. He also ordered to deduct money from the salaries of the responsible people, from the regiment commander down to the soldiers, and used such money to buy cows to replace the missing ones. The whole incident showed very clearly that he did not tolerate or cover for his subordinates in their wrongdoings like other commanders.")

He was also one among a very small number of generals, who did not have any political ambition, and who were never involved in political conspiracies and events. He rcserved all his time for military duties. Like General Thanh, General Trưởng was among a few generals of the ARVN, who has commanded combat units from the lowest to the highest levels:

• Commander of platoon: July 1954 (a platoon of the 5th Airborne Battalion)

• Commander of company: beginning of 1955 (1st Company, 5th Airborne Battalion)

• Commander of battalion: in 1961 (5th Airborne Battalion)

• Commander of Division: in 1966 (1st Infantry Division)

• Commander of corps: in 1972 (IV Corps and I Corps)

He had participated in many important battles while still serving in the Airborne, but he was most famous with the Battle of Hắc Dịch occurring in February 1965. At that time, he was still a Major and Commander of the 5th Airborne Battalion. Hắc Dịch was a secret zone of the 7th Viet Cong Division located in the dense forest North of Ông Trịnh Mountain, in the Province of Phước Tuy (formerly, Bà Rịa). This operation, attacking the Hắc Dịch secret zone, was organized by the III Corps, with the objective to annihilate the communist forces that had caused heavy damages to the 4th Marines Battalion in the Battle of Bình Giả (close to the Hắc Dịch secret zone) at the end of 1964 and the beginning of 1965. It was code-named Operation Nguyễn Văn Nho, (after the Commander of the 4th Marines Battalion, who had been killed in action at Bình Giả), and started on February 9, 1965. Among the forces participating in this operation, there was the 2nd Airborne Brigade under the Command of Lieutenant-Colonel Trương Quang Ân (later, Brigadier-General, Commander of the 23 Infantry Division, and killed in a helicopter accident on September 8, 1968). The 2nd Airborne Brigade included 3 battalions with the 5th Airborne Battalion of Major Ngô Quang Trưởng being the principal force. The 5th Airborne Battalion inflicted heavy damages to the two Viet Cong regiments of Q761 and Q762, with:

"hằng trăm xác cộng quân tràn ngập chung quanh tuyến phòng thủ, đầy dẫy hằng trăm vũ khí đủ loại từ AK47, súng trường CKC, súng chống chiến xa B40, B41 đến trung liên nồi, đại liên 12.8 ly, cối 61 ly, đạn dược quân trang quân dụng nhiều vô kể." [18]

(Translation:

"*hundreds of Communist soldiers killed around their defense lines, hundreds of weapons of all kinds from sub-machine guns AK-47, CKC rifles, antitank B-40, B-41, to 12.8-mm machine guns, to 61-mm mortars, and uncountable all kind of ammunitions and euipment.")*

Major Ngô Quang Trưởng was promoted at the battlefield to Lieutenant-Colonel and awarded Fourth-Class Bảo Quốc Huân Chương (National Order Medal). After this battle, he left the 5th Airborne Battalion, and was transferred to the Headquarters of the Airborne Brigade and served as its Chief of Staff, and, in the following year of 1966, when the Airborne Brigade was made a division, he was nominated Division Deputy-Commander.

However, for the majority of the people of the RVN, he was most famous for his victory of keeping Huế and recapture of Quảng Trị during the Communist general offensive called The Easter Offensive in the summer of 1972 when President Nguyễn Văn Thiệu appointed him Commander of I Corp replacing Lieutenant-General Hoàng Xuân Lãm.

Around noon of Thursday, March 30, 1972, during the Easter Holiday, Communist forces began their general offensive called the Easter Offensive all over the territory of the RVN. At the borders right at the south of the 17th Parallel, after a series of intensive artillery bombardments, three North Vietnamese main force divisions (Divisions 304, 308, and 320B), crossed the DMZ (Demilitarized Zone), attacked the northern and western areas of the Province of Quảng Trị. The responsibility for the protection of the Province of Quảng Trị belonged to the 3rd Infantry Division under the command of Brigadier-General Vũ Văn Giai (a graduate from the 10th Class of the Đà Lạt Inter-Arm Military Academy). The 3rd Infantry Division included three regiments (the 2nd, the 56th and the 57th), and was reinforced with two Marines Brigades (the 147th, and the 258th). All military installations and fire-support bases of the 3rd Infantry Division were tragically overrun with the surrender of the whole 56th Regiment at Camp Carroll under the command of Lieutenant-Colonel Phạm Văn Đính (a graduate of the 9th Class of the Thủ Đức Reserve Officer School in 1960), which made a great impact on the ARVN and the Allied Forces. On May 1st, 1972, the Province of Quảng Trị fell, the 3rd Infantry Division disintegrated and had to retreat toward Hue in the South. The population joined its retreat and were brutally attacked by the enemy, resulting in a horrible massacre, called ***"The Highway of Horror"*** on the part of the National Route No.1 between Quảng Trị and Thừa Thiên (Hue). The large and uncontrolled influx of people and soldiers also caused a total chaos in the imperial city of Huế, with a large number of undisciplined soldiers terrorizing the population by their stealing, and abusing. In addition to the chaotic situation in the city, the people of Huế were also afraid of the possibility of Huế falling into the enemy forces, and remembered the terrible massacre occurring in Huế during the Tết Offensive in 1968. As a result, they tried to escape from Huế by all means and, thus, made this chaotic situation much worse.

On May 3rd, 1972, President Nguyễn Văn Thiệu nominated Lieutenant-General Ngô Quang Trưởng Commander of I Corps to replace Lieutenant-General Hoàng Xuân Lãm. Right in the afternoon of that day, General Trưởng, together with his staff, flew immediately to Huế. On the next day, he issued two very important orders: 1) To establish the Forward Headquarters of I Corps at north of Huế, with the responsibility to stop all attacks of Communist forces; and 2) All soldiers, having left their units, missing their units, losing their units, must report immediately to the nearest military authority; any soldier refusing to obey this order will be shot on the spot. The order was re-established right away within the city. At the same time, rumor began circulating that ***"General Trưởng Is Back!"*** and the population were calmed down and stopped their escape from Huế. This was not a strange story since the people of Huế still remembered very clearly General Trưởng's determination and his military talent during the Tết Offensive when the whole city had fallen to the Communists and he kept fighting with his soldiers of the 1st Infantry Division from its headquarters in the Fort of Mang Cá within the imperial City of Huế, and later organized the counterattack to liberate Huế. During the whole course of the Vietnam War, one never witnessed this phenomenon: ***just one individual can make a clear change of the whole course of the war like this.***

After having stabilized the situation and stopped the enemy's attack into the Province of Thừa Thiên and the City of Huế, General Trưởng immediately planned the counterattack to recapture Quảng Trị.[19] The enemy forces occupying the Đinh Công Tráng Old Citadel of Quảng Trị Province resisted fiercely. General Trưởng had to use the two most combat-experienced divisions of the ARVN, the Airborne and the Marines Divisions, to recapture Quảng Trị. This battle became the bloodiest one for both sides during the Vietnam War. Finally, it was the soldiers of the 2nd Company, 3rd Battalion, 147th Brigade of the South Vietnamese Marines Division, who raised the RVN flag on top of the Đinh Công Tráng Old Citadel at:

"vào lúc 12 giờ 45 ngày 16/9/1972 sau 51 ngày đêm nhận lãnh trách nhiệm mà Sư Đoàn Dù giao lại và sau 78 ngày cuộc Hành quân tái chiếm Quảng trị được khởi sư."[20]

(Translation:

"at 12:45 pm of September 16, 1972 after 51 days and nights taking the responsibility turned over by the Airborne Division and after 78 days since the start of the operation to recapture Quảng Trị.")

General Trưởng's ability to lead and maneuver forces at great unit levels was not only famous among the South Vietnamese generals but also respected even by the American generals who had been fighting in Vietnam. The following comments by an American author succinctly but totally accurately described General Trưởng's personality and military talent:

"He was considered one of the most honest and capable generals of the South Vietnamese army during the long war in Southeast Asia. General Bruce Palmer described him in his book The 25-Year War as a "tough, seasoned, fighting leader" and "probably the best field commander in South Vietnam."[21]

After April 30, 1975, General Trưởng settled down in Virginia, USA. He passed away on January 22, 2007 in Fairfax, Virginia, USA, and his funeral was celebrated by the Vietnamese community very solemnly with all the honors reserved for a general of the ARVN. According to his wills, General Ngô Quang Trưởng's ashes were brought by his family back to Vietnam and spread over the Hải Vân Pass.[22]

Concluding Remarks

The history of the RVN lasted only about 20 years, and the RVN was constantly at war. Almost all families had their members serving in the armed forces. As the war was nearing the end, the role of the generals became more and more important. A not too small number of generals have been corrupted and have become rich, sometimes even on the sacrifices of the soldiers under their commands. The people were very dissatisfied with their corruptions. Therefore, they were very keen in their observations of the incorruptible generals, and finally "ranked" them in this order: ***"First Thắng, Second Chinh, Third Thanh, Fourth Trưởng."*** And all these four selected generals really deserved the people's admiration for them.

CHAPTER THREE

Heroic Defense of An Lộc in Summer 1972

The Summer of 1972 witnessed a general offensive of the Communist forces in South Vietnam on three fronts: 1) In the Province of Quảng Trị, right south of the DMZ (Demilitarized Zone) in Military Region I; 2) In the Province of Kontum in the Central Highlands of the Military Region II; and, 3) In the Province of Bình Long of the Military Region III. This Chapter discusses only the heroic defense of the ARVN in An Lộc, the capital town of the Province of Bình Long.

Orders of Battle

On the Communist side, there were the following units:

• 3 Divisions (the 5th, 7th, and 9th); each division had 3 regiments: the 5th had the E6, 174th, and 275th; the 7th had the 141st, 165th, and 209th; the 9th had the 271st, 272nd, and 95C

• 2 Independent Regiments: the 101st, and the 205th

• Artillery Division 69 with 2 Regiments, the 42nd and the 208th

• Anti-aircraft Regiment 271st

• Armored Regiment 203rd

• Special Weapons Regiment 202nd

• Sapper Group 429th

On the ARVN side, there were the following units:

• 5th Infantry Division with 2 Regiments (the 7th and 8th; the 9th Regiment had been erased after the Battle of Lộc Ninh)
• 52nd Regiment of 18th Infantry Division
• 3rd Ranger Brigade with 3 Battalions, the 31st, 36th, and 52nd
• Regional Forces and Militia units of Sub-District Bình Long
• Later: reinforcement included 1st Airborne Brigade (including 3 Battalions, the 5th, 6th, and 8th), 81st Commando Airborne Brigade, the whole 21st Infantry Division, and the 15th Regiment of the 9th Infantry Division

Summary of Information on Military Region III, Province of Bình Long and Town of An Lộc

The territory of Military Region III included 11 provinces of the Eastern part of Cochinchina under the defense responsibility of the III Corps with 3 infantry divisions located as follows:

• 5th Infantry Division: headquartered at Lai Khê, and responsible for the 3 Provinces of Bình Dương, Bình Long, and Phước Long
• 18th Infantry Division: headquartered at Xuân Lộc, and responsible for the 5 Provinces of Biên Hòa, Bình Tuy, Gia Định, Long Khánh, Phước Tuy, and the Special District of Vũng Tàu
• 25th Infantry Division: headquartered at Đồng Dù (Củ Chi), and responsible for the 3 Provinces of Hậu Nghĩa, Long An, and Tây Ninh

In April 1972, the Commander of III Corps was Lieutenant-General Nguyễn Văn Minh.[1] General Minh had been nominated on February 23, 1971 to replace Lieutenant-General (later, posthumously promoted to General) Đỗ Cao Trí, who was killed in a helicopter accident.

Figure 3.1. Lieutenant-General Nguyễn Văn Minh, Commander of III Corps

The 5th Infantry Division, responsible for the Province of Bình Long, under the command of Brigadier-General Lê Văn Hưng[2] and his Deputy, colonel Lê Nguyên Vỹ,[3] had 3 regiments:

- 7th Regiment, with Lieutenant-Colonel Lý Đức Quân as Commander, and headquartered in Phú Giáo
- 8th Regiment, with Colonel Mạch Văn Trường[4] as Commander, and headquartered in Dầu Tiếng
- 9th Regiment, with Colonel Nguyễn Công Vĩnh as Commander, and headquartered in Lộc Ninh

Figure 3.2. Brigadier-General Lê Văn Hưng, Commander of 5th Infantry Division

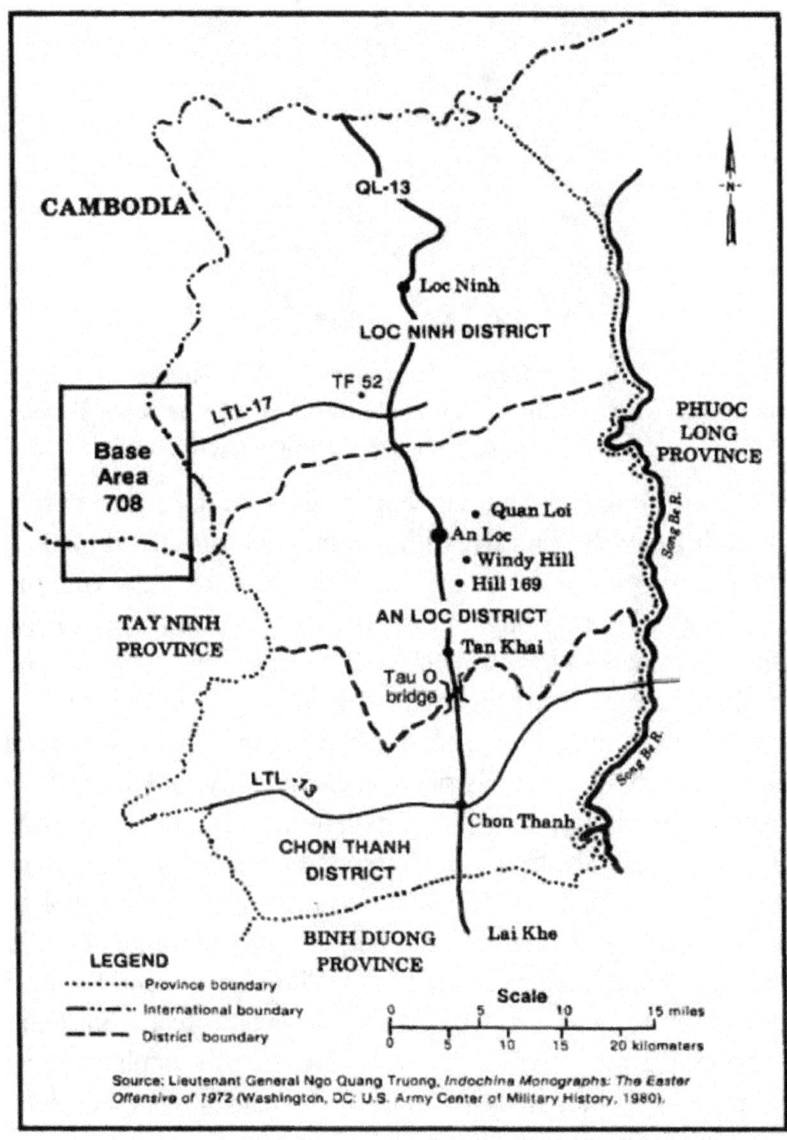

Figure 3.3. Map of Province of Bình Long

Figure 3.4. Brigadier-General Lê Nguyên Vỹ, Commander of 5th Infantry Division – At the time of the Battle of An Lộc, he was Colonel, Deputy-Commander of 5th Infantry Division

Bình Long was a province located at the northwest corner of the Military Region III, with a population of around 60,000, bordering with Cambodia on the north and northwest, with the Province of Phước Long on the east, with the Province of Bình Dương on the south, and with the Province of Tây Ninh on the south-east. It had three districts: Lộc Ninh in the north, An Lộc in the middle, and Chơn Thành in the South. The Town of An Lộc, located within the District of An Lộc, the capital town of the Province of Bình Long, with a population of around 15,000, was only about 100 km from Sài Gòn in the south. The main highway of Binh Long was the National Route 13, running north-south, from the Cambodian border, through the cities of Lộc Ninh, An Lộc, Tân Khai, Cầu Tàu Ô, Chơn Thành, and Lai Khê (belonging to the Province of Bình Dương) to reach Sài Gòn. Surrounding the Town of An Lộc were the rubber plantations, which occupied an area of around 75,000 acres. The Province Chief at the time of the Battle of An Lộc was Colonel Trần Văn Nhựt,[5] a former Marines officer with a lot of combat experiences. Later, Colonel Nhựt was promoted to Brigadier-General and appointed Commander of the 2nd Infantry Division.

Figure 3.5. Brigadier-General Trần Văn Nhựt, Commander of 2nd Infantry Division – At the time of the Battle of An Lộc, he was Colonel, Province and Sub-District Chief of Bình Long

After having received intelligence information regarding the most recent activities of the three 5th, 7th, and 9th Communist Divisions showing their intentions to make a large-scale attack of the Province of Bình Long, the Commander of the 5th Infantry Division, Brigadier-General Lê Văn Hưng (just promoted from Colonel to Brigadier-General by President Nguyễn Văn Thiệu on March 9, 1972), decided to move the Division's headquarters from Phú Lợi to Lai Khê in the north of the Province of Bình Dương, close to the southern border of the Province of Bình Long, and, at the same time, to locate the forward headquarters of the 5th Infantry Division to An Lộc under the command of Colonel Lê Nguyên Vỹ, his Deputy-Commander.

The main and reinforced units of the 5th Infantry Division were positioned as follows:

"- Trung Đoàn 7 Bộ Binh tại Phú Giáo do Trung Tá LÝ ĐỨC QUÂN chỉ huy, hoạt động dọc theo hành lang sông Bé ngăn chặn đường xâm nhập của Cộng Sản Bắc Việt vào chiến khu D.

- Trung Đoàn 8 Bộ Binh tại Dầu Tiếng (Quận Trị Tâm) do Đại Tá MẠCH VĂN TRƯỜNG chỉ huy hoạt động ngăn chặn các đoàn xâm nhập

Cộng Sản Bắc Việt từ biên giới Việt Miên theo hành lang sông Sài Gòn tiến vào Bình Dương.

- Trung Đoàn 9 Bộ Binh (trừ 1 Tiểu Đoàn) do Đại Tá NGUYỄN CÔNG VĨNH chỉ huy, được tăng phái Thiết Đoàn 1 Kỵ Binh (trừ 1 Chi Đoàn) do Trung Tá Kỵ Binh NGUYỄN ĐỨC DƯƠNG chỉ huy, và Tiểu Đoàn 74 Biệt Động Quân Biên Phòng, hợp thành Chiến Đoàn 9 Bộ Binh, trú đóng tại Quận Lộc Ninh tổ chức phòng thủ ngăn chặn địch từ Snoul (đất Miên) tiến đánh Việt Nam theo đường tiến sát Quốc Lộ 13.

- Trung Đoàn 52 Bộ Binh (trừ 1: gồm Tiểu Đoàn 2/52 và Tiểu Đoàn 1/48) do Sư Đoàn 18 Bộ Binh tăng phái và 1 Pháo Đội hỗn hợp (105 ly và 155 ly) do Trung Tá NGUYỄN BÁ THỊNH chỉ huy thiết lập căn cứ hoả lực tại Cầu Cần Lê (cách An Lộc 15 cây số, trên Quốc Lộ 13) để yểm trợ hoả lực cho An Lộc, Lộc Ninh và Căn Cứ Tống Lê Chân.

- Bộ Tư Lệnh Sư Đoàn 5 Bộ Binh đóng tại Lai Khê. Bộ Chỉ Huy Tiền Phương Sư Đoàn 5 Hành Quân đặt tại Tỉnh Lỵ Bình Long do Đại Tá Tư Lệnh Phó LÊ NGUYÊN VỸ chỉ huy." [6]

(Translation:

"- The 7th Regiment at Phú Giáo under the command of Lieutenant-Colonel LÝ ĐỨC QUÂN, and taking actions along the Bé River corridor against the Communist intention to move into the D War Zone.

- The 8th Infantry Regiment at Dầu tiếng (District of Tri Tâm) under the command of Colonel MẠCH VĂN TRƯỜNG, and taking actions against the Communist North Vietnamese infiltration convoys moving along the Sài Gòn River corridor from the Vietnam-Cambodia border into the Province of Bình Dương.

- The 9th Infantry Regiment (minus 1 battalion) under the command of Colonel NGUYỄN CÔNG VĨNH, reinforced with 1st Armored Calvary Squadron (minus 1 armored cavalry troop) under the command of Lieutenant-Colonel NGUYỄN ĐỨC DƯƠNG, and with 74th Border Ranger Battalion, forming the 9th Infantry Task Force, all positioned in Lộc Ninh District,

and taking actions against enemy forces (from Cambodia) moving into Vietnam along the roads leading to National Route 13.

- The 52nd Infantry Regiment (minus 1: including 2/52 Battalion and 1/48 Battalion) sent as reinforcement by the 18th Infantry Division, together with a Combined Artillery Company (105 mm and 155 mm) under the command of Lieutenant-Colonel NGUYỄN BÁ THỊNH to establish a fire-support base at Cần Lê Bridge (15 km from An Lộc, on National Route 13) to support An Lộc, Lộc Ninh, and Tống Lê Chân Base.

- The Headquarters of the 5th Infantry Division was located at Lai Khê, with its forward operational headquarters in the capital city of Bình Long under the command of its Deputy-Commander, Colonel LÊ NGUYÊN VỸ.")

Figure 3.6. Brigadier-General Mạch Văn Trường, Commander of 21st Infantry Division – At the time of the Battle of An Lộc, he was Commander of 8th Regiment, 5th Infantry Division

The Reasons for An Lộc Being Chosen as Objective of the Battle

The question was: Why was An Lộc, the capital town of Bình Long, a small province with a limited population, and having no economic potential, chosen by the Communists as one of the three main objectives of the Summer 1972 General Offensive? The answer was: The Paris Peace Talks, beginning since 1968, between the two fighting sides, had reached the point where it should be concluded. The Communists had created the Provisional Revolutionary Government of the Republic of South Vietnam (PRG) to represent the National Liberation Front of South Vietnam (NLF) at the conference table. This government was in need of a capital city, and for which the Communists had chosen An Lộc. At the same time, An Lộc was close enough for them to mount an attack of Sài Gòn.[7] The Communists, therefore, had assembled a large force and determined to seize An Lộc. On the opposite side, the ARVN, therefore, also determined to keep An Lộc at all cost.

Below is a table presenting the estimated total (35, 000) of Communist forces, which have engaged in the Battle of An Lộc:

5th VC Division		69th Artillery Division	
HQ & Support	4,680	HQ & Support	1,395
E6 Regiment	1,500	42nd Artillery Regiment	800
174th Regiment	1,500	208th Rocket Regiment	835
275th Regiment	1,500	271st Anti-Aircraft Regiment	800
Total	9,180	Total	3,830
7th NVA Division		Other Forces	
HQ & Support	4,100	205th NVA Regiment	1,250
141st Regiment	1,500	101st NVA Regiment	760
165th Regiment	1,500	203rd Tank Regiment	800
209th Regiment	1,500	Incl 202nd Special	
		Weapons Regiment	
Total	8,600	429th Sapper Group (–)	320
		Total	3,130
9th VC Division			
HQ & Support	4,680		
271st Regiment	2,000		
272nd Regiment	2,000		
95C Regiment	2,000		
Total	10,680		

Source: ***The Battle of An Loc*** / James H. Willbanks, p. 33

The Opening Battles

In fact, before the Battle of An Lộc began at the beginning of April 1972, MACV (Military Assistance Command – Vietnam), the General Staff of the RVN, as well III Corps (and thus, the 5th Infantry Division) were provided with intelligence information that it was Tây Ninh, not An Lộc, would be where the Communists wanted to seize in order to establish the capital city for the PRG.

At the Corps level, Major-General James F. Hollingsworth, Chief Advisor for III Corps, Commander of TRAC (Third Regional Assistance Command), directly provided advices for Lieutenant-General Nguyễn Văn Minh, Commander of the III Corps. Colonel William H. Miller, Chief Advisor, did the same thing for Brigadier-General Lê Văn Hưng, Commander of the 5th Infantry Division. At the beginning of February 1972, both American intelligence service and TRAC were thinking and believing Tây Ninh would be the objective of a big Communist attack in III Corps.[8]

In fact, before the beginning of the Battle of An Lộc:

"ngày 02 tháng 04 năm 1972, hai Trung Đoàn Cộng Sản có chiến xa và trọng pháo yểm trợ từ phần đất Miên xâm nhập đánh phá liên tục vào các căn cứ Lạc Long (cách Tây Ninh 35 cây số về phía Tây Bắc) và căn cứ Thiện Ngôn khiến quân trú phòng thuộc Sư Đoàn 25 Bộ Binh phải lui quân. Họ tung tin sẽ đánh chiếm Tây Ninh làm thủ phủ cho Mặt Trận Giải Phóng Miền Nam, khiến Quân Khu III phải điều toàn bộ Sư Đoàn 25 Bộ Binh phòng thủ giữ Tây Ninh và Sư Đoàn này mặc nhiên bị cầm chân tại đây." [9]

(Translation:

"on April 2, 1972, two Communist regiments, supported by tanks and heavy artillery, infiltrating from Cambodia, continuously attacked the bases of Lạc Long (about 35 km from Tây Ninh in the northeast) and Thiện Ngôn, forcing the defense troops belonging to the 25th Infantry Division to retreat. They spread rumors that they would capture Tây Ninh to make it the capital city of the NFL, forcing the III Corps to move the whole 25th Infantry Division to defend Tây Ninh, and, thus, this Division was kept there.")

Only after the communists began their large-scale attack of Lộc Ninh did the leaders of the ARVN, MACV, and TRAC change their views and believed that the Communists' intention and determination were to capture An Lộc.

In the early morning of April 5, 1972, all artillery units of the Communist 5th Division began to shell fiercely on the defense units of the 9th Regiment of the ARVN's 5th Infantry Division as well on the administrative buildings of the district center of Lộc Ninh. Right after the opening shelling, the two regiments of the Communist 5th Division, the 174th and the 275th supported by 25 tanks attacked Lộc Ninh from the west, concentration on the headquarters of the 9th Infantry Regiment located at the southern point of the airfield. The 9th Regiment forces fought vigorously waves after waves of the Communist attack, and successfully destroyed one enemy tank. At one point, artillery men of the forces defending Lộc Ninh have lowered their 105-mm canons and fired directly to the enemy infantrymen assaulting from the rubber plantations.

While the battle in Lộc Ninh was still raging, at the headquarters of the III Corps in Biên Hòa, both General Minh and General Hollingsworth realized that the objective of this general offensive was Bình Long; they no longer believed Tây Ninh was the objective. The air support was carried out immediately. U.S. planes, including A-37 jet fighters of the 8th Special Operations Squadron from Biên Hòa, Navy's jet fighters from the Constellation aircraft carrier, jet fighters F-4 and gunships AC-130 from Thailand, as well as the AFVN's fighters A-1 and jet fighters F-5, were sent in to provide continuous air support to the ARVN forces, which were fighting back fierce attacks from the Communists in Lộc Ninh. The air support for the Lộc Ninh battle front was also provided by the Cobra helicopters from the 9th Cavalry, U.S. 1st Cavalry Division.[10]

Brigadier-General Hưng and Colonel Miller boarded their helicopter, left the headquarters of thc 5th Infantry Division in Lai Khê and flew to the north right away. As they were approaching Chơn Thành, they got contact with the American advisors in Lộc Ninh. The advisors reported that the 9th Infantry Task Force's units in Lộc Ninh, although being strongly supported by U.S. and Vietnamese fighters and helicopters, had received heavy casualties caused by the enemy's artillery and tanks, and the situation had become very dire. The armored unit defending the northern side of Lộc Ninh had surrendered, and the Rangers units as well the 2nd Battalion of the 9th Regiment had fought their way back to Lộc Ninh. In the mean time, all units of the 9th Task Force defending Lộc Ninh, with the maximum support of US-Vietnamese air forces, had fought fiercely waves after waves of heavy attacks by infantry units of the Communist 5th Division.

General Hưng ordered Lieutenant-Colonel Nguyễn Bá Thịnh to move the 52nd Regiment (sent by the 18th Infantry Division and positioned at Cần Lê Bridge in the north of An Lộc) to reinforce Lộc Ninh. Lieutenant-Colonel Thịnh immediately order the 2nd Battalion to move north and provide support to Lộc Ninh. This Battalion was ambushed at a point close to the intersection of Inter-provincial Route 17 and National Route 13. Because all air support was concentrated at that time on Lộc Ninh battle front, the 2nd Battalion was not receiving any of these air support, and, finally, it had to move back to the departing point. On the next day, April 6, 1972, the headquarters of the 52nd Regiment was shelled and surrounded by enemy forces. In order to save this unit, which would be necessary for the defense of An Lộc in the near future, General Hưng ordered Lieutenant-Colonel Thịnh to abandon the fire-support base at Cần Lê Bridge, and move the 52nd Regiment back to An Lộc. All heavy equipment, tank and artillery were left behind, only infantrymen fought their way back, across the forest, to An Lộc. Only 600 out of a total of over 1,000 infantrymen of the 52nd Regiment finally reached An Lộc.[11, 12]

After several waves of attack, and although having suffered a lot of damages, caused by the fierce resistance from the defending forces as well as by the U.S. and South Vietnamese air support, including the U.S. gunships AC-130 and the horrible destruction by CBU-55 (CBU = Cluster Bomb Unit), the Communist forces of the 5th Division, finally, broke the defense lines of the 9th Regiment and overran Lộc Ninh. Colonel Nguyễn Công Vĩnh, Commander of the 9th Regiment, and Lieutenant-Colonel Nguyễn Đức Dương, Commander of the 1st Armored Cavalry Squadron, were captured by the enemy.[13] All 7 U.S. Advisors were reported as MIA (Missing in Action); in reality, except for Lieutenant-Colonel Richard S. Schott, who was seriously injured and killed himself so that his men could escape easily, all other advisors, one after another, were also captured by the enemy. They were: Major Albert E. Carlson, Major Thomas Davidson, Captain Mark A. Smith, Captain George Wanat, Sargent Howard B. Lull, and Sargent Kenneth Wallingford. On the ARVN side, more than one thousand soldiers were captured in Lộc Ninh; only about 50 soldiers escaped the siege and arrived back to An Lộc.[14] The 9th Regiment of the 5th Infantry Division was, in fact, wiped out.

Communist Attacks in An Lộc

ARVN's Preparations in Defense of An Lộc

As previously mentioned, when the battle of Lộc Ninh was still raging, Lieutenant-General Nguyễn Văn Minh, Commander of III Corps, saw right away that the real objective of the Communists in the Military Region III was to capture Bình Long, not Tây Ninh. He immediately ordered, on April 5, 1972, to airlift by helicopters to An Lộc the last reserve unit of III Corps, which was the 3rd Rangers Brigade.[15] On the next day, April 6, 1972, while the battle of Lộc Ninh was still raging, General Minh flew back to Sài Gòn to attend an important meeting at the Independence Palace. Present at this meeting were: President Nguyễn Văn Thiệu, General Cao Văn Viên, Chairman of the General Staff, Lieutenant-General Đặng Văn Quang, President Thiệu's Security Advisor, and all 4 Corps Commanders. General Minh presented his view of the serious situation in III Corps: if An Lộc were captured by the enemy to make it the capital city for the PRG, the political impact would be extremely disadvantageous for the RVN, and, thus, An Lộc should be safeguarded at all cost. Since there was no more reserve unit in III Corps, he proposed that alternatives should be found to reinforce An Lộc's defending forces. Both President Thiệu and Lieutenant-General Quang supported that point of view. Because all of the General

Reserve Units, such as the Airborne Division and the Marines Division, were already sent as reinforcements to the I and II Corps, the meeting reached the consensus that reinforcements for III Corps would be the 1st Airborne Brigade, the 81st Commando Airborne Brigade, and one division from the IV Corps. When asked for his ideas, Lieutenant-General Ngô Quang Trưởng, at that time Commander of IV Corps, recommended using the 21st Infantry Division for 2 reasons: 1) It had a lot of experiences with flexible mechanized combat; and, 2) It used to be under the command of General Minh. After discussion, everyone agreed with General Trưởng's recommendation.[16] After the meeting, President Thiệu issued an order to all ARVN's high-ranking officers present in An Lộc at the time that "An Lộc must be safeguarded ***at all cost.***"

As far as the 5th Infantry Division was concerned, General Hưng ordered Lieutenant-Colonel Lý Đức Quân to immediately move his 7th Regiment, located in Phú Giáo to protect the River Bé corridor, back to defend An Lộc. He also decided to move the division headquarters, having been already moved from Phú Lợi to Lai Khê, to An Lộc. On April 7, 1972, before flying into An Lộc, he had his helicopter landed in Dầu Tiếng to meet with Colonel Mạch Văn Trường, Commander of the 8th Regiment. He informed Colonel Trường of the serious situation of keeping An Lộc at all cost, of his decision to move the division headquarters to An Lộc, and of the fact that the 5th Infantry Division was no longer able to support the 8th Regiment, but demanded that Colonel should try his best to keep his position to protect the Sài Gòn River corridor. He also informed Colonel Trường that from that moment on, his 8th Regiment should report directly to the III Corps. After seeing General Hưng board his helicopter to fly into An Lộc, Colonel Trường immediately had a meeting with all unit commanders of the 8th to announce Gene ral Hưng's important decisions and ordered all units under his command to perform a total review of personnel and equipment, in particular the heavy guns such as the 57-mm recoilless guns, and the 81-mm mortars. During an operation searching an old base of the U.S. 1st Infantry Division (already sent back to the U.S.), the 1st Battalion of the 8th Regiment luckily discovered an ammunition cache of all kinds of ammo and 2,000 brand new M-72 LAW (Light Antitank Weapon) still in oiled wraps. These new M-72 antitank guns were immediately distributed to all units of the regiment. Three days later, April 10, 1972, General Minh, Commander of the III Corps, called Colonel Trường to the Corps headquarters in Biên Hòa, and after informing him of the grave situation in An Lộc, let him know his decision to return the 8th Regiment back to the 5th Infantry Division, and it would be helilifted to An Lộc the next day, April 11, 1972.[17]

Before the first Communist attack occurred on April 14, 1972, the defense forces in An Lộc were positioned as follows:

- The 8th Regiment defending the north
- The 3rd Rangers Brigade defending the east
- The 7th Regiment defending the west
- The 52nd Regiment (sent as reinforcement by the 18th Infantry Division) and the local units of the Sub-District of Binh Long defending the south

At that time, the reinforcements decided at the Independence Palace meeting of April 6, 1972, including the 1st Airborne Brigade, the 81st Commando Airborne Brigade and the 21st Infantry Division, were not sent to An Lộc yet.

Communist Preparations for their Attacks of An Lộc

For the Communists, after having captured Lộc Ninh, their objective was now to attack An Lộc, the capital town of the Province of Bình Long. As preparations for the attack, they had to carry out two operations: 1) Surrounding An Lộc; and, 2) Cutting all possible roads needed to send supplies and reinforcements for An Lộc.

The units of the VC 5th Division were ordered to move south and surround the northern side of An Lộc. The Bình Long provincial airfield in the north, and the Quản Lợi rubber plantation airfield in the northeast (about 5 km from An Lộc), necessary for the communication with and supplies for An Lộc, were continuously attacked by enemy artillery. The 7th Regiment, called back from Phú Giáo, dispatched one battalion to defend the Quản Lợi airfield. In the evening of April 8, 1972, several units of the VC Bình Long Division attacked and overran this airfield. The battalion dispatched by the 7th Regiment suffered heavy losses and had to retreat to An Lộc. After having captured Quản Lợi, the Communist artillery units occupied the high points, which gave them the advantage to precisely adjust their shelling of the main objectives in the town of An Lộc in the near future.

In the south, the units of the VC 7th Division have completely cut off National Route 13 from Chơn Thành. On April 7, 1972, the 1st Airborne Brigade was ordered to move from Lai Khê to Chơn Thành, with the objective to clear National Route 13. About 6 km past Chơn Thành, and still about 15 km south of An Lộc, the Brigade was completely stopped by several blockages of their 7th Division at a point near Tàu Ô Bridge.

An Lộc was completely surrounded, all ground and air ways for communications and supplies were cut off by the enemy. From July 7 to July 12, all supplies and medical evacuations were carried out by helicopters or by C-123 transport airplanes of the AFVN. The attack against An Lộc was to occur soon in the near future.

The First Attack: 13-15/April/1972

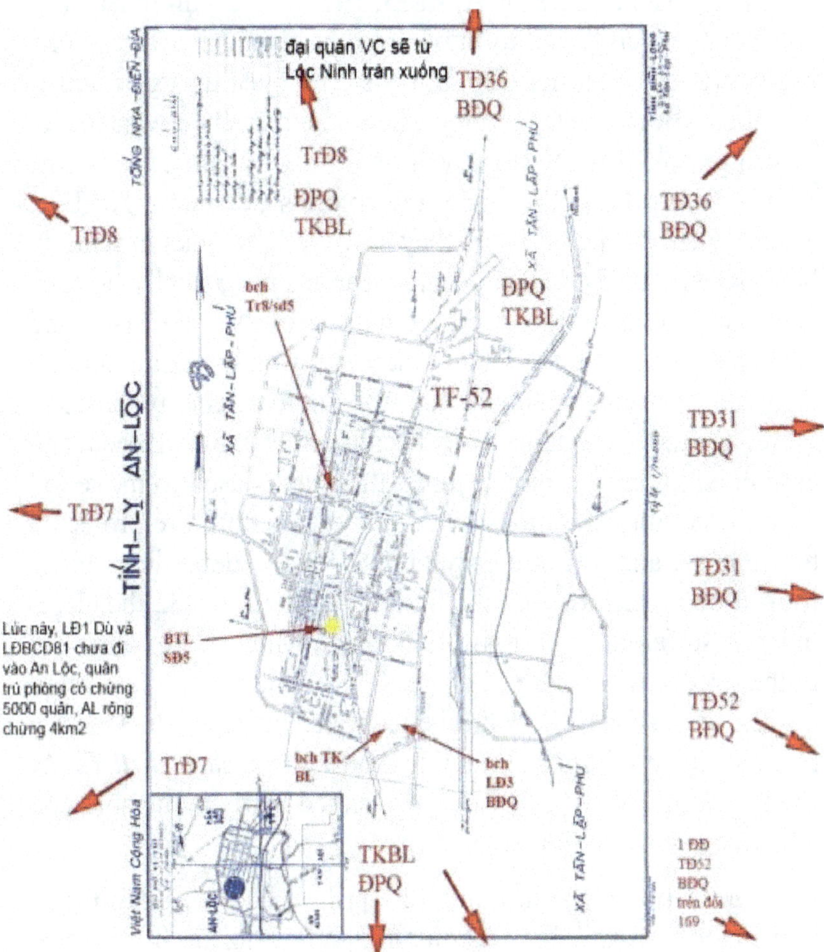

Figure 3.7. Defense Map of the ARVN in An Lộc

Source: ***Trận đánh An Lộc, Bình Long, ngày 13 tháng 4, 1972, …*** (The Battle of An Lộc, Bình Long, April 13, 1972 …), **online document at this URL:** https://kientruc5sj.wordpress.com/2014/08/18/tran-danh-an-loc-binh-long-ngay-13-thang-tu-1972-tran-bo-chien-cung-chien-xa-tien-cong-lan-dau-tien-cua-vc-vao-thi-xa-an-loc-bai-thu-5-by-duongtiden/

During the evening of April 12, as preparations for the infantry and tank attack in the morning, the Communists have shelled about 6,000 rounds of all kinds to the defense points in An Lộc. At exactly 6 am, Thursday April 13, 1972, the Communist tanks and infantrymen began to move into the town. It was the first big battle in which the Communists employed a large number of tanks. Both sides, therefore, had no experience whatsoever of using tanks (the VC) as well as fighting against tanks (the ARVN). On the ARVN side, the soldiers defending An Lộc, at first, were so scared when they saw the first tanks moving in because their individual and team weapons were totally useless. But after a soldier from the regional forces used an M-72 and destroyed the first enemy tank, the news was spreading among the defending forces, and no one was afraid of enemy tank any more. On the Communist side, because of lack of experience in combined infantry-armor combat, their tanks used to move too fast and get into situations where they were no more protected by infantry, and became easy targets for the defending forces in An Lộc. Therefore, on the first day of their attack, the Communists suffered heavy loss of 15 tanks, which were destroyed in the streets of An Lộc: 12 by the 8th Regiment's soldiers using M-72s, and 3 by U.S. Cobra helicopters. Afterwards, General Hưng ordered all units defending An Lộc to create ***"Kill Tanks Team"*** equipped with M-72s and manned by dynamic soldiers, who knew surrounding areas well.

The battle in the morning of April 13 had the main thrust in the North of An Lộc. A column of a few dozens T-54 tanks, moving in single file from north to south on the National Route 13, with infantrymen on both sides of the road, looked very menacing, appearing totally in control of the situation. They never knew that they were going to face Death.

The soldiers of the Regional Forces of the Sub-district of Bình Long as well as the infantrymen of the battalions of the 8th Regiment defending the northern side of An Lộc, a few days prior, have made all preparations needed for the fight against the attack they knew for sure would happen. The 105-mm canons of the 52nd Artillery Battalion (commanded by Major Hoàng Trung Liêm) belonging to the 8th Regiment, were ready with coordinates for concentration points for shelling established in advance. So were the 81-mm mortars of several units of the 8th Regiment.

When the enemy infantrymen and tanks reached the pre-established coordinates, all 105-mm guns and 81-mm mortars of the defending forces fired off immediately and simultaneously. The enemy infantrymen were panicked and ran away in total chaos. One T-54 tank was hit, exploded, turned sideway, blocking the way and forced the other tanks behind it to back off. About 15 tanks in front of the column could not back off and had no other choice to continue to move forward in to An Lộc, and, one by one, they were destroyed by the defenders of An Lộc with their M-72 antitank weapons, as can be seen in the following photo:

Figure 3.8. One T-54 tank destroyed in the Town of An Lộc
<u>Source:</u> *America's Last Vietnam Battle*, p. 392.

After having recovered from the debacle, at around 10 am, the Communists launched their second attack, still, with tanks and infantry, to An Lộc from the northwest. This time, although also having lost one T-54 tank, they did a lot better, and, at 11:30, they captured Bình Long airfield, and one section of the northern part of An Lộc. At mid-day, An Lộc was already cut into two parts: the northern part already fallen into the enemy's hands, and the southern part still under the defenders' control, and, of course, the middle part of the city was the hot battlefield where both sides were still fighting very hard for each street, each house.[18]

Throughout April 13 and the two following days, the fighting was almost continuous between the two sides. The attackers, in spite of having a much larger number of soldiers, could not control the battlefield because of the two following mean reasons:

• The fierce and effective resistance fighting of ***ALL*** defending units within the city, from the soldiers of the regional forces of the Sub-district of Bình Long to the soldiers of the two 7th and 8th Regiments of the 5th Infantry Division, the 52nd Regiment of the 18th Infantry Division, 3rd Rangers Brigade, and especially after Brigadier-General Lê Văn Hưng, Commander of the 5th Infantry Division, and also Commander of the An Lộc Battlefield, firmly announced: ***"ÔNG NHẤT QUYẾT TỬ THỦ AN LỘC VÀ SẼ NHẤT ĐỊNH CHẾT Ở ĐÓ NẾU THÀNH PHỐ NẦY BỊ CỘNG SẢN CHIẾM"***[19] (Translation: ***HE DETERMINED TO FIGHT TO THE DEATH TO SAFEGUARD AN LỘC, AND HE WILL DIE THERE IF THE TOWN IS CAPTURED BY THE COMMUNISTS."***

• The extremely effective of ground supports provided by both U.S. and ARVN air forces. On the AFVN side, Squadrons 221, 223, and 231, equipped with UH-1 Huey helicopters, Squadron 237 with CH-47 Chinook helicopters, and medivac

Flight 259E of Air Wing 43, have actively participated on a daily basis in bringing in reinforcement troops and supplies, and evacuating out injured soldiers. In terms of air tactical ground supports, the Observation Squadrons 112, 124, the Fighter Squadrons 514, 518, equipped with A-1 Skyraiders, of Air Wing 23, and Jet Fighter Squadron 522, with jet fighter Freedom Fighter F-5s (all belonging to Air Division 3 in Biên Hòa), have made hundreds of sorties to counter enemy attacks right in the An Lộc battlefield. All of these flights supporting the defense of An Lộc were carried out in the most dangerous conditions caused by an extremely heavy anti-aircraft network of the Communist attacking forces. A number of CH-47 Chinook helicopters were seriously damaged in the An Lộc battlefield, just like in the following report of a pilot from Squadron 237:

"Tình hình chiến sự mỗi lúc một gia tăng và mãnh liệt nhất là trận An Lộc, mùa Hè 72. Mỗi sáng, chúng tôi tất cả các trực thăng thuộc KĐ43CT đều sang standby tại Lai Khê chờ lệnh, UH-1 vào trước với các binh sĩ tinh nhuệ Nhảy Dù, Chinook vào sau với các khẩu trọng pháo 105 ly ở Đồi Gió, Tàu Ô, Tân Khai, bay cao, bay thấp đều bị bắn bằng đủ loại đạn, nhưng chúng tôi vẫn thi hành các phi vụ được giao phó. Hai Chinook đã tổn thất tại Tân Khai và Tàu Ô là PHĐ của Th/Tá Nguyễn Hữu Nhàn + Th/Úy Đặng Thiên Hiền, cơ phi Ch/Úy Kim, áp tải, xạ thủ đều hy sinh, Đ/Úy Trọng + Th/Úy Thanh bị bắt và được trao trả năm 73 nhưng cơ phi, xạ thủ và áp tải hy sinh.

Một Chinook của Tr/Úy Lê Quang Tiên và Đặng Đức Cường bị bắn cháy trên không, phải đáp khẩn cấp xuống phi trường An Lộc và được gunship bốc cứu. Phi cơ của Tr/Úy Sơn và tôi bị trúng một viên 12,7ly thủng bình xăng trái nhưng vô sự vì không phải đạn lửa và nhiều phi cơ khác bị đạn nhưng không đáng kể." [20]

(Translation:

"The war intensity was increasing and reached its peak in the Battle of An Lộc in the summer of 1972. Every morning, all of us, helicopter pilots of Tactical Air Wing 43, were at stand by in Lai Khê, waiting for orders for the day. UH-1 Huey helicopters were flying in first with combat-experienced Airborne

troops. Chinook helicopters were sent in next with 105-mm guns to important LZs like Đồi Gió, Tàu Ô, Tân Khai. No matter how high we flew, we were targets of the enemy heavy anti-aircraft guns of all kinds, but we still had to carry out our missions. We lost two Chinooks in Tân Khai: 1) in the first one, the whole air crew, including Major Nguyễn Hữu Nhàn as pilot; Second-Lieutenant Đặng Thiên Hiền as co-pilot; Warrant Officer Kim as flying mechanic, together with the loader and the gunner, were all KIA (killed in action); 2) in the second one, Captain Trọng as pilot, Second-Lieutenant Thanh as co-pilot were captured and exchanged in 1973, with the flying mechanic, the loader, and the gunner were all KIA.

The Chinook piloted by First-Lieutenants Lê Quang Tiên and Đặng Đức Cường, hit and burned in the air, had to make an emergency landing at An Lộc airfield and the crew was rescued by a gunship. The aircraft that First-Lieutenant Ly and I flew was hit by a 12.7 mm round that pierced the fuel tank but did not cause any explosion. Many other aircrafts were also hit but were not seriously damaged.")

On the USAF side, its support to the An Lộc battlefield was unprecedented and very effective will all kinds of aircrafts and with a very high number of sorties. B-52 strategic bombers, from U.S. airbases (52 aircraft) in U-Tapao in Thailand and in Andersen (31 aircraft) on Guam Island, made daily ***"carpet bombing"*** flights over concentration areas of enemy troops around An Lộc. Each B-52 flight always included 3 aircraft, each carrying up to 70,000 pounds of bombs, totalling around 100 tons of bombs. When a 3-aircraft B-52 flight ***"carpet bombed,"*** an area of 0.5 x 2 miles will be totally destroyed.[21] A note-worthy characteristic of the B-52 ***"carpet bombing"*** was that it was a total surprise and had a most horrific effect because the B-52 bombers were flying at a very high altitude (30,000 feet = 10,000 m = 10 km), and, thus, were invisible to the enemy forces; when they heard the explosions there was no escape for them. The Communists confirmed the level of destruction by B-52 ***"carpet bombings"*** as follows:

"Không quân Hoa Kỳ đã dùng B-52 để ném bom trải thảm dọn đường, ném bom tạo bãi đáp đổ quân cho các cuộc hành quân của kỵ binh bay, đánh vào các khu nghi ngờ tập trung quân và vào các khu hậu cần kho tàng của Quân đội Nhân dân Việt Nam và Quân Giải phóng Miền Nam Việt Nam và đã gây ra các huỷ diệt rất lớn, gây cảm giác rất ghê sợ, hãi hùng trong hàng ngũ đối phương và những người đã từng trải qua các trận bom B-52." [22]

(Translation:

"The American air force has used B-52s to carpet bomb, creating landing zones for the operations of their air cavalry forces, attacking areas they suspected of troop concentrations, and destroying the supply depots of People's Army and of the Army of the National Liberation Front, causing huge destructions, creating extreme fear within their enemy, and all people having experience of these B-52 bombings.")

In addition to the B-52s, the USAF also used other types of aircraft to provide ground supports to the An Lộc battlefield as follows:

- A-37 Dragonfly jet fighters
- AC-119 Stinger gunships
- AC-130 Spectre gunships
- Cobra attack helicopters

These types of aircraft have provided effective ground supports for the defenders of An Lộc. It was the Cobra helicopters that destroyed 3 T-54 tanks on the first day of the battle with their HEAT (**H**igh-**E**xplosive **A**nti**t**ank) missiles.

In the morning of April 15, the Communists tried again their ***"artillery before ground assault"*** tactical attack with infantrymen and tanks once more in An Lộc, but the results were again the same just like two days before, i.e., their attack was stopped by the fierce fighting back of the defenders with overwhelming ground supports by the American and South Vietnamese air forces. The intensity of the fighting was decreasing and was completely stopped in the evening, and, thus, the first wave of attacks of mid-April was over. The Communists were successful in capturing the northern part of the town of An Lộc, and the ARVN forces were still in control of the southern part of the town.

In order to have this temporary gain in the battle, the Communists have paid quite a high price with a big loss of soldiers and weapons. Just in terms of armored forces, the defenders of An Lộc have destroyed a total of 23 tanks, mostly Russian-made T-54. On the ARVN side, all 105-mm canons positioned in the town of An Lộc were destroyed.

Reinforcements for An Lộc in the Siege

The Nguyễn Trung Trực street, one of the principal streets of the northern side of the town of An Lộc, running east-west, was the demarcation line between the attacking and the defending forces. From their positions in the north and in the south of this line, the soldiers of both sides could see by eyes and follow the activities of their opponents in this very tense situation. The defenders knew very well that their enemy would attack again and that could happen any time. For their leaders, it was the time of make preparations for their next battle.

On the Communist side, they made criticism of the processes and results of their attacks of the past three days. They recognized the highly effective ground supports provided to the An Lộc defenders by the USAF and the AFVN, especially the great damages caused to their troop concentration points before their attacks. They also saw clearly that the big mistake of the attack plan of that time was the lack of close coordination between the infantry and the armored forces. And on top of that, they tried to regroup their forces for the next attack.[23]

On the ARVN side, it was the time for regrouping forces, repairing defense posts, and, of course, bringing reinforcements to An Lộc for the defense of the town.

Right from the beginning of April 1972, during the battle of Lộc Ninh, Lieutenant-General Nguyễn Văn Minh, Commander of III Corps, after the emergency meeting at the Independence Palace, had given order to the 1st Airborne Brigade, being responsible for the defense of the Capital City of Sài Gòn at that time, with Colonel Lê Quang Lưỡng as Commander[24] (Colonel Lưỡng was later promoted to Brigadier-General and was the last Commander of the Airborne Division), including 3 battalions, the 3rd, the 5th and the 6th, to move to Lai Khê immediately. On April 7, 1972, the 1st Airborne Brigade began its operation from Lai Khê to Chơn Thành, along the National Route 13, with the objectives to remove all blockages defended by the VC 7th Division from Chơn Thành to An Lộc. Just past Chơn Thành 6 km in the north, still about 15 km south of An Lộc, they were stopped at the Tàu Ô Creek by a whole regiment of the VC 7th Division with several solidly well-prepared defense outposts.

Figure 3.9. Brigadier-General Lê Quang Lưỡng, Commander of the Airborne Division – At the time of the Battle of An Lộc, he was Commander of the 1st Airborne Brigade

On April 14, 1972, after the meeting in Lai Khê with Lieutenant-General Dư Quốc Đống, Commander of the Airborne Division, and Colonel Lê Quang Lưỡng, Lieutenant-General Nguyễn Văn Minh, decided that the 1st Airborne Brigade should be helilifted to An Lộc. Colonel Lưỡng flew to An Lộc right away to discuss with General Hưng for the best plan to move his brigade to An Lộc. The plan was approved by General Hưng and was carried out immediately. Colonel Lưỡng then discussed the details of the plan with Major Nguyễn Văn Ức, Commander of the Helicopter Squadron 221, Tactical Air Wing 43, Air Division 3.[25, 26] The landing of the whole 1st Airborne Brigade was safely completed in two days, July 14 and 15, and reported as follows:

"Sau cuộc họp, Đại Tá Lưỡng bay quan sát vị trí trận địa để chọn bãi đổ quân. Sau năm vòng bay, vị sĩ quan Lữ Đoàn Trưởng quyết định đổ quân xuống ấp Srok Ton Cui, cách An Lộc 4 cây số về phía Đông. Theo kế hoạch, Tiểu Đoàn 6 Nhảy Dù sẽ xuống trước để khai quang bãi đáp. Rồi ngày hôm sau, 15 tháng 04/1972, hai Tiểu Đoàn 5 và 8 cùng Bộ Chỉ Huy Lữ Đoàn 1 Nhảy Dù sẽ được trực thăng vận xuống khu vực này. Sau khi đã hoàn tất cuộc đổ quân, hai Tiểu Đoàn 5 và 8 sẽ chia làm hai cánh tiến quân vào An Lộc." [27]

(Translation:

"After the meeting, Colonel Lưỡng took a helicopter flight to observe the terrain in order to pick a landing zone. After five flying rounds, the Brigade Commander decided to land his troops at the Srok Ton Cui hamlet, about 4 km east of An Lộc. According to the plan, the 6th Airborne Battalion would land first to clear the landing zone. On the next day, July 15, 1972, the two Battalions, the 5th and the 8th, together with the 1st Airborne Brigade commanding staff would be helilifted to this area. After the landing was completed, the 5th and 8th Battalions would move into An Lộc in a two-pronged advance.")

After the 1st Airborne Brigade was successfully brought into An Lộc as reinforcement to the defenders inside, next came the 81st Commando Airborne Brigade under the command of Lieutenant-Colonel Phan Văn Huấn, who, after the Battle of An Lộc, was promoted to Colonel. The helitransport of the 81st Commando Airborne Brigade was carried out on April 16, 1972, again by the Helicopter Squadron 221, as follows:

"Đến ngày 16 tháng 04 năm 1972, Liên Đoàn 81 Biệt Cách Dù, được tăng viện cho An Lộc, và khởi phát cuộc phản công tái chiếm lại ½ lãnh thổ phía Bắc An Lộc.

Từng đoàn trực thăng HU-1D cất cánh từ căn cứ Lai Khê vào trưa ngày 16 tháng 04 năm 1972 đưa 550 Biệt Cách Nhảy Dù đến chiến trường An Lộc một cách an toàn.

Bãi đổ quân được chọn trên một khoảng ruộng trống, về phía Tây, Tỉnh lộ 245, cách Đồi Gió 1 cây số về phía Đông Bắc.

Hợp đoàn trực thăng từng đợt 30 chiếc HU-1D cho mỗi đợt đổ quân, có 4 trực thăng võ trang hộ tống bao vùng. Đợt đầu thả Bộ Chỉ Huy Liên Đoàn, do Trung Tá Phan Văn Huấn chỉ huy và 4 toán trinh sát của Liên Đoàn 81 Biệt Cách, do Trung Úy Lê Văn Lợi chỉ huy, cùng Đại Đội 1 do Đại Úy Nguyễn Ích Doàn chỉ huy và Đại Đội 2 do Đại Úy Nguyễn Sơn chỉ huy; chuyến thứ nhì gồm có Liên Đoàn Phó, Thiếu Tá Nguyễn văn Lân, cùng Đại Đội 3 do Đại Úy Phạm Châu Tài (có biệt danh là Hổ Xám) chỉ huy, và Đại Đội 4 do Đại Úy Đào Minh Hùng chỉ huy.

Sau khi được an toàn nhảy xuống trận địa, kiểm điểm quân đầy đủ, Trung Tá Huấn liền cho lệnh các đơn vị di chuyển đến chiếm cứ Ấp Srok Gòn, cận kề bên bãi đổ quân, bố trí xong xuôi, Trung Tá Huấn mở tần số truyền tin, liên lạc được với Tướng Hưng (Bộ Chỉ Huy Mặt Trận) và Đại Tá Lưỡng (Lực Lượng Dù) ở phía Nam để được hướng dẫn lộ trình an toàn cũng như tránh ngộ nhận giữa quân bạn trước khi tiến quân vào thành phố." [28]

(Translation:

"On April 16, 1972, the 81st Commando Airborne Brigade was sent into An Lộc as reinforcements for the counter-attack to recapture the northern side of An Lộc.

In the afternoon of April 16, 1972, flight after flight of UH-1D helicopters, taking off from Lai Khê base, safely brought 550 commando airborne troops to An Lộc battlefield.

The selected landing zone was selected in a bare rice field in the west, along Provincial Route 245, about 1 km northeast of Đồi Gió (Windy Hill).

The helitransport of these troops was carried out by two waves of UH-1D helicopters, each wave having 30 aircraft. The first wave brought in the Brigade's Command Staff headed by Lieutenant-Colonel Phan Văn Huấn, together with 4 reconnaissance groups under the command of First-Lieutenant Lê Văn Lợi, the 1st Company of Captain Nguyễn Ích Đoàn, and the 2nd Company of Captain Nguyễn Sơn. The second wave of troops included Major Nguyễn Văn Lân, Deputy-Commander of the Brigade, the 3rd Company under the command of Captain Phạm Châu Tài (nicknamed Grey Tiger), and the 4th Company under the command of Captain Đào Mộng Hùng.

After the safe landing of all of his men, Lieutenant-Colonel Huấn ordered them to move immediately to secure Srok Gòn Hamlet, adjacent to the landing zone. When all units had already taken positions, he communicated with both General Hưng (Battlefield Commander) in the town center, and Colonel Lưỡng (1st Airborne Brigade Commander) in the south in order to be guided on the safe entrance into the town as well as to avoid false encounter with friendly troops before his men began to move into the town.")

Figure 3.10. Colonel Phan Văn Huấn, Commander, 81st Commando Airborne Brigade

With these reinforcements, the number of defenders in An Lộc increased by almost 3,000, and, more, much more importantly, it helped boost the defenders' morale to a higher level since these two groups of reinforcement were among the most combat-experienced units of the ARVN. In addition, the 1st Airborne Brigade also achieved two very important milestones for An Lộc: 1) Establishing a very secure LZ not only for medical evacuations of wounded soldiers but also for bringing in supplies of foods, ammunitions, and more reinforcement troops; and, 2) Bringing in a battery of six 105-mm guns to establish in place and in time a new fire-support base for the defenders since, at that time, all big guns of An Lộc had already been destroyed. All ARVN units inside An Lộc were ready for a new attack of the Communists. They did not have to wait for long.

Second Wave of Attacks: 19-22/April/1972

Again, like in the first attack, using the same tactic of ***"artillery before ground assault,"*** from midnight of April 18 to early morning of April 19, the artillery units of the VC 9 thDivision have shelled thousands of rounds of their big guns as well as of missiles to the positions of the defenders of An Lộc, and the main thrust with tanks and infantrymen began immediately after the shelling stopped.

There were a couple of important points in this wave of attacks. First, because they had captured the northern half of the town in the first wave, the Communists thought and believed that they would be able to swallow the whole town in this second wave. Hà Nội radio, therefore, had made the announcement that An Lộc had already been "liberated" and the PRG would be officially presented itself in An Lộc on April 20, 1972.[29] Second, this wave of attacks, although occurring at several points in An Lộc, was clearly concentrated on positions held by the new reinforcement forces, i.e., the 1st Airborne Brigade, with the objective to destroy this unit in order to affect the defenders' morale.

The 275th Regiment of the 5th Division and the 141st Regiment of the 7th Division, with the support of a group of 6 tanks, had a co-ordinated attack against positions of the 1st Airborne Brigade at Windy Hill, Hill 169, and Srok Ton Cui Hamlet. The Brigade's unit under the highest pressure from the enemy was the 6th Battalion at Windy Hill under the command of Lieutenant-Colonel Nguyễn Văn Đĩnh. The Windy Hill was also the location of the fire-support base with the 6 105-mm guns of the 1st Airborne Brigade.

"Trước áp lực quá nặng của địch quân, Đại Tá Lưỡng cho phép Trung Tá Nguyễn Văn Đĩnh, Tiểu Đoàn Trưởng Tiểu Đoàn 6 Nhảy Dù, được toàn quyền quyết định về kế hoạch triệt thoái.

Trung Tá Đĩnh cùng với hai Đại Đội 60 và 62 di chuyển theo ngọn đồi xuống ấp Srok Ton Cui, nơi đóng quân của Đại Đội 61. Trong khi đó, hai Đại Đội 63 và 64 còn lại do Thiếu Tá Phạm Kim Bằng chỉ huy vẫn tiếp tục án ngữ cao địa. Cánh quân do Trung Tá Đĩnh chỉ huy bị Cộng quân chặn đánh. Những binh sĩ Nhảy Dù này đổi hướng và triệt thoái về hướng Nam. Sau đó, họ được trực thăng của Không Quân Việt Nam bốc về Lai Khê. Cánh quân còn lại của Tiểu Đoàn 6 Nhảy Dù và Bộ Chỉ Huy Lữ Đoàn rút vào An Lộc. Riêng pháo đội đại bác 105 ly với 6 khẩu được lệnh phá hủy tất cả súng trước khi rút lui." [30]

(Translation:

"Realizing the great pressure from the enemy on the 6th Battalion, Colonel Lưỡng gave its commander, Lieutenant-Colonel Đĩnh, the total authority to make decision regarding his unit's retreat.

Lieutenant-Colonel Đĩnh together with two Companies 60 and 62 moved down hill to Srok Ton Cui Hamlet where Company 61 was stationed. Meanwhile, the two remaining Companies 63 and 64, under the command of Major Phạm Kim Bằng, still held the high position on top of the hill. The group with Lieutenant-Colonel Đĩnh was attacked, had to change direction and moved south, and finally were picked up by AFVN helicopters and transferred to Lai Khê. The remaining force of the 6th Battalion together with the Command Staff of the 1st Airborne Brigade retreated into An Lộc. The artillery unit received order to destroy all of the six 105-mm guns before their retreat.")

Although having achieved one part of their objective, which was the destruction of the 6-105-mm-gun fire-support base of the 1st Airborne Brigade, and the forced retreat of the 6th Airborne Battalion from the Windy Hill, the Communists could not destroy the 1st Airborne Brigade. The Brigade was successful to keep most of its soldiers and was able to safely move into An Lộc. Besides, during this wave of attacks, the six tanks deployed by the Communists were all destroyed by the airborne troops.

In the meantime, all attacks by several units of the VC 9th Division, at different locations inside An Lộc, were all pushed back by the defenders. The southern side of the town was still under the control of the defending units. April 20, 1972 quietly passed. The objective of this second wave of attacks by the Communists, i.e., capturing An Lộc to create the capital city for the PRG, was not achieved. They still tried to mount another attack on April 21 from the south without any success in front of the fierce fighting back by the 5th and 8th Airborne Battalions. The second wave of attacks against An Lộc by the Communists came to an end in the evening of April 22, 1972.

Hell On Earth In An Lộc

An Lộc, during the time of the Communist siege, was described by an American author as a hell on earth in an article printed in the U.S. Army journal ***Pacific Stars and Stripes***, issue of May 1, 1972, under title: ***"An Lộc: a battlefield in hell."*** [31] An Lộc, with an area of just about 4 square kilometers, was pounded everyday by thousands of shells of all kinds of guns, from 105 / 155-mm howitzers to mortars, to 122-mm missiles. There were days, in preparations before the main attacks with tanks and infantrymen, when the shelling reached the levels of 5,000 or 6,000 rounds, and, on May 11, 1972, An Lộc was hit with more than 8,000 shells,[32] which all international war correspondents termed the fiercest artillery attack of this Indochina War.

With that level of intensity of the shelling together with the fierce raging of all the fighting inside the town accompanied by involvements of tanks from the attackers and air supports provided by USAF and AFVN for the defenders, almost all houses and buildings were destroyed or heavily damaged, as in the photo below:

Figure 3.11. Center of An Lộc after first wave of attacks

Because they had captured high positions surrounding the town, such as the Quản Lợi airfield and Đồng Long Hill in the north, Windy Hill and Hill 169 in the northeast, the Communist artillery forces were very precise in their shelling. One U.S. advisor present in An Lộc said that the chance of survival in the open in five minutes was just about 50%.[33] In such battlefield conditions, everyone in An Lộc, civilians and soldiers, had to live in shelters, of all kinds, from the heavily fortified bunkers of the command posts of regiments, brigades, division to makeshift shelters of civilians. In spite of these protections, the casualties of civilians and soldiers from the enemy shelling were not insignificant. Corpses, of humans and animals, were scattered everywhere, with chopped-off body parts, arms, legs being blown everywhere, even on branches of those trees that were still standing. A large part of these corpses were not properly buried, and, after a while, were rotted causing a serious air pollution with an extremely horrible stench.

Before the battle, An Lộc had a population of about 15,000. After Lộc Ninh fell, the town's survivors escaped to the south, and An Lộc's population, during the siege, was estimated at around 20,000. Of course, people also knew that An Lộc would certainly be the next target of the Communist attack, but they were not able to get out of An Lộc because the National Route 13 had already been cut off. During the battle, the leaders of both Catholic and Buddhist people have tried quite a few times to help their people to leave An Lộc without success because the Communists always shelled directly to the evacuees, causing heavy casualties. An officer of the 3rd Rangers Brigade gave the following report of the massacre:

"Có một ngày vào buổi sáng, khi ngớt pháo, tôi vừa chui lên nóc trung tâm hành quân để quan sát chung quanh thì thình lình… tôi nghe tiếng loa phóng thanh phát lên yêu cầu hai bên ngưng chiến. Loa phóng thanh được phát ra từ một đoàn người rất đông và rất dài, dẫn đầu bởi các nhà sư và các cha Công Giáo với cờ trắng trên tay phất qua phất lại. Lúc đó, Thiếu Tá Lạc, tiểu đoàn trưởng 36 BĐQ vừa gặp Trung Tá LĐT xong, nghe la hét cũng đến gần tôi trên nấp hầm trung tâm hành quân để quan sát.

Đoàn người đi trên con đường trước mặt và hướng đông BCH/LĐ tiến về hướng Nam định rẽ qua QL.13 để di tản về hướng Nam. Khi đoàn người đi về hướng gần phòng tuyến tiểu khu thì bỗng nghe tiếng pháo nổ ầm ầm hướng đó. Quan sát kỹ thì tôi thấy đích thị địch đã không ngưng pháo, mà còn cố tình pháo thẳng vào đoàn người di tản trên. Đoàn người trúng đạn pháo kêu la thảm thiết, tiếng khóc của trẻ con vang dội đến khu tôi đang đứng.

Thiếu Tá Lạc thấy cảnh tượng kinh hoàng vì Việt Cộng quá dã man đối với người dân. Ông nói cả Cha, Thầy, lẫn đàn bà con nít bọn chúng vẫn không tha thì quả thật là man rợ. Lần pháo này dường như chúng có điềm chỉ nên đạn pháo rót chính xác vào đoàn người làm thân xác họ văng tung tóe, tay chân văng máng trên các cành cây ven đường bởi dân chúng trên đường không có gì tránh né. Một số họ chỉ chạy nằm sát gần những gốc cây lớn mà thôi. Sau đợt pháo đó, dân chúng và cả Cha lẫn Thầy đều tan hàng trở về chốn cũ của mình." [34]

(Translation:

"One day, in the morning, when the shelling stopped, I got out of the operation center, reached to the top of the bunker in order to make some observation. Suddenly, I heard some callings for ceasefire emitted from some loudspeaker. The callings were from a large and long crowd, led by some monks and priests carrying and waving white flags. Right at that moment, Major Lạc, Commander of the 36th Rangers Battalion, just finished his meeting with the Lieutenant-Colonel Commander of the Brigade, also heard the callings, and came to lay down next to me.

The crowd was on the road right in front of us and on the east of the Brigade's command post, marching south, about to turn into the National Route 13 with the intention to evacuate to the south. When the crowd was close to the defense line of the sub-district regional units, we suddenly heard many explosions in that direction. I saw very clearly that the enemy deliberately shelled directly into the crowd. Being hit and injured by the shells, people, including a large number of children, were calling one another, shouting and crying pathetically.

Major Lạc found the scene extremely horrific by the Communists' savage treatment of the people. He could not believe that they could kill people in cold blood and indiscriminately like this: monks, priests, women and children. This time it seemed that the shelling was guided by some informant and, thus, very accurate, right on top of the crowd, making their shattered body parts flying everywhere, falling on branches of the trees on both sides of the road. The people did not have anywhere to hide; a number of them did the only thing that they could do: ran and laid down close to the stumps of big trees. After the shelling, the crowd broke up, and the people, including the monks and the priests, had to go back to where they had left.")

The people of An Lộc as well as the refugees from Lộc Ninh did not have any other choice than to find any ways and means to survive with the defenders inside this hell on earth.

Because the National Route 13, the main communication and supply way for An Lộc, had been cut off in the south, and both airfields, Bình Long and Quản Lợi, had been captured by the enemy, An Lộc could only be supplied by means of parachuting. However, since the Communist anti-aircraft system was very intensive and effective, the supplying for An Lộc by parachutes provided by transport aircrafts faced with a lot of difficulties. The supplies had to be dropped from an altitude of 5,000 feet or sometimes even higher. During the period of the enemy first wave of attacks, after 27 flights operated within 48 hours, only 34 of 135 tons of supplies were getting into the hands of the defenders.[35] The shortage of foods and other kinds of supplies was a fact of life, which lasted throughout the whole period of several months of the battle. The people and soldiers of An Lộc lived together in the shelters and shared together the meager foods available. During these 20 years of the Vietnam War, the people-soldier relationship has never been that close. The treatment of injuries for civilians and soldiers became more and more difficult because the Bình Long provincial hospital had been completely destroyed by the enemy's shelling and there was a serious shortage of all kinds of medical equipment and drugs. The nylon threads taken from the sandbags were boiled and reused by surgeons in stitching cuts after surgeries. Once in a while, taking advantage of pauses between the enemy's waves of shelling, the defenders used bulldozers to dig the ground for huge mass graves (from 300 to 500 corpses) for dead civilians and soldiers.

"Kiểm tra tình trạng quân số và thương binh thì từ ngày 13-04-72 bắt đầu cuộc chiến đến nay, tổn thất thương vong các tiểu đoàn gần phân nửa. Số người tử thương thì đã giải quyết chôn tại chỗ. Số bị thương thì tồn đọng rất nhiều vì ngày nào cũng có nhiều thương binh nhưng không tản thương được. Vì thế, quân y tạm thời giải quyết như sau: số người bị thương nhẹ còn đi đứng được thì sau khi băng bó xong cho trở về đơn vị, địch vào cầm súng bắn nữa. Do đó có người bị thương 2 hoặc 3 lần hoặc nhiều lần. Có người lần trước bị thương nhẹ, lần sau bị thương

nặng. Cũng có những thương binh nhẹ sau đó lại tử thương! Còn những thương binh nặng để nằm đó chờ tản thương sống thoi thóp rồi có người mòn mỏi chết dần. Đại Đội 52 Quân Y báo cáo khu vực Trung Đoàn 8 có cả ngàn quân nhân và thường dân bị thương nặng chờ tản thương nằm chật cả một dãy phố Đại Lộ Hoàng Hôn. Những người còn lành mạnh thì rất mệt mỏi và gầy ốm vì phải chiến đấu hết ngày này sang ngày khác, không thì giờ nghỉ ngơi, thiếu ngủ, thiếu ăn, tinh thần lúc nào cũng căng thẳng, sinh mạng không biết sẽ chết lúc nào. Lại nữa mùi hôi thối từ xác chết rất khó thở, ruồi lằn sinh sản nhanh kinh khủng! Nước không đủ uống, lấy đâu mà tắm giặt, dơ bẩn, khó chịu, nhưng họ cũng phải ráng chịu, phấn đấu sống để mà chiến đấu, để bảo vệ quê hương và dân tộc không lọt vào tay Cộng Sản." [36]

(Translation:

"A review of the level of strength of all units, from the beginning of the battle on July 13, 1972 up to the present, showed that the casualty level of battalions was at almost 50%. The dead soldiers were buried in place. The number of the injured ones increased day by day because the medivac was impossible. The unit surgeons, therefore, decided to resolve the issue as follows: those soldiers who were lightly injured would be released back to their units so that they could continue to fight. This decision las led to the fact that some soldiers could be injured two or three times, or even several times. In some cases, the second injury was more serious than the first one. In other cases, the second injury was fatal. There were also cases in which the soldiers with serious injuries, while waiting for medivac, became weaker and weaker and died. The 52nd Company of Medical Services reported that within the area responsible by the 8th Infantry Regiment there were thousands of seriously injured soldiers and civilians, who occupied many houses on Sunset Boulevard, waiting for medivac. The uninjured soldiers were losing weight and totally exhausted because they had been uninterruptedly fighting for days, without a break, a rest, lacking of sleep, of foods, under constant pressure, and under threat of being killed at any time. In addition, the stench of rotted

corpses made breathing extremely difficult. Another terrible fact of the polluted environment was that flies were everywhere. Water was so scarce, not enough for drinking, let alone bathing, washing clothes. Everyone was feeling very uncomfortable but they had no choice: they must continue to fight to survive, and to keep the country out of the Communist control.")

Third Wave of Attacks: 11-15/May/1972

After more than two weeks of regrouping, getting reinforcements and new supplies, as well as re-equipping with new guns and tanks, the Communists launched a new wave of attacks, starting in the morning of May 11, 1972. One day before that, there was an important change in the defenders' side: Colonel Miller, Chief Advisor of General Hưng, ended his tour of duty in Vietnam, and was replaced by Colonel Walter Ulmer, a West Point graduate with combat experience after two previous one-year tours of duty in Vietnam. This change would have a good effect to General Hưng's work because, unlike Colonel Miller, Colonel Ulmer was calmer, more sensitive, and more understanding.

At exactly 4:30 am of May 11, 1972, the tremendous shelling into An Lộc, which had been continuous since 1 am, suddenly stopped: the defenders knew right away that the attack with infantrymen was about to begin. And they were right. The infantry units of the VC 5th started their attack from the north while the infantry units of the 9th Division did the same from the west, with the support of 40 tanks.[37] The fighting resumed in the same form and with the same intensity just like the two previous ones. One thing new in this wave of attacks was the fact that the Communists, for the first time, used the Russian-made surface-to-air infrared-homing-guided SA-7 Strela missiles to fight back the aircraft employed by the USAF and the AFVN for ground supports, especially targeting the US Cobra gunships.

In the north, the 8th Infantry Regiment and the 81st Commando Airborne Brigade were under great pressure by the VC 5th Division but they fought back ferociously and still kept their positions. In the west, the 7th Infantry Regiment was also under fierce attack by the 272nd Regiment of the VC 9th Division. The defending forces destroyed 2 tanks, but the enemy forces still advanced, closing in on the Command Headquarters of the 5th Infantry Division of General Hưng. The 3rd Infantry Battalion had to retreat to keep its forces. The situation in An Lộc was extremely grave. General Hưng ordered the 5th Airborne Battalion to rush from the south in order to break the siege at the Division's Headquarters. In a phone conversation with Colonel Trường, Commander of the 8th Regiment in the north, General Hưng said:

"Nếu địch tràn ngập Bộ Tư Lệnh Sư Đoàn 5 trước khi tiểu đoàn Dù tới thì tôi sẽ tự sát chớ không để cho địch bắt. Vậy khi tôi chết rồi thì anh dắt Trung Đoàn 8 đi theo Liên Đoàn 81 Biệt Cách Dù rút về Chơn Thành." [38]

(Translation:

"If the 5th Infantry Division's Headquarters were overrun by the enemy before the 5th Airborne Battalion arrives, I would commit suicide, not letting myself captured by the enemy. After my death, you should lead the 8th Regiment and move with the 81st Commando Airborne Brigade to Chơn Thành.")

Fortunately, right at that moment, the attacking forces committed a big mistake. The units of the 272nd Regiment of the VC 9th Division, instead of advancing to the southeast, moved to the northeast, attacking, overrunning, and capturing the office of the Bình Long provincial Department of Public Works.[39] After that, thanks to the arrival of the 5th Airborne Battalion from the south, of one Rangers battalion from the east, and of the 8th Reconnaissance Company of the 8th Infantry Regiment from the north, the 5th Infantry Division's Headquarters was secured.

In the meantime, under the very effective maneuver of the

US Chief Advisor, Colonel Ulmer, the number of USAF flights of tactical supports for An Lộc was greatly increasing. Just for May 11, there was a total of 297 tactical support flights carried out over An Lộc. After that, during the next 4 days, there were about 260 flights. Regarding the strategic B-52 bombers, within 24 hours of May 11, there was a total of 30 flights, including the 5 flights that General Hollingsworth had "borrowed" from the II Corps. This time, the ***"carpet bombing"*** by the B-52s was accurate beyond imagination, sometimes just a few hundred meters from the defenders' positions. In one of these B-52 flights, the ***"carpet bombing"*** was executed just 600 yards from the 81st Commando Airborne Brigade's positions and was successful in saving the Brigade when it was surrounded and almost overrun by a whole regiment of the VC 5th Division. This regiment was almost completely wiped out.[40]

Toward the evening of May 15, 1972, the Communist third wave of attacks of An Lộc was considered as a complete failure: ***they did not capture An Lộc***. A large number of their 40 T-54 tanks were destroyed right inside the town, with some still intact but abandoned by their soldiers, who tried to escape by running away. Most of their infantry units were decimated by the defenders and by these tactical support flights. The remaining soldiers were terrified by these US-South Vietnamese air forces' tactical bombings, completely losing their morale, escaping by running away into the rubber plantations around An Lộc, with a quite large number of them being victims of these B-52's ***"carpet bombings."*** In the following days, the Communists still launched a few attacks but they have already lost their momentum. In the evening of May 15, all of the remaining units of their attacking forces left An Lộc area for good.

This third wave of attacks was completely broken, but the fighting was still on since the enemy still tried to keep the areas surrounding An Lộc they had captured.

ARVN's Counterattack and Breaking the Siege of An Lộc

In the northern side of An Lộc, on June 10, 1972, the 81st Commando Airborne Brigade, despite its quite heavy casualties, launched a search-and-destroy operation against all enemy resistance outposts in the streets they had captured before. Two days later, after having gained the total control of this area, the Brigade began another operation to recapture Đồng Long Hill, about half a kilometer north of An Lộc, which had been captured by the enemy for the past two months. Following is a recount of the operation by Captain Lê Đắc Lực of the 81st Commando Airborne Brigade:

"Đích thân Trung Tá Chỉ Huy Trưởng Phan Văn Huấn đã điều động Đại Đội 2 và Đại Đội 3 chia làm hai cánh, Đại Đội 3 do Đại Úy Phạm Châu Tài chỉ huy, sẽ tiến quân từ hướng Đông và Đại Đội 2 do Đại Úy Nguyễn Sơn chỉ huy, phối hợp cùng hai Toán Thám Sát do Thiếu Úy Lê Văn Lợi chỉ huy, sẽ tiến quân từ hướng Nam, tất cả lợi dụng vào nửa đêm trời tối, âm thầm, kín đáo bò sát lên đỉnh đồi, nằm ém quân tại chỗ, đợi cho đến khi trời vừa hừng sáng, sau khẩu lệnh xung phong của Đại Úy Sơn, tất cả đã đồng loạt nổ súng xối xả, tấn công vào các pháo tháp, hầm trú ẩn của địch quân, bọn địch dù đông, công sự phòng thủ vững chắc, nhưng quá bất ngờ, không kịp trở tay trước lối đánh thần tốc, táo bạo của Biệt Cách Dù, nên một số đã bị sát hại, số còn lại vừa định thần đã phản ứng chống trả, nhưng không ngăn cản được quyết tâm tái chiếm đồi Đồng Long của các Chiến sĩ Biệt Cách Dù, cuối cùng chúng cũng đã bị tiêu diệt, hay đã phải buông súng đầu hàng.

Hai Toán Thám Sát đã không chậm trễ, khai triển đội hình công hãm và thanh toán cứ điểm cuối cùng của địch trên chóp đỉnh, bốn tên địch quân ngoan cố cầm cự trong tuyệt vọng, để rồi phải phơi thây thảm khốc. Thiếu Úy Lợi và các Toán viên đã mừng rơi nước mắt, cùng cầm Quốc Kỳ Việt Nam Cộng Hòa cắm xuống ngay trên đỉnh Đồi Đồng Long." [41]

(Translation:

"It was our Commander, Lieutenant-Colonel Phan Văn Huấn, who deployed two companies, the 2nd and the 3rd, divided in 2 wings, the 3rd Company under the command of Captain

Phạm Châu Tài moving from the east, and the 2nd Company under the command of Captain Nguyễn Sơn moving from the south, in co-ordination with 2 Reconnaissance Teams under the command of Second-Lieutenant Lê Văn Lợi moving from the south. All units, taking advantage of the night, quietly crawled to the top of the hill, lied down there in total silence, and waited. At the first morning light, after Captain Sơn's order for assault, all soldiers fired off their weapons, fiercely attacked all enemy outposts, bunkers. Although they outnumbered the Brigade and were in solidly protected positions, the enemies were completely surprised by the Brigade's lightning fast, and daring assault. A large number of them were killed. The remaining enemy force tried to regroup and fight back but was unable to stop the Brigade's determination of recapturing Đồng Long Hill. At the end, most of them were eliminated, and the rest surrendered.

The two Reconnaissance Teams were quick in their attack of the enemy last outpost on top of the hill. The group of four enemy soldiers in that outpost stubbornly fought back and were also killed. Second-Lieutenant Lợi and his men could not hold back their tears when they put up the RVN's flag right on the top of Đồng Long Hill.")

With the recapture of Đồng Long Hill, the town of An Lộc was considered as completely liberated. On June 16, 1972, Lieutenant-General Nguyễn Văn Minh, Commander of III Corps, flew to An Lộc, and promoted "at the battlefield" Lieutenant-Colonel Phan Văn Huấn, Commander of the 81st Commando Airborne Brigade, to Full Colonel.

Figure 3.12. Temporary cemetery in An Lộc for the fallen soldiers of the 81st Commando Airborne Brigade
(Source: ***An Lộc Địa*** by Lê Đắc Lực)

Figure 3.13. Cemetery in An Lộc, rebuilt after the battle, for the fallen soldiers of the 81st Commando Airborne Brigade
(Source: Same as Figure 3.12)

It was right here, on the common tombstone of the town cemetery, was engraved Ms Nguyễn Thị Pha's poem (a school teacher in An Lộc), which has now become part of the History of South Vietnam:

An Lộc địa sử ghi chiến tích
Biệt Cách Dù vị quốc vong thân

(Translation:

History Recorded Victory in the Land of An Lộc Commando Airborne Soldiers Fell for Fatherland

In the south, the clearance of National Route 13, from Chơn Thành to An Lộc, faced many difficulties due to the blockages by the VC 7th Division, which cut off National Route 13 at many points between Lai Khê and Chơn Thành, and between Chơn Thành and An Lộc, as illustrated in the following map:

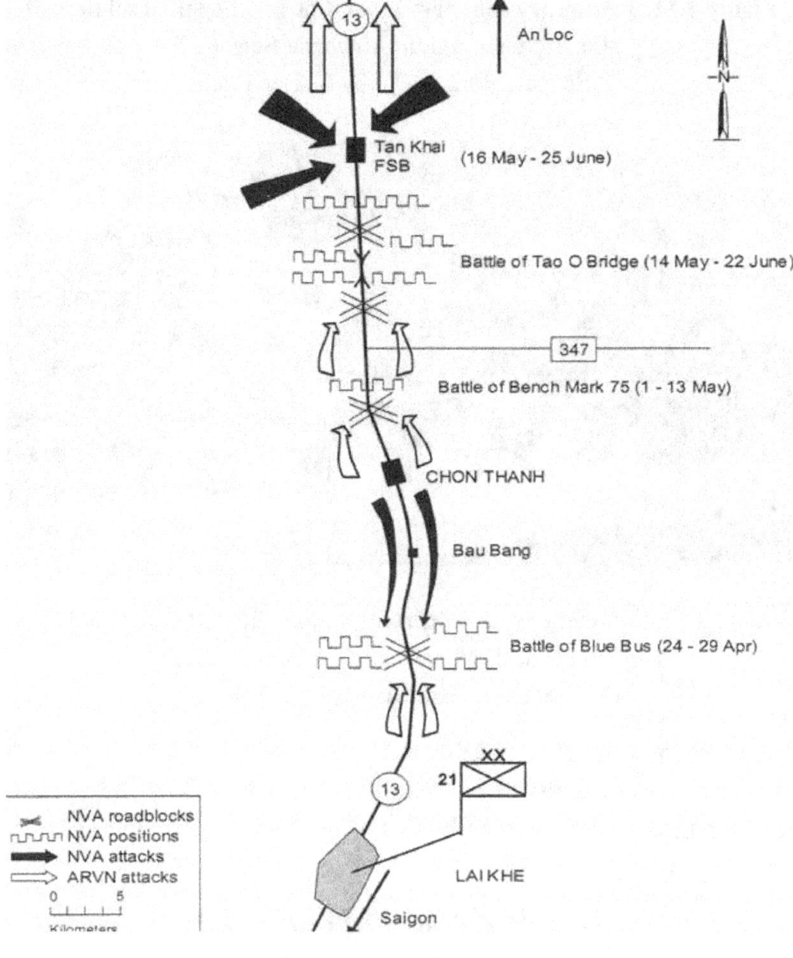

Figure 3.14. Map of National Route 13 with "blockages" by VC 7th Division between Lai Khê và Tân Khai

After the meeting at the Independence Palace of April 6, 1972, the 21st Infantry Division, under the command of Major-General Nguyễn Vĩnh Nghi,[42] was ordered to move immediately from the IV Corps as reinforcements for the III Corps. The whole division had been present in Lai Khê since April 12 and was positioned as follows: 1) The 31st Regiment in Suối Tre Hamlet area; 2) The 32nd Regiment in the south of Chơn Thành; 3) The 33rd Regiment in the north of Lai Khê; and, 4) The 9th Armored Cavalry Squadron right in Lai Khê.

With a determination to completely lock the National Route 13 from Lai Khê to An Lộc, in order to deny the 21st Infantry Division' s move to reinforce and break the siege, several units of the two regiments, the 165th and the 209th, of the 7th Division (after mid-may 1972, the 9th Division dispatched several more units as reinforcements), had positioned many blockages, causing a lot of difficulties for the 21st Infantry Division, which had to engage in several big battles along the National Route 13 during the period of April-May-June 1972. (See the map above). Both sides suffered many casualties as follows: 1) For the 21st Infantry Division, up to May 26, 1972, out of 12,000 soldiers, the casualty rate has already reached 50%, including a high-ranking officer, Colonel Trương Hữu Đức (posthumously promoted to Brigadier-General), Commander of the 52nd Task Force, killed in Chơn Thành when his C & C helicopter was hit and downed; 2) On the Communist side, several companies (usually with 150-200 men) of the 209th Regiment was down to 10 men.[43] From mid-May 1972, with the big difficulties which the 21st Infantry Division was facing on National Route 13, the 9th Infantry Division's 15th Regiment (under the command of Colonel Hồ Ngọc Cẩn[44]), was ordered to move from the IV Corps to reinforce the 21st Division.

Tân Khai was a village about 9 km southeast of An Lộc. Its terrain was quite flat and bare, totally unfit for erecting blockages, and thus, not occupied by the enemy. Recognizing this advantage, on May 15, Lieutenant-General Minh created a new Task Force and placed it under the command of Colonel Cẩn. This Task Force included the 9th Armored Cavalry Squadron, 1 infantry battalion extracted from the 15th Regiment, and a battery of three 105-mm howitzers extracted from the 93rd Artillery Battalion. The Task Force was ordered to bypass the enemy blockage at Tàu Ô Creek, and moved north to capture Tân Khai. At the same time, another battalion, also of the 15th Regiment, was helilifted to a point about 1.5 km east of Tân Khai. This unit searched and secured the area in preparation for future moves of troops to Tân Khai. In the following days, the remaining units of the 15th Regiment were all helilifted to Tân Khai. In the mean time, AFVN's Chinook helicopters and U.S. Sikorsky helicopters brought in the 105-mm and 155-mm guns to establish the Long Phi fire-support base in Tân Khai to provide support to An Lộc. On May 18, 1972, the 15th Regiment was already in total control of the area surrounding the Long Phi fire-support base in Tân Khai.

Having noticed their big mistake regarding Tân Khai, the Communists immediately launched their counter-attack. In the morning of May 20, the VC 141st Regiment of the 7th Division, supported by tanks, immediately attacked the fire-support base in Tân Khai. The fighting lasted several weeks and both sides suffered high casualties.

In the morning of June 4, 1972, the 6th Airborne Battalion, after having regrouped, reinforced, re-equipped, was helilifted to Tân Khai, and, together with other battalions of the 15th Regiment, divided in 2 wings, immediately moved to clear National Route 13, from Tân Khai to An Lộc. After four days of fierce fighting, the 6th Airborne Battalion was successful in removing all blockages by the 7th Division, and:

"đúng 17 giờ 15 ngày 8 tháng 6, Đại Úy Ngô Xuân Vinh, Đại Đội Trưởng Đại Đội 62, đứng lên mặt đường nhựa, ngã ba vào xã Thanh Bình (đồn điền Xa Cam), bắt tay với Đại Úy Trương Ngọc Ni, Đại Đội Trưởng

81 Nhảy Dù, đơn vị cực Nam của An Lộc, để đánh dấu một chiến thắng quan trọng ngày giải toả AN LỘC." [45]

(Translation:

"at exactly 17:15 on June 8, Captain Ngô Xuân Vinh, Commander of the 62th Company, standing up on the asphalted road, at the intersection to Thanh Bình Village (Xa Cam plantation), shook hand with Captain Trương Ngọc Ni, Commander of the 81st Company of the 8th Airborne Battalion, the unit defending the southernmost point of An Lộc, and, thus, marked an important victory of the day An Lộc was liberated.")

The connection of the two airborne battalions as well as the one of the units of the 15th Regiment with the units defending the southern side of An Lộc, marked the beginning of the complete clearance of An Lộc. The defending perimeter of An Lộc was expanded, and the helicopter flights were carried out safely for medical evacuations, supplies and troop reinforcements. On June 13, the 48th Regiment of the 18th Infantry Division was brought in by helicopters from Lai Khê to An Lộc to replace the units of the 5th Infantry Division, which had suffered high casualties, and were extremely tired, almost exhausted after three months of almost continuous fighting. On June 17, the units of the 48th Regiment launched their first operation, capturing the hills south of An Lộc, and, from the advantageous positions of these hills, have guided effectively the USAF and AFVN aircraft in their bombings of the remaining VC outposts north and west of An Lộc, Thanks to these activities, the 81st Commando Airborne Brigade and the 3rd Rangers Brigade were able to recapture the whole northern side of An Lộc, and the 7th Regiment of the 5th Infantry Division was also able to recapture the western side of the town, which had been captured by the enemy since May 11.[46] Although there was some sporadic shelling by the enemy, and with An Lộc now being flattened, the whole town was now under the total control of the ARVN units.

Figure 3.15. Aerial view of An Lộc being flattened

On June 18, Lieutenant-General Nguyễn Văn Minh, Commander of III Corps, after his flight to An Lộc with his Chief US Advisor, Major-General Hollingsworth two days before, officially announced that the Communist siege of An Lộc was completely over. On June 24, the 81st Commando Airborne Brigade and the 1st Airborne Brigade were ordered to leave An Lộc, going to the I Corps to reinforce the Quảng Trị battlefront.

On July 7, 1972, President Nguyễn Văn Thiệu flew to An Lộc to visit and console the soldiers, and decorate and promote a number of commanders of the defending forces there. At the same time, he also made the historic decision in the history of the ARVN to give the promotion by one rank to ***ALL*** soldiers present during the time of the heroic fighting in An Lộc.

Figure 3.16. Photo taken on 7-July-1972 at President Thiệu's visit of An Lộc

From left to right: Lieutenant-General Nguyễn Văn Minh, Commander of III Corps, Colonel Bùi Đức Điềm, Operation Assistant to Commander of 5th Infantry Division, General Cao Văn Viên, Chief of General Staff of ARVN, Brigadier-General Lê Văn Hưng, Commander of 5th Infantry Division, President Nguyễn Văn Thiệu, and Colonel Trần Văn Nhựt, Province Chief and Sub-District Chief of Bình Long.

Concluding Remarks

The Battle of An Lộc, from April to June 1972, with an unprecedented intensity, ended with a glorious, worth of admiration victory of the ARVN heroic soldiers, who wowed to fight to the death to defend the town. Both sides have suffered huge casualties and lost tremendous armaments. The most tragic thing about the battle, however, was the great loss of lives and properties of the local people trapped in An Lộc during the whole time of the fighting, as shown in the following painful and horrible story of two little girls, who miraculously survived the battle:

"Để chuẩn bị cho cuộc tấn công tái chiếm Đồi Đồng Long, trong lúc khai triển đội hình khi đến gần chân đồi với đầy dẫy cây rừng hoang dại, các Chiến Sĩ Đại Đội 2 Biệt Cách Dù đã phát hiện một căn hầm, nằm khuất lấp dưới những tấm ván gỗ và những cỏ cây xác xơ vì bom đạn. Các Binh sĩ áp sát đến miệng hầm, họ nghe vài ba tiếng động sột soạt nhỏ phát ra từ bên trong. Rất thận trọng, họ chưa vội nổ súng hay tung lựu đạn

mà chỉ phát lời kêu gọi đầu hàng, đồng thời cấp báo ngay về Bộ Chỉ Huy Hành Quân, Trung Tá Chỉ Huy Trưởng Phan Văn Huấn ra lệnh Đại Úy Sơn cho Binh sĩ quan sát kỹ càng, có thể là địch quân mà cũng có thể là đồng bào, nhưng bất kể họ là ai, với hơn hai tháng chiến trận xảy ra nơi đây, không lương thực, nước uống, thì đâu còn sức đề kháng để chống cự, phải tìm mọi cách đưa họ ra khỏi căn hầm đó. Và thật không thể tưởng tượng được, chỉ vài ba phút sau đó, có hai em bé gái khoảng chừng 6, 7 tuổi bò ra, trên người chỉ còn những mảnh vải rách nát, tả tơi che thân, đất bùn, ghét bẩn bám đen xì trên thân thể khô cằn, còm cỏi, chỉ còn da bọc xương, hai mắt sâu hoắm trên một khuôn mặt hốc hác, ngây dại, thờ thẫn, giọng nói khàn đục, thiểu não, nhìn hai bé chẳng khác gì hai bộ xương biết đi, thật quá đổi thương tâm, đau lòng, không ai có thể cầm được nước mắt.

Trung Tá Chỉ Huy Trưởng đã mang hai bé về Bộ Chỉ Huy Hành Quân và giao cho Ban Quân Y của Bác Sĩ Nguyễn Thành Châu khám nghiệm, chữa trị, chăm sóc cho đến khi hai bé tạm bình phục và hai bé đã kể lại mọi sự việc như sau: "Hai cháu tên là Hà Thị Loan và Hà Thị Nở, con của Trung Sĩ Hà Văn Hiến, phục vụ tại Tiểu Khu. Khi Việt Cộng tấn công, pháo kích vào An Lộc, Mẹ cõng em trai 4 tuổi và dắt hai cháu chạy giặc, thì bất ngờ Mẹ bị trúng đạn pháo chết ngay tại chỗ, em trai bị thương nặng ở chân. Chúng cháu liền cõng em trai chạy xuống ẩn trú trong một cái hầm kế cận chân đồi Đồng Long, trong đêm hôm đó em trai cháu chết, quá khó khăn để chôn cất, nên chúng cháu để xác em trai nằm bên cạnh cho đến thối rửa chỉ còn bộ xương. Chúng cháu trốn ở đó suốt hơn hai tháng, lúc đầu may nhờ có một số cơm gạo sấy của ai bỏ lại đã ăn dần, về sau ăn sống luôn mấy con gà con lạc mẹ đang trốn chung trong hầm. Cạn kiệt lương thực, đói quá ban đêm khi không còn nghe tiếng đạn pháo kích, thì mò ra khỏi hầm kiếm rau cỏ mà ăn. May nhờ đến ngày hôm nay được các bác tìm thấy mà cứu sống các cháu." [47]

(Translation:

"While preparing for the counter-attack to recapture Đồng Long Hill, in their approach to the foot of the hill covered with wild brushes, the soldiers of the 2nd Commando Airborne Company discovered an underground shelter, hidden under wooden boards covered with debris made of pieces of grasses and

tree branches shattered by bombings. They crawled close to the opening of the shelter, and heard some very faint sounds emitting from inside. Acting carefully, they neither fired their guns nor threw grenades into the shelter. They just made calls for surrender, and at the same time reported to the operation command post. The commander, Lieutenant-Colonel Phan Văn Huấn, ordered Captain Sơn's men to observe carefully, to find out for sure if that was the enemy or our people. He insisted that whatever the case, enemy or our people, after more than two months of the battle, and without food and water, they would not have enough strength to resist, and they must be taken out of the shelter. And something unimaginable happened: after just two or three minutes, two little girls, 6 or 7 years old, crawled out of the shelter. Their clothes were torn in pieces. Their bodies were just skin-and-bones blackened with dirt. They looked haggard with deep eye sockets and with hoarse voices. Looking at them, just like two walking skeletons, the soldiers could not hold back their tears.

The Commander brought them back to the Brigade's headquarters and delivered them to Dr. Nguyễn Thành Châu's Medical Section for examination, treatment and caring. After they have somewhat recovered, they told their story: ***"We are Hà Thị Loan and Hà Thị Nở, the children of Sargent Hà Văn Hiến, serving at the Sub-District. When the VC attacked, shelled into An Lộc, Mother carried our 4-year- old younger brother on her back and led us run for shelter. Suddenly Mother was hit and killed on the spot, and our younger brother had his foot injured. We carried our brother to hide in an underground shelter close to the foot of Đồng Long Hill. Our brother died that evening. Unable to bury him, we just laid him down there. His body was rotting away until it became just a skeleton. We were hiding there for more than two months. At first, thanks to some dried rice left by someone, we had something to eat; after that we had to eat raw, without cooking,***

some strayed baby chickens that were hiding in the shelter with us. At the end, without any food, we had to wait until the shelling stopped then we crawled out of the shelter, searched and ate any vegetables or even grass we found. We are lucky to be found and saved by you, uncles."

CHAPTER FOUR

Recapture of Quảng Trị: The Bloodiest Battle of the Vietnam War

On March 30, 1972, three North Vietnamese divisions crossed the DMZ (Demilitarized Zone), attacked defense outposts of the ARVN (Armed Forces of the Republic of Vietnam) north and west of Quảng Trị Province, in I Corps. This Summer 1972 General Offensive, called ***The Easter Offensive*** by the US media, really began. Two weeks later, three other North Vietnamese divisions attacked An Lộc, the capital city of Bình Long Province, in III Corps, 60 km north of Sài Gòn. And around the same time, on April 14, 1972, Kontum Province in II Corps was also attacked by two North Vietnamese divisions. In I Corps, on May 2, 1972, the Communists captured Quảng Trị Province after Brigadier-General Vũ Văn Giai, Commander of the 3rd Infantry Division, decided to retreat from the Đinh Công Tráng Citadel. The north of Thừa Thiên Province and Huế was gravely threatened. On the next day, May 3, 1972, President Nguyễn Văn Thiệu nominated Lieutenant-General Ngô Quang Trưởng,[1] the then-current Commander of IV Corps, to replace Lieutenant-General Hoàng Xuân Lãm as Commander of I Corps. In the afternoon of the same day, General Trưởng, together with some senior high-ranking officers of his staff, immediately flew to Huế. From Phú Bài airfield, news of ***"General Trưởng Is Back"*** was spreading fast and Huế was like reborn. After a really swift stabilization of the bad situation in Huế, General Trưởng organized the great operation code-named ***Operation Lam Sơn 72*** with the objective of recapturing Quảng Trị. This operation officially ended when the ARVN achieved a total victory, recapturing the Đinh Công Tráng Citadel on September 15, 1972. This Chapter tries to recount this operation: the bloodiest battle of the 20-year Vietnam War.

Political Importance of the Battle

When Mr. Richard M. Nixon was inaugurated as U.S. President on January 20, 1969, the U.S. was having more than half a million troops in the RVN (Republic of Vietnam), already with 31,000 KIA (Killed in Action), and the Vietnam War had become the cause of the most serious division within the U.S. population since the end of the Civil War (1861-1865) more than one hundred years ago. President Nixon had to find a way to help the U.S. disengage from the war without being accused of abandoning its ally, the RVN. The solution he found was called the Vietnamization of the War: a planned, gradual, and phased withdrawal of U.S. troops from South Vietnam, going hand in hand with the preparation of the ARVN to take full responsibility in this defensive war. The first test of this policy was the Operation Lam Sơn 719 (February and March 1971) carried out by the ARVN with their attack across the Laotian border, aimed at destroying North Vietnamese supply depots on the Hồ Chí Minh Trail. The ARVN achieved some of the objectives of this important operation but also had to pay a high price with some heavy losses. North Vietnam maintained that they had defeated the ARVN, and, therefore, Nixon's Vietnamization policy had failed. For North Vietnam, this Summer 1972 General Offensive was to prove to the whole world that the Vietnamization policy of the U.S. was, undeniably, a total failure.

From mid-1968, after the Tet Offensive, the U.S. and North Vietnam, then later also with the participation of both the RVN and the NFL (National Liberation Front, i.e., VC = Viet Cong) had begun the peace talk in Paris, France. The negotiations had lasted 4 years, and now had to be concluded. Both sides wanted to have the upper hand in the military front in order to obtain concessions from the opponents in the diplomatic front. The battle of Quảng Trị became a very important card game, and, for both sides, it should be "a must win."

For the RVN and the U.S., the recapture of Quảng Trị had to be done at all cost. The most combat-experienced units of the ARVN, therefore, were put under the command of Lieutenant-General Ngô Quang Trưởng, Commander of I Corps. The U.S. also wanted to see the ARVN recapture Quảng Trị, and, thus, tried the best to provide the ARVN with the most effective air and artillery supports at the battlefield. Never before were the U.S. air and artillery supports carried out at that level of intensity. In addition to the maximum air and artillery supports from battleships of the U.S. Pacific Fleet offshore of the East Sea (i.e., South China Sea), there were continuous "carpet bombings" by B-52 strategic bombers from Andersen base in Guam and from U-Tapao base in Thailand. U.S. Air Force statistics showed that, in the 3 months, April-June 1972, during the Battle of Quảng Trị, there was a total of 2,700 sorties of B-52 with 57,000 tons of bombs dropped in these "carpet bombings."[2] On the U.S. Navy side, the unit participating in the battle was the Task Force 77 of the 7th Fleet, with two aircraft carriers, the Hancock and the Coral Sea (later reinforced with 4 more aircraft carriers, the Kitty Hawk, the Constellation, the Midway and the Saratoga) and several destroyers and cruisers. Each aircraft carrier had an air wing with about 90 jet fighters of different types such as F-4 Phantom, A-7 Corsair, and A-6 Intruder. [3] Of course, the casualties of the North Vietnamese by these air and artillery supports from the U.S. forces were horrible.

Figure 4.1. "Carpet bombing" by a flight of B-52 in 1972 in Quảng Trị
Source: Internet

From the North Vietnamese side, in order to prove that Vietnamization was a complete failure, they had to keep Quảng Trị at all cost. The order to ***fight to the death*** was imposed to the commanders of all units occupying Quảng Trị. On June 28, 1972, when General Trưởng gave the order to launch the Operation Lam Sơn 72 for the counter-attack aimed at recapturing Quảng Trị, the City of Quảng Trị and the Đinh Công Tráng Citadel had been under the enemy's control for almost two months. North Vietnamese forces had more time than they needed to organize their defense: digging traffic trenches, building underground shelters, arranging obstacles, setting up pre-arranged coordinates for artillery, positioning air defense network, etc. All units of the Airborne and Marine Divisions of the ARN would have to pay with their blood to recapture each square meter of land, each house, each street. Never before in the 20-year Vietnam War have these South Vietnamese combat-experienced units sustained casualties that high.

Orders of Battle of Both Sides

North Vietnamese Army (NVA) forces defending Quảng Trị included the following units:

• 2 regiments of the 320B Division: the 48th Regiment and the Triệu Hải Regiment

• 1 regiment of the 325th Division: the 95th Regiment

• 1 regiment of the 308th Division: the 88th Regiment

• 2 local battalions of Quảng Trị

• Later, reinforcements were: the 312th Division, and the remaining units of the 325th Division

On the South Vietnamese side, the attacking forces to recapture Quảng Trị included the following units:

• 2 brigades of the Airborne Division: the 2nd and the 3rd Brigades

• 3 brigades of the Marine Division: the 147th, the 258th, and the 369th Brigades

• 81st Commando Airborne Brigade

• 2 Armored Cavalry Squadrons: the 7th and the 18th Squadrons

• Artillery battalions of the Airborne Division and the Marine Division

From the U.S. side, there was absolutely no involvement of ground combat troops, but there were tremendous air and artillery supports, including B-52 strategic bombers.

Counter-Attack Plan by General Trưởng

The counter-attack plan to recapture Quảng Trị by Lieutenant-General Ngô Quang Trưởng, newly appointed Commander of I Corps, included two main parts:

• Part I: stabilizing the situation in Huế

• Part II: launching attack to the north to recapture Quảng Trị

Stabilizing and Safeguarding Huế

Figure 4.2. Lieutenant-General Ngô Quang Trưởng, Commander of I Corps

After the fall of Quảng Trị, together with the North Vietnamese pursuit of the retreating units of the ARVN between Quảng Trị and Thừa Thiên Provinces, causing the indiscriminate massacre of innocent people on National Route 1 (called the ***Đại Lộ Kinh Hoàng = Highway of Horror*** by South Vietnamese media), the city of Huế had to bear the heavy military pressure by the enemy from outside and to face with tremendous difficulties from inside caused by the presence of tens of thousands of refugees coming from Quảng Trị as well as by the bad and undisciplined actions of the soldiers of these retreating units.

In order to stabilize the situation and to calm down the people of Huế, General Trưởng's first action was to issue two very important orders: 1) Establish the Advanced Command of I Corps in the north of Huế with the responsibility to stop all attacks of the North Vietnamese forces; and, 2) Order that all wandering soldiers, either having left their units or having losing contact with their units, or having their units disintegrated, must present themselves to currently existing military authorities in the city. Those soldiers refusing to comply with this order would be shot to death on the spot. Only after a few days were the situation and the morale of the people of Huế completely stabilized.

General Trưởng decided to assign the responsibility of defending the north of Thừa Thiên Province and the imperial city of Huế to the two most combat-experienced of the Advanced Command of I Corps. The Marine Division, with the new Commander, colonel Bùi Thế Lân,[4] had the responsibility to defend the north and northwest of Huế. The 1st Infantry Division, under the command of Major-General Phạm Văn Phú[5], had the responsibility to defend the south and southwest of Huế, stopping all Communist attacks from A Shau Valley.[6]

In the north of Huế, the defense line of the South Vietnamese Marine Division ran along the south bank of Mỹ Chánh River, with the 147th Brigade on the left, and the 369th Brigade on the right. The 147th Brigade, with Lieutenant-Colonel (later promoted to Colonel) Nguyễn Năng Bảo as Commander, included the following units: the 1st Battalion (called Quái Điểu = Monster Bird), the 4th Battalion (called Kình Ngư = Whale Shark), the 7th Battalion (called Hùm Xám = Gray Tiger), and the 1st Marine Artillery Battalion (called Lôi Hỏa = Thunder Fire). The 369th Brigade, with Lieutenant-Colonel (later also promoted to Colonel) Nguyễn Thế Lương, included the following units: the 3rd Battalion (called Sói Biển = Sea Wolf), the 6th Battalion (called Thần Ưng = Sacred Hawk), the 9th Battalion (called Mãnh Hổ = Strong Tiger), and the 3rd Marine Artillery Battalion (called Nỏ Thần = Sacred Crossbow). These two brigades had the responsibility to stop all attacks from the north by the units of the North Vietnamese 304th, 325th, and 308th Divisions.

In the west and southwest of Huế, the units of the 1st Infantry Division, under the command of General Phạm Văn Phú, had the responsibility to stop all attacks from A Shau Valley of the North Vietnamese 324B Division.

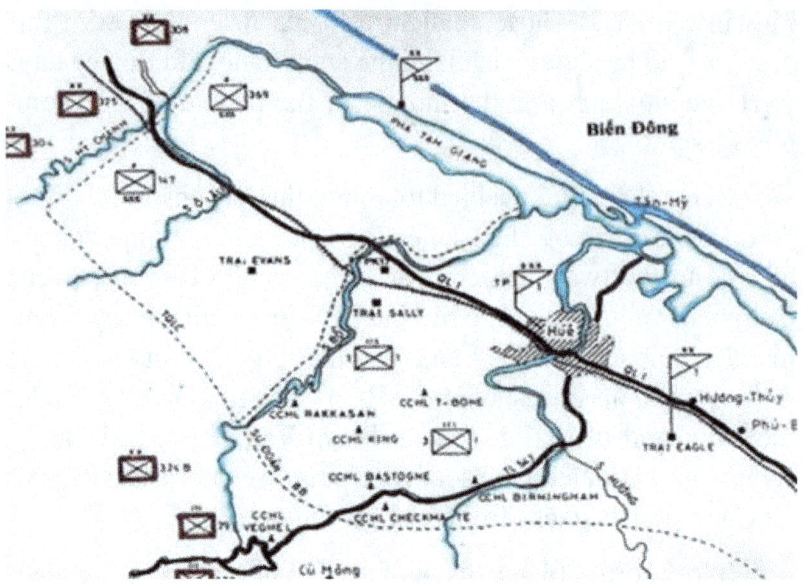

Figure 4.3. Defense map of Quảng Trị – Thừa Thiên at the beginning of May 1972

After almost two months of organizing the defense and stabilizing the situation in Huế, General Trưởng decided that it was about time to launch the counter-attack to recapture Quảng Trị.

Counter-Attack to Recapture Quảng Trị

Preparations Before Launching Operation Lam Sơn

The operation to recapture Quảng Trị, code-named ***Operation Lam Sơn 72***, officially began on June 28, 1972, and ended on September 16, 1972 when the South Vietnamese Marines raised the flag of the Republic of Vietnam on top of the Quảng Trị Old Citadel (also known as the Đinh Công Tráng Citadel).

Because of the great importance of this operation, its preparations were carried out very carefully with three phases: [7]

• The first 10 days of June 1972: all units on the battlefront were regrouped, inspected, getting combat-ready.

• From June 11 to June 18: in the west, the 1st Infantry Division launched an attack in the direction of the Veghel fire-support base; in the north, units of the Airborne and Marine Divisions began operations in the north bank of Mỹ Chánh River to test the strength of the enemy.

• From June 19 to June 27: two diversion operations were launched with the Airborne attacking Cam Lộ, and the Marines landing in Cửa Việt.

Two days before Operation Lam Sơn 72 began, General Trưởng launched a fierce bombardment at all North Vietnamese outposts, their artillery locations and their supply depots as well. In addition to the AFVN and artillery units, there were also the very active involvement of the U.S. counterparts, including the battleships offshore, and the B-52 strategic bombers coming from Thailand (U-Tapao airbase) and Guam (Andersen airbase), as demonstrated in the following map:

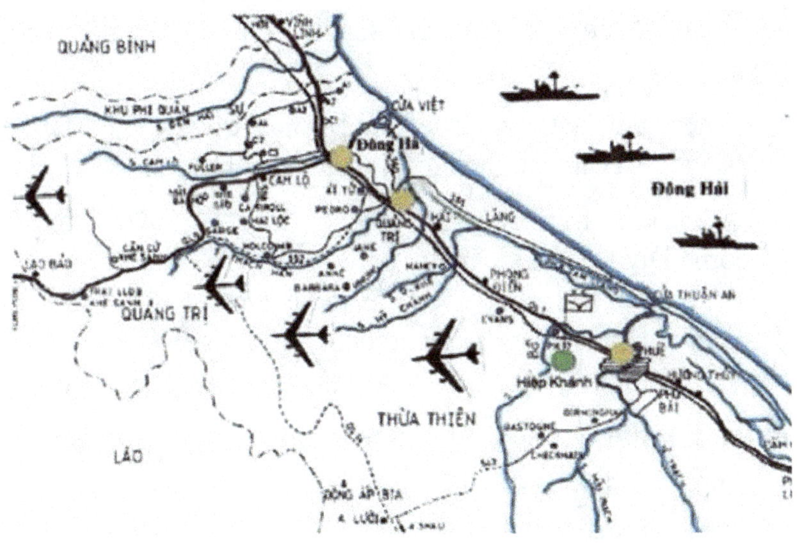

Figure 4.4. Map of Quảng Trị in Summer 1972

<u>Source</u>: Internet

Operation Lam Sơn 72

On June 28, 1972, ***Operation Lam Sơn 72*** officially began with two main thrusts in the north, in coordination with a secondary thrust southwest of Huế. Because he started his career in the airborne service (his first commission, in July 1954, was a Second-Lieutenant, platoon commander, 5th Airborne Battalion[8]), General Trưởng decided to assign the Airborne Division to take the main thrust in this important operation. The direction of the Airborne Division's attack would be southwest of National Route 1 toward La Vang. The second thrust in the north was assigned to the Marine Division, along Local Road 555, toward Triệu Phong. The third thrust southwest of Huế was the responsibility of the 1st Infantry Division. On the southern side of Hải Vân Pass, the defense of Đà Nẵng was given to the 3rd Infantry Division, which was being re-equipped and re-trained under the newly appointed Commander, Brigadier-General Nguyễn Duy Hinh.[9]

The counter-attack carried out by the Airborne and Marine Divisions to recapture Quảng Trị included 2 phases:

• Phase 1: from June 28, 1972 to July 27, 1972 with the Airborne Division as the main force

• Phase 2: from July 27, 1972 to September 16, 1972 with the Marine Division as the main force, resulting in the total victory of recapturing the Đinh Công Tráng (Quảng Trị) Citadel

Phase 1 of the Counter-Attack with the Airborne Division

After having assumed the command of I Corps, General Trưởng requested that the General Staff give him some reinforcements to replace the loss of the 3rd Infantry Division, and he was given two brigades of the Airborne Division: the 2nd and the 3rd. The 2nd Airborne Brigade, under the command of Colonel Trần Quốc Lịch (later promoted to Brigadier-General and appointed Commander of the 5th Infantry Division [10]), arrived in Huế on May 8,1972 and was immediately deployed by General Trưởng to the battlefront with the responsibility to defend the south bank of Mỹ Chánh River, together with the 258th Marine Brigade under the command of Colonel Ngô Văn Định. The 3rd Airborne Brigade, under the command of Colonel Trương Vĩnh Phước, was also sent to I Corps on May 22, 1972. Right after that, the whole Command Staff of the Airborne Division, including the Division Commander, Lieutenant-General Dư Quốc Đống, also flew to I Corps, and took position at Landing Zone (LZ) Sally south of Bồ River, next to National Route 1.[11]

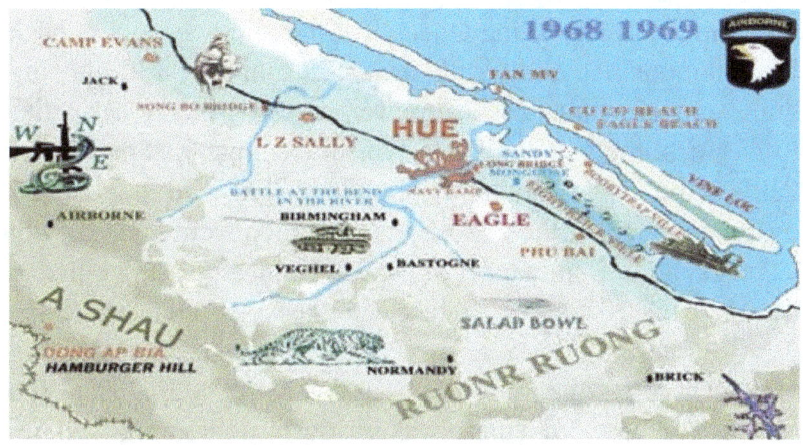

Figure 4.5. Map showing location of LZ Sally in Quảng Trị

<u>Source</u>: Internet

At exactly 3 am, June 28, 1972, Colonel Trần Quốc Lịch ordered the three battalions of his 2nd Airborne Brigade to cross Mỹ Chánh River, launching the counter-attack: the 2nd Battalion with Major Nguyễn Đình Ngọc as Commander on the left, the 1st Battalion with Major Lê Hồng as Commander in the middle, and the 3rd Battalion with Major Trần Văn Sơn as Commander on the right. Thanks to the factor of surprise, these three battalions obtained some encouraging results, breaking the North Vietnamese's defense line, attacking directly the command post of the 203rd Armored Regiment, seizing several heavy equipment, such as 62-mm and 81-mm mortars, 37-mm and 57-mm anti-aircraft guns, and even three T-54 tanks as well. The Airborne forces continued to push north, with the 3rd Battalion turning to the east with objective to capture Hải Lăng District. In the early morning of the same day, two additional Airborne battalions, the 9th Battalion (with Lieutenant-Colonel Trần Hữu Phú as Commander), and the 11th Battalion (with Major Lê Văn Mễ as Commander) were helilifted to land at north of Nhùng River. These two battalions were going in parallel, pushing to the north, and removing all enemy blockages. Certainly, the North Vietnamese knew right away that this ARVN's counter-attack was aimed at recapturing Quảng Trị, they fiercely fought back by continuous shelling with their 122-mm and 130-mm big guns, and 107-mm missiles as well, causing heavy casualties to the Airborne battalions. A typical example was that in the battle at the Tân Lệ hamlet, Phước Môn Village, all four company commanders of the 9th Airborne Battalion were injured, with Captain Ngưu, Commander of the 94th Company, being killed in action. After 10 days of fighting with the North Vietnamese, the 3rd Airborne Battalion was successful in re-capturing Hải Lăng District at 4 pm of July 7, 1972. In this battle, Major Trần Văn Sơn, Battalion Commander was seriously injured and was replaced by Major Võ Thanh Đồng, Deputy-Commander of the 9th Airborne Battalion.[12] With the re-capture of Hải Lăng, the road to the north in the direction of the Quảng Trị Citadel was greatly shortened but the advance of the ARVN airborne units was still not easy at all. The reason was quite simple: the enemy units occupying Quảng Trị had received the fight-to-the-death order to defend Quảng Trị. For the whole three weeks, from July 7 to July 27, the Airborne battalions (reinforced by the 5th Airborne Battalion, which was sent to Quảng Trị immediately after the end of the Battle of An Lộc) were moving very slowly in that piece of land between Nhùng River and Thạch Hãn River because of the extremely fierce resistance of the North Vietnamese. Only after the "carpet bombing" by B-52 at the northern bank of Thạch Hãn River, could the 5th Airborne Battalion cross the river, moved up to position in the area of An Thái village, just about 3 km southwest of the Đinh Công Tráng Citadel.

The battle to re-capture the City of Quảng Trị and the Đinh Công Tráng Citadel really began on July 17, 1972, with all the attacking airborne battalions being deployed as follows:

• The 7th Battalion on the west of the city

• The 11th Battalion from Thạch Hãn River to Long Hưng crossroad

• The 9th Battalion on the south of the city

• The 6th Battalion on the east of the city

• The 5th as the main force attacking the Đinh Công Tráng Citadel

Lieutenant-Colonel Nguyễn Chí Hiếu, Commander of the 5th Airborne Battalion, decided that the whole battalion would attack the Citadel the next day, July 18, 1972, with the objective of capturing at least half of its perimeter in two days.

The Đinh Công Tráng Citadel was built in 1823 under the reign of Emperor Minh Mạng (1820-1840). At first, the citadel was built in dirt; in 1838, it was rebuilt with bricks. It was a square with about 500 m each side, and, thus, the perimeter was about 2,000 m. The walls of the citadel were 9.4 m high, with their base measuring 12 m across. Surrounding the citadel was a moat 4 m wide, 8 m deep, with 4 high and extruding forts at the 4 corners. When the Battle of Quảng Trị began on March 30, 1972 the main office of Sub-District of Quảng Trị and the Headquarters of the 3rd Infantry Division were located in the Citadel (the Advanced Headquarters of the 3rd Infantry Division was positioned in Ái Tử base).[13]

Figure 4.6. Aerial photo of the Đinh Công Tráng Citadel in 1967
Source: Internet

With such a solid structure of the Citadel, and with the determination of "fighting to the death" of the enemy defending forces, together with the maximum support of their tanks, artillery, and anti-aircraft weapons, the airborne battalions had to suffer heavy casualties. But at the same time, with waves after waves of bombardment from the U.S. Navy and Air Force, including "carpet bombings" by B-52 strategic bombers, the North Vietnamese forces defending the Đinh Công Tráng Citadel were also paying an extremely high price.

Lieutenant-Colonel Nguyễn Chí Hiếu, Commander of the 5th Airborne Battalion, the main force of the attack, assigned the 51st Company, with Captain Trương Đăng Sỹ as Commander, and the 52nd Company, with First-Lieutenant Hồ Tường as Commander, to push first in parallel columns. The move was very difficult because of the fierce resistance by the enemy. Following is the recap of the attack by Captain Sỹ (later promoted to Major):[14]

"Từ làng Trí Bưu, về hướng Tây Bắc, mục tiêu kế tiếp là Nhà Thờ Trí Bưu. Tôi và Hồ Tường song song bung đội hình từng bước tiến lên,

nhường làng Trí Bưu lại cho Bộ Chỉ huy Tiểu đoàn. Đoạn đường từ đây đến Nhà Thờ Trí Bưu khoảng vài trăm thước cũng không phải dễ đi ...

Tôi đã sử dụng tất cả hỏa lực yểm trợ: 18 khẩu 105 ly, cơ hữu Nhảy Dù, 4 khẩu 155 ly, 2 khẩu 175 ly của Quân đoàn 1...

Ngày nào cũng có ít nhất hai phi tuần oanh tạc. Ban đêm, thỉnh thoảng còn được hải pháo từ Đệ Thất hạm đội bắn yểm trợ. Nếu cần thiết, còn được 18 khẩu 105 ly của Thủy quân Lục chiến tăng cường. Ngày nào ít lắm cũng có một hay hai lần bắn "T.O.T". [Time On Target = Pháo yểm trợ có phối hợp trước để diễn ra cùng một lúc]

Có lúc chúng tôi phải tiến quân trong mưa bụi của pháo binh, mục đích không cho địch quân ngóc đầu khỏi hố. Tôi áp dụng chiến thuật từng bước nhảy vọt. Hồ Tường tiến tới từ 50m đến 100m thì dừng lại bố trí, 51 tiến lên qua mặt 52, rồi lại tiến lên 50m đến 100m dừng lại hầm hố bố trí, cứ thế tiến dần ...

Nhưng sức kháng cự của địch quân còn quá mạnh, nhất là bên cánh phải còn khu làng nhỏ sát bờ sông Thạch Hãn, địch bắn qua quá rát. Ban đêm đôi lúc chúng tôi còn nghe cả tiếng chiến xa địch."

(Translation:

"From Trí Bưu Village, to the northwest, the next target was the Trí Bưu Church. Hồ Tường and I gradually moved in parallel formation, ceding the Trí Bưu Village to the battalion to set up its command post. The road to the Trí Bưu Church was only a few hundred meters but was not an easy road...

I used all fire support available: eighteen 105-mm howitzers of the Airborne, four 155-mm and two 175-mm big guns of I Corps...

There were at least two flights of bombers. At night, occasionally there were some fire supports from the U.S. 7th Fleet. When needed, there were also fire supports from the eighteen 105-mm howitzers of the Marine Battalions. Everyday, there were at least one or two "T.O.T. = Time on Target" fire supports.

Sometimes we had to move under the dust rains caused by

our artillery, with the objective not to let the enemy raise their heads from their shelters. I applied the one-by-one-step tactic. Hồ Tường moved from 50 m to 100 m then stopped and positioned his men, the 51st moved up, passed the 52nd, moved up 50 m to 100 m more, and then stopped and positioned...

But the enemy's resistance was still very strong, especially from the right side of the small village area next to the bank of the Thạch Hãn River. At night, occasionally we could even hear the noises from the enemy tanks.")

Before such reality of the battlefield, many units were brought in as reinforcements for the attacking push of the 51st and 52nd Companies of the 5th Airborne Battalion as follows:

• The 2nd Reconnaissance Company of the Airborne Division

• One company of the 11th Airborne Battalion (called ***"Song Kiếm Trấn Ải = Two Swords Defending Border Fort"***)

• Two companies of the 81st Commando Airborne Brigade (just having finished their job in the breaking of the An Lộc siege, becoming famous with the praise of An Lộc people through the poem: ***"An Lộc địa sử ghi chiến tích, Biệt Cách Dù vị quốc vong thân = History Recorded Victory in the Land of An Lộc, Commando Airborne Soldiers Fell for Fatherland"***)

In spite of these reinforcements, the attacking push against the Đinh Công Tráng Citadel by the Airborne units still faced with many difficulties caused by the fierce resistance by the enemy. Captain Sỹ had tried twice to provide his men with an opportunity to raise the RVN's national flag on top of the Citadel but in both times it could not last long. At the first try, he used a team of eight volunteers led by Corporal Trần Tâm, with Private Second Class Hồ Khang, who was born and grew up in Quảng Trị, to raise the flag. This group of volunteers started moving at midnight, and at sunrise they succeeded to raise the RVN flag, but, immediately, the enemy concentrated their artillery to shell at the point where the flag was raised. The 51st and 52nd Companies moved up right away to rescue the volunteer group. When they were approaching the Citadel's wall, they were stopped by the 4-meter-wide moat. In the evening, Captain Sỹ was reported by reconnaissance soldiers that, four men in the volunteer group had been killed, the rest was considered as MIA (Missing in Action). In the following morning, he called for air support and a flight of three AFVN A-37 jet fighters was sent and they were able to knock down part of one corner of the wall, and thus, filled up that part of the moat. The airborne units crossed the moat, moved in and safeguarded that part of the knock downed wall. Captain Sỹ ordered his men to raise the RVN flag the second time, but, unfortunately, right at that moment, another A-37 flight mistakenly dropped bombs on the Airborne units, causing heavy casualties for almost half of these units. The attack of the Đinh Công Tráng Citadel by the 5th Airborne Battalion was temporarily suspended. On the next day, July 26, 1972, Lieutenant-General Ngô Quang Trưởng ordered the Airborne Division to hand over the responsibility of attacking the Citadel to the Marine Division.[15]

Phase 1 of the Attack by the Marine Division

At the beginning of May 1972, after having nominated Lieutenant-General Ngô Quang Trưởng to replace Lieutenant-General Hoàng Xuân Lãm as I Corps Commander on May 2, 1972, President Nguyễn Văn Thiệu also, on May 4, 1972, nominated Colonel Bùi Thế Lân, at that time Deputy-Commander of the Marine Division, to take over the command of the Marine Division, replacing Lieutenant-General Lê Nguyên Khang. On May 28, 1972, Colonel Lân was promoted to in-service Brigadier-General. The promotion ceremony was presided over by President Nguyễn Văn Thiệu, who himself pinned the star on Colonel Lân's collar at the Command Post of the Marine Division in Huế.

Right from the first day of Operation Lam Sơn 72, May

26,1972, carrying the order from Lieutenant-General Ngô Quang Trưởng, Brigadier-General Bùi Thế Lân, new Commander of the Marine Division, immediately deployed 4 battalions, the 3rd Battalion, the 5th Battalion, the 7th Battalion, and the 8th Battalion, to the north, along the coast, on the east of National Route 1, in parallel with the Airborne Division. The Marine battalions met tough resistance by the units of the North Vietnamese 304th Division, which had created a whole series of blockages in solid concrete bunkers.

On June 29, 1972, two Marine battalions, the 1st Battalion and the 4th Battalion, with a total of 1,450 soldiers, were helilifted (by U.S. Marine Corps CH-46 and CH-53 giant helicopters) to the northeast of the City of Quảng Trị, along Local Road 555, at two landing zones, the Flamingo LZ and the Hawk LZ. Thanks to the air and artillery supports, including "carpet bombings" by B-52 strategic bombers, the Marine battalions did not meet strong resistance of the enemy at these LZs. However, after the landing was over, the North Vietnamese units tried many times to surround the Marine battalions by infantrymen having tank support. Their efforts were broken by naval bombardments from the U.S. battleships, about 4 km offshore. At the end of June 1972, the Marine battalions have caused significant casualties to the enemy: 1,515 killed, 15 captured, and 18 tanks destroyed.[16]

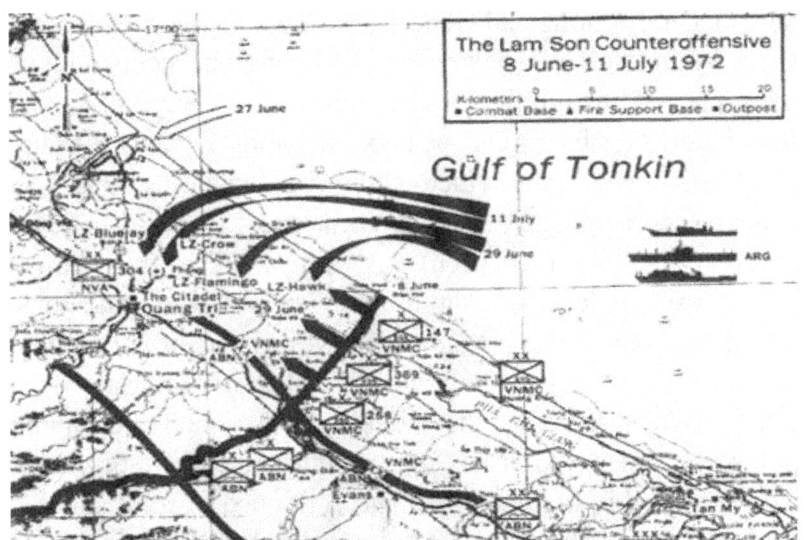

Figure 4.7. Operational map to re-capture Quảng Trị (1)
<u>Source</u>: *U.S. Marines in Vietnam: the war that would not end, 1971-1973*, p. 109.

During the first two weeks of July 1972, the Marine battalions were ordered to regroup and maintain the areas they had captured from the enemy. General Lân then realized the need to launch one more operation aimed at placing one more battalion farther north to prevent possible reinforcements from the enemy. The objective of this operation would be to cut off Local Road 560, about 17 km long, from Cửa Việt base (an old ARVN base) to the City of Quảng Trị, being used as the main supply conduit by the enemy defending forces in the City of Quảng Trị and the Đinh Công Tráng Citadel. On July 11, 1972, General Lân launched his new helilifting operation, bringing the 1st Marine Battalion (called Quái Điểu = Monster Bird), under the command of Major Nguyễn Đăng Hòa, to land in Triệu Phong District, at the two landing zones Blue Jay and Crow. It was a very risky and dangerous operation because the landing of troops was carried out right inside the enemy territory, and, thus, would be met with the enemy's fierce resistance. Therefore, both General Trưởng and General Lân were themselves present to see Major Hòa off, shaking his hand before he stepped in his helicopter. Although the landing zones were "prepared" carefully in advance by air and artillery, including B-52s, the group of 32 helicopters (all provided by the U.S., including 17 CH-53 helicopters, carrying 60 soldiers each, and 15 CH-46 helicopters, carrying 20 soldiers each) was "welcomed" by the enemy's air defense network of 23-mm and 37-mm anti-aircraft guns. The helicopter carrying Major Hòa was hit but was still able to land. But as soon as he jumped off the aircraft, Major Hòa was hit by a shrapnel of the enemy's 57-mm shell and injured in his right thigh. After having his injury taken care of, Major Hòa remained in the battlefield and continued to command his battalion. One CH-53 helicopter was hit and exploded in the air, killing most of the 60 soldiers on board, with only 12 of them having survived. When the landing was finished, the 1st Marine Battalion suffered a casualty of over 100 soldiers, killed and injured. After three days of continuous and fierce fighting with the enemy having the support of their tanks, the 1st Marine Battalion was successful in stopping all counter-attacks by the enemy, destroying many of their tanks with M-72 anti-tank guns, safeguarding the frontline, and achieving well the objective of the operation. After that, the 1st Marine Battalion was replaced by the 2nd Marine Battalion (called Trâu Điên = Crazy Buffalo, with Major Trần Văn Hợp as Commander), which continued to move north, expanding the battlefront to Ba Bến Bridge, helping the Marine Engineers to build a floating bridge for the first group of M48 tanks of the 20th Armored Cavalry Squadron to cross the Vĩnh Định River, taking positions to defend the areas, which had been captured by the 1st Marine Battalion. After having accomplished its duty, on July 14, 1972, the 1st Marine Battalion was ordered to move back to Huế to have a break and to regroup.[17]

On July 22, 1972, General Lân again launched another

operation in the north and east of the City of Quảng Trị, with the objective to cut off all supply conduits and communications channels of the enemy. It was an operation of two Marine battalions of the 147th Marine Brigade in co-ordination with several armored and infantry units. The companies of the 5th Marine Battalion were helilifted to Lima and Victor landing zones (see the map below), about 3 km northeast of the City of Quảng Trị. They met only a rather weak resistance from the enemy, but, on the contrary, the armored and infantry units faced with very fierce enemy resistance before they were able to connect with the Marine units. By mid-afternoon, the two Marines battalions of the 147th Marine Brigade were able to make connection with each other and the enemy was pushed back to the Cửa Việt River. In the ensuing fighting during the next two days, the Marine units eliminated all enemy blockages, causing big casualties for the enemy: 133 killed, 5 tanks destroyed, and a 100-bed field hospital erased.[18] This operation ended the first phase of Operation Lam Sơn 72, in which the Marine Division only had a secondary role. In accordance with General Trưởng's decision, from July 27, 1972, the Airborne Division handed over the main role to the Marine Division in the effort to re-capture, at all cost, the City of Quảng Trị with its symbol being the Đinh Công Tráng Citadel.

Figure 4.8. Operational map to re-capture Quảng Trị (2)
Source: *U.S. Marines in Vietnam: the war that would not end, 1971-1973*, p. 120.

Phase 2 of the Attack by the Marine Division

On July 27, 1972, Brigadier-General Bùi Thế Lân presented the following plan for the operation to re-capture the Đinh Công Tráng Citadel:

• The 258th Brigade, with Colonel Ngô Văn Định as Commander, providing the main thrust of the attack, with a huge force including the following units:

o 7 Marine combat battalions (1st, 2nd, 3rd, 5th, 6th, 8th, and 9th)
o 1st Marine Artillery Battalion with 105-mm howitzers
o 17th Armored Cavalry Squadron (commanded by Lieutenant-Colonel Nguyễn Viết Thanh) with M-113 personnel carriers, and a group of M48 tanks
o There would always be at the Command Post of the 258th Brigade a team of 10 U.S. advisors under the command of Major Gordon Keiser, USMC, Chief Advisor of the 258th Brigade; this advisor team would be respon-

sible for planning the fire-support provided by the U.S. Navy and Air Force units of the U.S. 7th Fleet's Task Force 77 offshore and by the B-52 strategic bomber flights from Guam and Thailand.[19]

• The 147th Marine Brigade, as the secondary force of the attack, with Lieutenant-Colonel Nguyễn Năng Bảo as Commander, including three combat battalions and the 2nd Marine Artillery Battalion, was responsible for the northeast part of the Citadel, and for preventing the enemy reinforcements from the north.

• The 369th Marine Brigade, with Colonel Nguyễn Thế Lương as its new Commander (replacing Colonel Phạm Văn Chung just promoted to Chief of Staff of the Marine Division), was the reserve force.

Figure 4.9. Colonel Ngô Văn Định (left) and Brigadier-General Bùi Thế Lân (right)

In terms of tactic, General Lân decided to opt for "xa luân chiến = rotation fighting tactic" as follows:

"Các Tiểu Đoàn TQLC từ 1 đến 9 thay phiên nhau trực thuộc Lữ Đoàn lên tuyến đầu chiến đấu, rồi lui về sau bổ sung nghỉ ngơi. Nhờ vậy các Tiểu Đoàn TQLC đều được bổ sung đều đặn, khả năng chiến đấu không quá suy giảm vì tổn thất." [20]

(Translation:

"The Marine battalions, from the 1st Battalion to the 9th Battalion, took turn to place themselves under the command of the Brigade, move up to the battlefront, fight, and then retreat to take a break. Thanks to this tactic, every Marine battalion had time to regroup, reinforce, and did not loose its fighting capability.")

The counter-attack operation of the 258th Marine Brigade included three phases:

- Phase One: From July 27 to August 29, 1972
- Phase Two: From August 29 to September 9, 1972
- Phase Three: From September 9 to September 16, 1972

Phase One: From July 27 to August 29, 1972

During this phase, the 258th Brigade had 3 battalions: the 3rd, the 5th, and the 9th. Colonel Ngô Văn Định decided to deploy these units as follows:

- The 3rd Battalion, under the command of Major Nguyễn Văn Cảnh, was responsible for the southeast of the Citadel, in the area of the Trí Bưu Church
- The 9th Battalion, under the command of Lieutenant-Colonel Nguyễn Kim Đễ, took care of the south of the City of Quảng Trị, in the area of the Long Hưng crossroad
- The 5th Battalion, under the command of Major Hồ Quang Lịch, was the reserve force, also positioned at the Long Hưng crossroad

In the morning of July 27, 1972, the 3rd Marine Battalion moved up to replace the units of the 5th Airborne Battalion in the area south of the Citadel, about 200 meters from the Citadel's wall. All units of the 3rd Marine Battalion faced with the same fierce resistance from the defenders, exactly like the case of the 5th Airborne Battalion. After two weeks of fighting, with a casualty rate of almost 50% (400 out of 700 soldiers), the 3rd

Marine Battalion was ordered to retreat to Cù Hoan close to the Command Post of the 258th Marine Brigade to take a break and to regroup. The 8th Marine Battalion moved up to replace the 3rd Battalion. After two weeks of fighting, the 8th Battalion also suffered heavy casualties, and was ordered to retreat, and the 3rd Battalion, after having been reinforced, went back to take over from the 8th Battalion. This time the 3rd Battalion was successful in removing all enemy blockages, and expanding the area under its control right to the Citadel's wall.

During this Phase One, the units of the 9th Marine Battalion took turn to attack, removing all enemy blockages in the areas of the Long Hưng crossroad, the Hospital, the Bồ Đề School, on the bank of the Thạch Hãn River, along Trần Hưng Đạo Street leading to the City of Quảng Trị. The casualties suffered by the 9th Battalion were also very heavy, totaling around 300. After that, the 9th Battalion was ordered to move back to the area of Gia Đằng for a break and regrouping, and was replaced by the 1st Battalion.

With all these gains paid by heavy casualties of the 3rd and 9th Battalions, the road to the City of Quảng Trị and the Đinh Công Tráng Citadel was widely opened to other Marine units. But the battle was still far from over, and the Marines would still pay more with their blood.

Phase Two: From August 29 to September 9, 1972

During this Phase Two, the 258th Marine Brigade was reinforced and employed up to five combat battalions, the 1st, the 3rd, the 5th, the 6th, and the 8th Battalions.

This time, the fierce fighting of the Marine battalions, with as much high casualties as in Phase One, was caried out right inside the City of Quảng Trị. The objectives of all Marine battalions were: 1) to destroy all enemy blockages; 2) to safeguard all administrative offices of the City; and, 3) to prepare for the last battle: attack and re-capture the Đinh Công Tráng Citadel.

Colonel Định divided the responsibilities among the battalions as follows:

• The 1st Battalion, replacing the 9th Battalion, would attack from the area of the Hospital to the north, to re-occupy the Police Station, the Electricity Station, the school for girls, and the barracks of the Field Police Units.

• The 3rd Battalion, replacing the 8th Battalion, continued to safeguard the southeast of the Citadel

• The 5th Battalion was responsible for the southeast of the Long Hưng crossroad

• The 6th Battalion (with Lieutenant-Colonel Đỗ Hữu Tùng as Commander) was responsible to annihilate all enemy forces north of the Long Hưng crossroad, and to move to the southwest of the Citadel

• The 8th Battalion (with Major Nguyễn Văn Phán as Commander), after handing over the area to the 3rd Battalion, was ordered to move back and become the reserve force.

During the whole two weeks of this Phase Two, the Marine battalions had always to face with the fierce resistance by the enemy. The urban fighting tactic (employed and improved by the Marine units in Huế and Sài Gòn during the Tet Offensive of 1968) was used again by these four Marine battalions. They fought close combat with the enemy to re-gain each quarter, each street, each house. Besides, the enemy artillery units, positioned outside the city, continued to shell, causing many difficulties and heavy casualties to the Marines units. In spite of all these problems, the Marine battalions, in the end, were able to accomplish their missions, and came close to the walls of the Đinh Công Tráng Citadel.

Phase Three: From September 9 to September 16, 1972

This was the last phase of Operation Lam Sơn 72, with the objective to re-capture the Đinh Công Tráng Citadel. General

Lân decided to deploy two brigades in this important attack:

• The 147th Brigade in the northeast, including the 3rd and the 7th Battalions, with Lieutenant-Colonel Nguyễn Năng Bảo as Commander, and Lieutenant-Colonel Nguyễn Xuân Phúc as Deputy-Commander

• The 258th Brigade in the southwest, including the 1st, the 2nd, the 5th, and the 6th Battalions.

The two main targets for the 258th Brigade, the Residence of the Quảng Trị Province Chief and the Administrative Main Office of the Province of Quảng Trị, were assigned to the 2nd Battalion, with Major Trần Văn Hợp as Commander and Captain Phạm Văn Tiền as Deputy-Commander, and with its Command Post positioned at the Long Hưng crossroad, right at the intersection of Lê Duẫn Street and National Route 1.

The attack to capture these two targets was assigned by Major Hợp to the 4th Company under the command of Captain Lê Quang Liễn, and the 5th Company under the command of First-Lieutenant Huỳnh Văn Trọn. It was quite certain that the enemy defending forces were not unaware of the intentions of the Marine units already present within the City of Quảng Trị. Therefore, right from the early morning of September 14, 1972, they already sent a "welcome greeting" to the 4th and 5th Companies of the 2nd Marine Battalion with a big shelling of their 130-mm big guns, but, luckily, did not cause any serious damages to the attackers. After the shelling was over, the 4th Company launched its attack and captured two targets: first the Phước Môn School, and then the Teresa School, together with a number of prisoners. Through the interrogation of the prisoners, Captain Liễn knew that they belonged to a unit of the North Vietnamese 320B Division that had just crossed the Thạch Hãn River the night before as reinforcement for the existing enemy defending force in the city. In that evening, Captain Liễn had a meeting with his Deputy, First-Lieutenant Nguyễn Hữu Hào, and First-Lieutenant Trọn, Commander of the 5th Company. They discussed and planned the attack for the next morning, September 15, 1972, and the target was the Administrative Main Office of the Province of Quảng Trị. With the supports provided by two M48 tanks and two M-113 personnel carriers, the 4th and 5th Companies of the 2nd Marine Battalion, in spite of the fierce resistance at each of the enemy blockages, have finally accomplished their mission at 8:30 am, July 15, 1972: the capture of the Administrative Main Office of the Province of Quảng Trị, as reported in the following account by Captain Liễn:

"Riêng Đại Đội 4 đã tịch thu được một số lớn chiến lợi phẩm và một kho tiếp liệu gồm:

• 412 súng cá nhân

• 102 súng cộng đồng

• 40 thùng lương khô do Trung Cộng sản xuất

• 23 máy truyền tin của Trung Cộng

• 18 tù binh

• Nhiều hố chôn tập thể và xác quanh khu vực Tòa Hành Chánh và khu hầm ngầm bên trái Tòa Hành Chánh, khoảng 30 xác.

Bộ Chỉ Huy Tiểu Đoàn 2 Thủy Quân Lục Chiến phải dùng 6 đợt thiết vận xa M113 để chuyển tù binh và chiến lợi phẩm về Bộ Chỉ Huy." [21]

(Translation:

"The 4th Company has captured a large number of spoils of war and an enemy supply depot that included:

• 412 individual weapons

• 102 community weapons

• 40 boxes of dried foods produced by the Chinese

• 23 communications devices also produced by the Chinese

• 18 prisoners

• Many mass graves in the area surrounding the Administrative Main Office, and about 30 corpses in the underground shelter in the left wing of the Administrative Main Office

The 2nd Marine Battalion had to use 6 waves of the M-113

personnel carriers to move all of these prisoners and spoils of war back to its Command Post.")

The 147th Brigade was given the responsibility to attack from the northeast, and its main objective was to eliminate all remaining enemy blockages in the Đinh Công Tráng Citadel, which had already been tremendously damaged because of the bombardments for the past two months. This main responsibility was assigned to the 3rd Marine Battalion with Major Nguyễn Văn Cảnh as Commander and Major Trần Kim Độ as Deputy-Commander.

Major Cảnh deployed two companies of his battalion, the 2nd Company with Captain Giang Văn Nhân as Commander, and the 3rd Company with Captain Nguyễn Văn Thạch as Commander, to remove these enemy blockages. In the early morning of September 15, 1972, the 3rd Company moved first, broke the enemy defense line at the Right Portal of the Citadel. All of its platoons immediately and overwhelmingly filled up the top of the wall, and thrust into all portals of the citadel. The 22nd Platoon occupied the Main Portal looking out to Lê Văn Duyệt Street. The defenders' resistance was rather weak, and they retreated to defend the Left Portal looking out to Phan Đình Phùng Street, but it was too late. All units of the two companies assaulted at once and, together, they cleared all defense posts of the enemy in this area of the Citadel. Noises from the enemy guns in their resistance gradually faded, and finally died out. The 3rd Marine Battalion has accomplished its mission brilliantly. The Đinh Công Tráng Citadel inside the City of Quảng trị was now under the total control of the South Vietnamese Marine units. This Citadel with walls 9.4 m high, and with the base of the walls 12 m wide, severely damaged by the U.S. and ARVN terrible bombardments, was then a total ruin as can be seen in the following photo:

Figure 4.10. Solidly walled Đinh Công Tráng Citadel now a total ruin

<u>Source</u>: *U.S. Marines in Vietnam* (Note no. 16, p. 119)

"Sau gần 24 giờ chiến đấu không nghỉ, những người lính của Đại Đội 2 Tiểu Đoàn 3 TQLC đã dựng ngọn cờ trên cổng thành cửa Tả vào mờ sáng ngày 15 tháng 9 năm 1972." [22]

(<u>Translation</u>:

"After almost 24-hour nonstop fighting, the soldiers of the 2nd Company of the 3rd Marine Battalion raised the flag on the Left Portal of the Citadel in the early morning of September 15, 1972.")

Figure 4.11. Soldiers of the 3rd Marine Battalion raising the RVN Flag on Đinh Công Tráng Citadel (Quảng Trị)

Source: Article by Colonel Ngô Văn Định (Note no. 19)

The official flag raising ceremony was carried out the next day, at 12:45 pm, September 16, 1972. The Operation Lam Sơn 72, started on June 28, 1972, ended with the most glorious victory of the Marine Division of the ARVN: the re-capture of the Province of Quảng Trị that had been captured by the enemy since May 1, 1972.

Concluding Remarks

In this bloody and decisive battle, ***"Bên Thắng Cuộc"*** (The Winning Side), i.e., the Communist North Vietnam (according to the way Huy Đức, a North Vietnamese author, called North Vietnam in his book entitled with these same three words), has lost in a big way, and ***"Bên Thua Cuộc"*** (The Losing Side), i.e., South Vietnam, won also in a big way. Both sides, however, suffered huge casualties. It is really hard to know accurately the total casualties of both sides in this Battle of Quảng Trị, from June 29 to September 16, 1972, especially for the North Vietnamese forces, that had fought to the death and were buried under the completely ruined City of Quảng Trị and the Đinh Công Tráng Citadel caused by the tremendous bombardments by aircraft from the U.S. 7th Fleet and the AFVN, and from the B-52 carpet bombings.

On the South Vietnamese side, just for the 258th Marine Brigade, the total casualties were: 3,911, including 637 killed, and 3,274 injured.

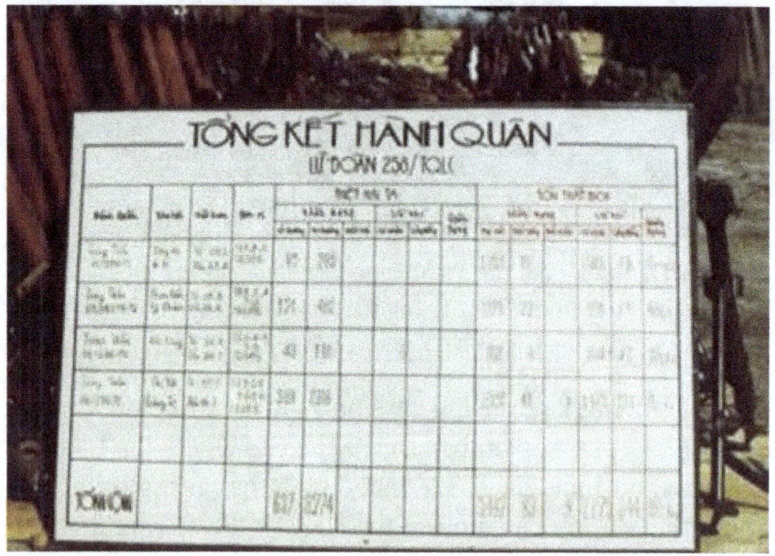

Figure 4.12. Report of casualties of the 258th Marine Brigade
<u>Source:</u> Article by Colonel Ngô Văn Định (Note no. 19)

Of course, these figures ***did not include*** the casualties of the other two Marine brigades, the 147th Brigade and the 369th Brigade, as well as the casualties of the Airborne Division, and the other ARVN services, such as the Rangers, the Commando Airborne, the Armored Cavalry, etc. In his book, author Dale Andradé (Note no. 18; p. 196), said:

"... the South Vietnamese marines suffered more than 5,000 casualties since June, 3,658 of them during the seven-week battle to recapture the citadel. Almost one out of every four marines in the entire division was wounded or killed."

On the North Vietnamese side, it is also very difficult to know exactly the official total casualties. However, it is almost 100% correct to say that the two regiments, the 48th Regiment and the Triệu Hải Regiment of the 320B Division, having fought to the death inside the City of Quảng Trị and the Đinh Công Tráng Citadel, had suffered extremely heavy casualties, and could be considered as completely wiped out. In a recent official Vietnamese document, ***"công bố tại mít tinh kỷ niệm 40 năm = made public at the meeting commemorating the 40th anniversary"*** of the battle, North Vietnam recognized that they had lost a total of 36,000 soldiers, and that, in fact, the 48th Regiment and the Triệu Hải Regiment were wiped out. The Triệu Hải Regiment, starting the battle with 1,500 men, and ended with less than a section (about 12 soldiers), and the 48th Regiment had a casualty rate of more than 80%.[23] In terms of personal memory, Colonel Vũ Trung Thướng, Political Commissar of the 5th Company, 2nd Battalion, 48th Regiment of the 320B Division during the 1972 Battle of Quảng Trị, recounted as follows:

"... từ ngày 28/6 đến ngày 16/9/1972, Đại đội 5 của tôi từ 120 quân, nhưng sau đó chỉ còn 17 người sống sót." [24]

(Translation:

"... from June 28 to September 16, 1972, my 5th Company, from 120 soldiers, was reduced to only 17 survived men.")

Most recently, on January 1, 2018, the 584th Team for the Collection of Remains of Fallen Soldiers of the Military Command of the Province of Quảng Trị, announced that 12 additional such remains were just discovered in Tân Mỹ Hamlet, Hải Lệ Village, City of Quảng Trị.[25] It is certain that in the future there would be more, many more such discoveries of remains of the North Vietnamese fallen soldiers, who were killed and buried in other areas within the City of Quảng Trị and the Đinh Công Tráng Citadel during this bloodiest battle of the Vietnam War.

CHAPTER FIVE

Vindicating and Honouring the ARVN

The Vietnam War ended on April 30, 1975. The Republic of Vietnam (RVN) and its army, The Armed Forces of the Republic of Vietnam (ARVN) have both ceased to exist. Since then, the majority of research studies to evaluate the war by American historians of the ***"orthodox"*** school have determined that the U.S. lost the war because of many reasons, one of which was its undeserving ally, the ARVN itself: ***the ARVN was a cowardly and incompetent army***. Recently, this erroneous and even insulting judgment of the ARVN was completely rejected by a new generation of American authors and researchers of the ***"revisionist"*** school. This Chapter summarizes the revisionist authors' arguments, judgments, and conclusions in their efforts to vindicate and honor the ARVN.

Erroneous Judgment on the Nature of the ARVN

In an article about the two schools of thought, "orthodox and revisionist," author Mark Moyar, of the "revisionist" school, has determined that one of the worst mistakes of the "orthodox" American historians was that they had been deeply and badly influenced by the suspicious journal articles and books of the trio of authors Halberstam + Sheehan + Karnow, who happened to be all famous U.S. correspondents in the 1960s. The common judgment on the RVN and the ARVN of the "orthodox" authors was:

"America's South Vietnamese allies were corrupt and cowardly, in contrast to the patriotic and dedicated North Vietnamese and Viet Cong." [1]

The ARVN was seen as cowardly and incompetent just because they lost the Battle of Ấp Bắc (January 1963), which was reported in minute details by that trio of authors in their best-seller books, in particular Sheehan's ***A Bright shining lie***. [2, 3, 4] In his book, Sheehan has reserved a whole chapter for this battle, entitled ***Book III: The Battle of Ap Bac***, from page 201 to page 265, in which he used every opportunity to praise the Viet Cong leaders and to badmouth and disparage the ARVN leaders. Following is just one typical example:

" ... the captain in charge of the M-113s, [referring to Captain Lý Tòng Bá, Commander of the 7th M-113 Armored Cavalry Company] ***who had been one of the few decent officers of this stinking army, was behaving like the rest of the cowardly bastards."*** [5]

In his book, ***Vietnam, a history: the first complete account of Vietnam at war***, author Karnow, although reserving only 3 pages for the Battle of Ấp Bắc in Chapter 7, entitled ***Vietnam is the place***, also did not save his words in disparaging the ARVN right in the Introduction as follows:

"The Diem's army's shortcomings became dramatically apparent in January 1963 near Ap Bac, a village in the Mekong delta forty miles southwest of Saigon, where an inferior Vietcong contingent mauled a South Vietnamese division that could have scored a victory had it not been led by pusillanimous officers." [6]

The above sentence by Karnow, in addition to the use of words intended to disparage and humiliate the ARVN, also contained some misinformation, which caused regrettable misunderstanding for the readers. The operation at Ấp Bắc was in fact planned by the 7th Infantry Division, but the units deployed in the battle were only at the battalion level, not even at the regiment level, let alone ***"a South Vietnamese division"*** mentioned by Karnow in that sentence.

Author Halberstam, in his book, ***The Making of a quagmire: America and Vietnam during the Kennedy era***, has also reserved one whole chapter, ***Chapter 6: Disaster: The Battle of Ap Bac***, from page 77 to page 92, for this battle. Although he did not use disparaging and humiliating words for the ARVN like Sheehan and Karnow, Halberstam also caused some misunderstanding about the role of Captain Lý Tòng Bá in the battle, for example his insubordination, refusing to carry out the order from Colonel Bùi Đình Đạm, Commander of the 7th Infantry Division. Here is what Halberstam wrote in page 85:

" ... at this moment he refused to move his APC's ... Colonel Vann, circling in a light spotter plane, radioed Ba's unit that Dam had ordered it to advance. But Ba refused to move..." [7]

From the ancient time to the present, military wise, winning or losing is just normal, sometimes we win, other times we lose. The reasons for winning or losing depend on many important factors such as intelligence, tactics, supplies, etc. During the second half of 1962 (from July 1 to December 31, 1962), according to the chronology book by serious and highly respected author Đoàn Thêm, ***Hai mươi năm qua: việc từng ngày (1945-1964)*** (The Past twenty years: daily events (1945-1964)), there were dozens of battles between the ARVN and the Viet Cong, and, in fact, the ARVN won most of them, with the following statistics (compiled by yours truly, based on the figures given in Đoàn Thêm's book):

- ARVN: 94 killed, and 119 injured
- Viet Cong: 2,413 killed, and 438 captured

Among the battles in up to 1964, in the operation codenamed "Bình Tây" (meaning Pacification in the West), of August 21, 1962, in Bàu Sáng, Gia Rai (Province of Ba Xuyên), the VC Phú Lợi Battalion was badly defeated with heavy casualties: 166 killed, and 25 captured.[8] The books by that trio of U.S. correspondents did not mention the above battle at all but all had detailed yet ***not accurate*** descriptions of the Battle of Ấp Bắc of January 2, 1963, which was a battle that the ARVN had lost with fairly big casualties: 83 killed, more than 100 injured, with 3 U.S. advisors killed, 8 injured, and five CH-21 helicopters shot down; for the VC, they had 18 killed, and 39 injured.[9] This fact has shown very clearly the total bias of these 3 U.S. correspondents in their reporting. Moreover, they all had not been at the battlefield, and they just wrote their articles based on what they had heard from the U.S. advisors. The ARVN officer, present at the Battle of Ấp Bắc, was Captain Lý Tòng Bá, a courageous armored cavalry officer always fighting together with his subordinates, who later became the Brigadier-General, Commander of the 25th Infantry Division, and who did not desert his unit and his men, fought to the last minute and, finally, was captured by the enemy on April 29, 1975 after his division was defeated. Following is a paragraph taken from General Bá's Memoir:

"Đến đây, tôi tưởng cần nói rõ sự thật trận đánh diễn tiến của nó không giống như NEIL SHEEHAN viết kể trong quyển sách của anh – cuốn "A BRIGHT SHINING LIE" xuất bản năm 1988. Những điểm chính yếu cùng lý do chính đáng từng diễn tiến của trận đánh không được trình bày, mà tác giả chỉ viết phần tổng quát theo lời kể, lời tường thuật một cách hời hợt và thiếu sót của JAMES SCANLON – Đại Úy Cố Vấn đơn vị. [tr. 65] ***... Tôi xin đặt một câu hỏi theo lời trình bày của Neil Sheehan trong "A BRIGHT SHINING LIE," làm sao tôi dám cãi lệnh Tư Lệnh Sư Đoàn*** [là Đại Tá Bùi Đình Đạm, Tư Lệnh Sư Đoàn 7 BB] ***để thi hành lệnh của Trung Tá*** [Chuẩn Tướng Bá đã nhớ sai, lúc đó ông Thơ mới mang lon Thiếu Tá] ***Tỉnh Trưởng Mỹ Tho Lâm Quang Thơ không chịu vượt kinh truy kích địch.*** [tr. 68]***"*** [10]

(Translation:

"Now, I think I need to set the record straight because the battle did not happen like NEIL SHEEHAN wrote in his book – ***"A BRIGHT SHINING LIE"*** *published in 1988. The main points as well as the appropriate reasons for each step of the battle were not presented; instead the author has only given a*

general description, based on the perfunctory and defect recount by JAMES SCANLON – the U.S. Advisor of the unit [page 65] ... *Based on the presentation of Neil Sheehan in his book,* ***"A BRIGHT SHINING LIE,"*** *question I have the following: how could I disobey the order given by a Division Commander* [i.e. Colonel Bùi Đình Đạm, Commander of the 7th Infantry Division] *and carry out an order from the Lieutenant-Colonel* [Brigadier-General Bá has made a mistake here: at that time Mr. Thơ was only a Major] Province Chief Lâm Quang Thơ not to chase after the enemy? [page 68].")

Author Mark Moyar, in his important work, ***Triumph forsaken: the Vietnam War, 1954-1965***, has written very clearly as follows:

> ***"Colonel John Paul Vann, a U.S. Army advisor and the central figure in Sheehan's book A Bright Shining Lie, was more dishonest in dealing with the press than Sheehan ever acknowledged. Vann fed the journalists an extremely misleading version of the Battle of Ap Bac, one that the journalists transformed into the accepted version of the battle."*** [11]

However, because of their status as recipients of the U.S. prestigious Pulitzer Prize, the books by that trio of correspondents all became best-sellers, and were used as main referenced documents by a whole generation of U.S. historians and researchers of the "orthodox" school. This fact means that their negative judgments regarding the fighting capability of the ARVN have become the norms, which have been repeated again and again by the "orthodox" authors, and have been exploited to the maximum by the members of the anti-war movement. One more noteworthy point was that the majority of the "orthodox" authors were also university professors. A number of their students later have become university professors too, and they continued to convey these negative judgments to the next generations of students. During that period of almost forty years, the U.S. media and movie industry have also actively participated in that movement of badmouthing and disparaging the ARVN.

The unavoidable result was that, for a very large majority of the American people, the ARVN was seen as a cowardly and incompetent army. Where is the truth?

Heroic Nature and High Competence of the ARVN

The truth, which has now become undeniable, has been shown through the two Communist general offensives in 1968 (Tet Offensive) and 1972 (Easter Offensive), especially during the latter when almost all U.S. ground combat troops had already been withdrawn, and the ARVN had to fight alone.

In the Communist general offensive of 1972, which was later referred to by the U.S. media as ***The Easter Offensive***, the ARVN has fought very heroically at all three battle fronts: Quảng Trị in I Corps, Kontum in II Corps, and An Lộc in III Corps. And the ARVN has won all of them and caused heavy casualties to the Communists. Of course, the ARVN also had to pay a high price for these victories.

When writing about the Battle of Quảng Trị, American author Dale Andradé has written as follows:

> ***"… the South Vietnamese marines suffered more than 5,000 casualties since June, 3, 658 of them during the seven-week battle to recapture the citadel. Almost one out of every four marines in the entire division was wounded or killed."*** [12]

Fighting to re-capture a city that had been occupied for almost two months by the enemy, who have had enough time to organize its defense with a determination to fight to the death, the ARVN, with such heavy casualties, has demonstrated very clearly its heroic nature, definitely not being a cowardly army like in the judgment repeated by the "orthodox" authors for almost four decades. The bloody Battle of Quảng Trị is presented in details in Chapter Four of this book.

In the An Lộc battle to the death, the situation was a lot more difficult. The town of An Lộc had been surrounded by a very big Communist force that included 3 infantry divisions (the 5th, the 7th, and the 9th Divisions), an artillery division (the 69th Artillery Division), and several support regiments of air-defense, armored cavalry, special weapons, sappers, etc. The ARVN, with a much smaller defending force (even the 5th Infantry Division had only 2 regiments), has heroically resisted with a determination to fight to the death against waves after waves of enemy attacks supported by T-54 tanks. Throughout the whole time of the battle, the ARVN units had to stand through horrible enemy shelling, someday up to thousands of rounds of big guns. In his book, ***The Battle of An Loc***, author James H. Willbanks stated clearly as follows:

> ***"The ceaseless shelling, estimated at over 78,000 rounds during the three-month period, had reduced the city to almost total ruins. ... The ARVN defenders in the city had sustained 5,400 casualties, including 2,300 killed or missing. One battalion of the 5th ARVN was down to 26 effectives from an original strength of 300 soldiers."*** [13]

This heroic Battle of An Lộc (Province of Bình Long) is presented in details in Chapter Three of this book.

The heroism and high competence of the ARVN were demonstrated once more, and also the last time in the Vietnam War, at the town of Xuân Lộc, the door to Sài Gòn, the capital city of the RVN, in mid-April 1975. After having captured both Military Region II and Military Region I of the RVN, and broken the Phan Rang defense line of the Advanced Headquarters of the III Corps, North Vietnamese forces advanced toward Sài Gòn with a unstoppable momentum. The town of Xuân Lộc was the last outpost of the ARVN at the gate of Sài Gòn. The Communists thought that they would capture Xuân Lộc very easily. They were wrong. A whole army of theirs, the 4th Army, under the command of General Hoàng Cầm, including 3 divisions, the 6th, the 7th, and the 341st Divisions, was stopped by just one ARVN division, the 18th Infantry Division, under the command of General Lê Minh Đảo, for almost two weeks, from April 9 to April 21, 1975.

Applying their familiar ***"artillery before ground assault"*** tactic, North Vietnamese artillery units have fiercely bombarded Xuân Lộc and turned this small town into a ruin. Following was a report fielded by a U.S. correspondent:

"Almost every building has been damaged, and the town center reduced to rubble. The streets are pocked with 130-millimeter shells that come whistling in from the green, brooding hills to the north. What were once houses are now heaps of pulverized stone and charred timbers. The market, its tin-roofed stalls twisted into weird shapes, looks like a junk yard, and the bus station, where the initial fighting took place, is recognizable as such only by the blackened skeletons of a few buses..." [14]

In spite of these attacks, just like the units of the ARVN defending An Lộc in summer 1972, the units of the 18th Infantry Division have heroically sustained that fierce shelling, waited for the enemy infantry assault into the town, fought them back really hard and caused heavy casualties to them. Two American authors, George J. Veith and Merle L. Pribbenow, have written a very lengthy article (a total of 51 pages), describing in details the Battle of Xuân Lộc. Following is a quotation they took from General Hoàng Cầm's Memoir itself:

"During the first three days of the battle 7th Division suffered 300 casualties and the 341st Division suffered 1,200 casualties ... Virtually all of our 85 mm and 57 mm artillery pieces had been destroyed." [15]

Concluding Remarks

Through the works of the U.S. authors of the "revisionist" school, today the American people have a more accurate picture of the ARVN, the U.S. ally during the Vietnam War. They now know clearly that ***The ARVN definitely was NOT a cowardly and incompetent army.*** This Chapter only reviews a number of the writings of the "revisionist" authors, who, on behalf of a majority of the honest American people, have decided that they had to vindicate and honor the ARVN, an army now belonging to History. In the concluding section of their above-mentioned lengthy article about the Battle of Xuân Lộc, the two American authors Veith and Pribbenow have quoted the famous statement by Major-General Lê Minh Đảo, Commander of the 18th Infantry Division:

"Please do not call me a hero. My men who died at Xuan Loc and a hundred battles before are the true heroes." [16]

PART TWO

AN ARMY UNJUSTLY ABANDONED AND LEFT FOR DEAD

CHAPTER SIX

"The Vietnam War Was an Unwinnable War": Right or Wrong?

It is safe to say that the Americans, not the Vietnamese, that have produced the most writings about the Vietnam War. The volume of documents written in English by the Americans on the Vietnam War is monumental. The contributions by the Vietnamese authors were quite modest. Today, the American authors are divided clearly into two schools of thought: 1) The majority belongs to the "orthodox" school; and, 2) The minority belongs to the "revisionist" school. In general terms, their positions are totally opposite: for the "orthodox" authors, ***"the Vietnam War was an unwinnable war"*** while the "revisionist" authors believe that the Vietnam War could have been won and at a much lower cost had the U.S employed a more appropriate strategy. This Chapter is an effort to understand, analyze, and evaluate that judgment by the "orthodox" authors that ***"the Vietnam War was an unwinnable war."***

Origin of the Phrase "An Unwinnable War"

The phrase "an unwinnable war," which later was used by some of the "orthodox" authors even in the titles of their books, (for example: ***Autopsy of an unwinnable war: Vietnam*** written by William C. Haponski and Jerry J. Burcham, and published by Casemate in 2019; and, ***Vietnam: the history of an unwinnable war, 1945-1975*** *written by* John Prados, and published by University Press of Kansas in 2009), was probably insinuated for the first time by Mr. George Ball (1909-1994), Assistant Secretary of State in the administration of President Lyndon B. Johnson, who advised the President to resolve the war by negotiations because he did not believe that the U.S. would be able to win the war. In his memo to President Johnson, dated July 1, 1965, he presented very clearly his thoughts on the Vietnam War, with the objective to advise President Johnson not to escalate the war. Right in the opening paragraph of his memo, under the heading ***"A Losing War,"*** he gave the following statement:

"The South Vietnamese are losing the war to the Viet Cong. No one can assure you that we can beat the Viet Cong or even force them to the conference on our terms, no matter how many hundred thousand white, foreign (US) troops we deploy." [1]

At that time, President Johnson did not listen to this advice, and still decided to escalate the war. Later, after President Johnson's death and the Lyndon B. Johnson Presidential Library had been built, during a recorded oral interview made by the Library, Mr. Ball used the phrase "unwinnable war" for the first time:

"... But each one was addressed at some particular proposal for escalation, challenging the proposal and arguing that we were losing the war, that it was an unwinnable war, that we could commit any number of – 500,000 I think the figure I used at one point in a memorandum – and that we still would not win." [2]

Arguments for the Judgment

In order to clearly understand this negative judgment on the Vietnam War, we must go back to the period when the U.S. government decided to escalate the war. That was the beginning of 1965, two years after the military coup overthrowing the Ngô Đình Diệm regime, with the continuous power struggle among the ARVN generals leading to the internal political chaos and the rapid and strong development of the Communist forces in South Vietnam. This unwanted enemy growth has gradually turned into a very serious threat that forced the U.S. government to make the decision to send ground combat troops to the RVN in order to reverse that dangerous situation.[3, 4] At that time, except for Mr. George Ball as previously mentioned, almost all close advisors of President Johnson, in particular Secretary of Defense Robert S. McNamara, agreed on the policy of escalating the war in South Vietnam. The escalation of the Vietnam War was carried out through two simultaneous military action programs: 1) Massive build-up of U.S. ground combat troops in South Vietnam; and, 2) Sustained bombings of North Vietnam with Operation Rolling Thunder, by jet fighters from Đà Nẵng Airbase, from the aircraft carriers offshore, and by B-52 strategic bombers from Guam and Thailand. And for the 3-year period (1965-1967), the intensity of the Vietnam War has increased to the unimaginably horrible level. Following is what Mr. McNamara said in his memoir:

"Between 1965 and 1967, U.S. and South Vietnamese air forces dropped over a million tons of bombs on the South, more than twice the tonnage dropped on the North. ... Sorties against North Vietnam grew from 25,000 in 1965 to 79,000 in 1966 to 108,000 in 1967, and the tonnage of bombs dropped rose from 63,000 to 136,000 to 226.000." [5]

In addition to the objective of reversing the bad situation in South Vietnam at the beginning of 1965, the U.S. government's decision to get itself directly involved in the war and to escalate the war also had another objective, which was to show North Vietnam its determination to defend the South, and to inflict great damages to the North so that they would have to renounce its intention to conquer the South militarily. The U.S. would never be able to achieve this second objective. It is also in his memoir that Mr. McNamara admitted the failure of the Operation Rolling Thunder:

"... as Rolling Thunder intensified, U.S. intelligence estimated that infiltration increased from about 35,000 men in 1965 to as many as 90,000 in 1967, while Hanoi's will to carry on the fight stayed firm." [6]

From that moment on, Mr. McNamara started having second thought about the U.S. ability to win the war. He began to have disagreements with the American senior generals of the Joint Chiefs of Staff (JCS) [7] on the Vietnam War, especially on the policy of the sustained bombing of North Vietnam. On May 2, 1967, he recommended that President Johnson reject JCS's request to reinforce and expand Operation Rolling Thunder. Then on May 19, 1967, he sent a memo to President Johnson containing his pessimistic judgment on the Vietnam War as follows:

> ***"… Continuation of our present moderate policy, while avoiding a larger war, will not change Hanoi's mind, so is not enough to satisfy the American people; increased force levels and actions against the North are likewise unlikely to change Hanoi's mind, and are likely to get us in even deeper in Southeast Asia and into a serious confrontation, if not war, with China and Russia; and we are not willing to yield. So we must choose among imperfect alternatives."*** [8]

The disagreement between the Mr. McNamara and the JCS was gradually getting more and more serious. Only one day after that memo, i.e., on May 20, 1967, the JCS sent Mr. McNamara a memo in which they referred even to the use of nuclear weapons. Mr. McNamara recounted it in his memoir as follows:

> ***"On May 20, they sent me another memo repeating their views that invasions of North Vietnam, Laos, and Cambodia might become necessary, involving the deployment of U.S. forces to Thailand, and, quite possibly, the use of nuclear weapons in South China. All of this, they emphasized, highlighted the need to mobilize U.S. reserves. Their continued willingness to risk a nuclear confrontation appalled me."*** [9]

Having lost the confidence in the JCS' way of thinking, Mr. McNamara turned to the Central Intelligence Agency (CIA) and asked them to evaluate the option of bombing of North Vietnam. The CIA frankly responded as follows:

"We do not believe that any of the programs... is capable of reducing the flow of military and other essential goods sufficiently to affect the war in the South or to decrease Hanoi's determination to persist in the war." [10]

Mr. McNamara has then taken a further step in the re-evaluation of the situation of the Vietnam War. He and Mr. Paul Nitze, the Secretary of the Navy, unofficially established a special research group inside the Navy called ***Navy Vietnam Appraisal Group***, which included 10 admirals of the Navy and one brigadier-general of the U.S. Marine Corps, headed by Rear-Admiral Gene R. LaRocque, and sent to Vietnam to study the situation on the spot. In the period of six months, this group tried to understand, studied and evaluated a series of programs, plans, capabilities that could be used as options for the Vietnam War, including the possibility of U.S. troops landing and attacking directly North Vietnam. Its final conclusion was that the U.S. would not be able to win militarily. Mr. McNamara has recorded in his memoir as follows:

"These and other options examined were evaluated as insufficient to achieve a military victory." [11]

With his ingrained pessimistic thoughts and now with the above mentioned totally pessimistic conclusions of the CIA and the research group of the Navy, Mr. McNamara reached the conclusion that the U.S. had already failed in the Vietnam War. He has written the following statement in his memoir:

"By now it was clear to me that our policies and programs in Indochina had evolved in ways we had neither anticipated nor intended, and that the costs—human, political, social, and economic—had grown far farther than anyone had imagined. We had failed." [12]

The Tet Offensive by the Communists (from January 30, 1968), although actually a military defeat of the Communists with a very heavy loss, on the contrary has helped Mr. McNamara to think that he was right in his pessimistic thoughts: the Communists had won. He resigned from his position as

Secretary of Defense at the end of February 1968. And his last decision before his resignation was to reject General Westmoreland's request of February 27, 1968 for an additional 200,000 U.S. troops in Vietnam.[13]

On March 31, 1968, President Johnson announced that he would not run for re-election, stopped the bombing of North Vietnam, and called Hà Nội to come to the conference table. After his ascending to the power, President Richard M. Nixon began the implementation of his policy of ***Vietnamization of the War***, started the withdrawal of U.S. troops, continued the peace talk with North Vietnam, and finally signed Paris Peace Accords on January 27, 1973. U.S. Congress began to implement measures to tie the hands of the Executive, decreased and finally cut off all military aids to the RVN. On April 30, 1975, the RVN had to surrender. The Communists won the Vietnam War.

Developments of the Judgment

After 1975, the American people have suffered from the ***Vietnam syndrome*** for several decades. In 1995, Mr. McNamara published his memoir. The memoir has caused a lot of discussions among the American scholars and research, who had studied the Vietnam War. Of course, there were praises and attacks as well. In spite of all these remarks, Mr. McNamara maintained that his memoir has shown only one side of the evaluation of the Vietnam War. He wanted to know what and how the other side (i.e., the Communists) has seen and thought of the war. He sought help from Mr. Leslie Gelb, who was then President of the Council on Foreign Relations (CFR),[14] a non-profit think tank on foreign policy and issues in international relations. He asked the CFR to sound out whether Hà Nội wanted to exchange experience of the Vietnam War with the U.S. The timing was good since the U.S. Government had lifted the embargo against Vietnam in February 1994, re-established diplomatic relations between the two countries in 1995, and on April 11, 1997, Mr. Douglas "Pete" Peterson, a former American pilot shot down in North Vietnam and held as a prisoner of war in Hỏa Lò Prison in Hà Nội for more than 6 years, would be nominated by President Bill Clinton to serve as the first American Ambassador in Vietnam after the Vietnam War.

In the period from November 1995 to February 1998, there was a total of six waves of meetings in Hà Nội, between the American and Vietnamese scholars and former civilian and military officials, which included the two most important persons in both sides: Secretary of Defence Robert S. McNamara, and North Vietnamese General Võ Nguyên Giáp. Several documents were prepared on the topics of discussions for those meetings. After that, all of them were put together in a folder of documents used for discussions at an international conference called ***"The Vietnam War Re-examined: Its History and Lessons"*** organized by Rockefeller Foundation in Bellagio, Italy, from July 27 to July 31, 1998, with the participation of American and Vietnamese scholars and former officials together with a number of international scholars. After the conference, in 1999, that document folder was published in New York as a book by Public Affairs Publisher under title ***"Argument without end: in search of answers to the Vietnam tragedy."*** [15] This book included 8 chapters and presented the conclusions of all topics of discussions in the meetings in Hà Nội. Chapter Seven, under the title ***U.S. Military Victory in Vietnam: A Dangerous Illusion?*** from page 313 to page 371, will help us understand very clearly the basic argument for the negative judgment on the Vietnam War of Mr. McNamara and his supporters. The whole Chapter Seven, except for the Introduction by Mr. McNamara, was written by former Colonel Herbert Y. Schandler.

Mr. Herbert Y. Schandler (1928-2015) was a veteran and a researcher on the Vietnam War. He graduated from Westpoint Military Academy in 1952, had served two tours of duty in Vietnam in the Special Forces, and retired from the U.S. Army as a Colonel. He obtained a Ph.D. in Public Administration from

Harvard University, and was the author of two following famous books on the Vietnam War:

• ***The Unmaking of a president: Lyndon Johnson and Vietnam***, published by Princeton University Press in 1977

• ***America in Vietnam: the war that couldn't be won***, published by Rowman & Littlefield in 2009

Dr. Schandler was assigned by Mr. McNamara the responsibility to answer the principal question used as the title for Chapter Seven: ***U.S. Military Victory in Vietnam: A Dangerous Illusion?*** Anh his answer was as follows:

"The achievement of a military victory by U.S. forces in Vietnam was indeed a dangerous illusion." [16]

In his explanation of why he thought that the U.S. military victory in Vietnam was an illusion, he wrote very clearly as follows:

"The heart of the illusion is the failure of the U.S. military and civilian leaders alike to understand the nature of the war in which they became involved in Vietnam. It was a people's war – a civil war. Fundamentally, therefore, it was not simply a war of North Vietnamese aggression, as we viewed it at the time." [17]

Criticism of Arguments for the Judgment

The most important foundation of the arguments for the negative judgment of the Vietnam War was originated from the failure of the French Expeditionary Forces in the Indochina War (1945-1954), i.e., the resistance war of the Vietnamese people against the evil intention of the French to come back and impose again their domination in Vietnam. The authors of the "orthodox" school all saw the Vietnam War as the continuation of the Indochina War, and the U.S. troops, like the French soldiers, as a foreign army, and as such, would be hated by the Vietnamese people and, in the end, would be defeated just like the French Expeditionary Force. This point of view was the origin of all wrong arguments of the "orthodox" school of thought regarding the nature of the Vietnam War. The "orthodox" authors have based on the thoughts and conclusions of Mr. McNamara, the architect of the American military policy in Vietnam. And they were that the U.S. had done everything possible militarily and still could not win; therefore, the Vietnam War was indeed ***"an unwinnable war."*** We will try to evaluate each of all these arguments of this negative judgment.

Arguments on the Nature of the Vietnam War

Let's begin with a discussion of Dr. Schandler's affirmation that the Vietnam War was a ***"people's war,"*** and, thus, it was ***"an unwinnable war."*** This argument by Dr. Schandler showed that he had been much influenced by the Communist line of thinking. The concept of people's war was synthesized by Communist General Võ Nguyên Giáp from the thousand-year experience of the Vietnamese people in resistance wars against foreign invaders. It was completely appropriate in talking about the Indochina War when the entire Vietnamese people stood up to fight against the French Expeditionary Forces. But it was completely wrong in talking about the Vietnam War with the intention to tie the U.S. forces a role similar to the one of the French forces, and to see the South Vietnamese people just like the Vietnamese people in the Indochina War. ***It is quite clear that the American people did not understand Vietnamese contemporary history at all.*** The "orthodox" authors often said that the U.S. political and military leaders did not understand North Vietnam (and that's why Mr. McNamara had to go to Hà Nội several times, during 1995-1998, enduring humiliation to get to understand North Vietnam, though too late), but, in reality, ***these people did not understand even their ally, the RVN, either.***

It can be said that the majority of the American people, who have tried to get some knowledge of Vietnam, including the "orthodox" authors as well as the political and military leaders, believed that North Vietnam, represented by the Vietnamese

Communist Party (VCP), was the only legitimate representative of the Vietnamese people, and also had the merit of defeating the French Expeditionary Force and obtaining the independence for Vietnam. Biased by this incorrect thinking, despite the fact that the RVN was one of the U.S. allies in the Cold War against the expansion of the Communists in Southeast Asia, the Americans did not really completely respect the RVN, and sometimes even openly showed their contempt. ***They did not spend enough time to understand clearly how the RVN was born and why the RVN, from the government to the people, just could not accept to live together with the Communists.*** The below presentation will show Vietnamese contemporary historical events leading to the establishment of the country called the RVN.

"During the French domination in Vietnam, in terms of political organizations and parties, the VCP was neither the first nor the only one to fight against the French. In the latter part of the 19th century there were already many anti-French resistance movements, e.g., Cần Vương (Response to the Call of the Emperor), Văn Thân (Movement of the Intellectuals), Đông Du (Journey East), etc. At the beginning of the 20th century, many political parties were created, e.g., Việt Nam Quốc Dân Đảng (Vietnam Nationalist Party), Đại Việt Đảng (Greater Viet Party), Duy Dân Đảng (Populist Party), Tân Việt Cách Mạng Đảng (New Viet Revolutionary Party), etc. The Yên Bái Uprising launched by the Vietnam Nationalist Party occurred even before the creation of the VCP in 1930. As a person, Hồ Chí Minh was neither the first nor the only one patriot to fight against the French. As Vietnamese, we have learned and known (from elementary schools) the names of our anti-French patriots and heroes: Nguyễn Trung Trực, Thủ Khoa Nghĩa, Thủ Khoa Huân, Phan Đình Phùng, Nguyễn Thiện Thuật, Hoàng Hoa Thám, etc. of the 19th century; and Phan Bội Châu, Phan Châu Trinh, Kỳ Ngoại Hầu Cường Để, Tạ Thu Thâu, Nguyễn An Ninh, Phan Văn Hùm, etc. of the early 20th century." [18]

Even before the VCP succeeded in the August Revolution in Hà Nội (from August 14 to August 30, 1945), the people of South Vietnam (at that time it was still known as Nam Kỳ or Nam Bộ) had enthusiastically participated in different organizations or movements involved in the struggle for the independence of Vietnam.

"Ngày 18 tháng 3, 1945 tức hơn một tuần sau ngày Nhật đảo chánh 9 tháng 3, lần đầu tiên ở Sài Gòn đã có một cuộc biểu tình khổng lồ, công khai, trên 50.000 người ở sân thể thao Vườn Ông Thượng. Dân chúng Sài Gòn đã nô nức hưởng ứng lời kêu gọi của Hồ Văn Ngà tham dự lễ tưởng niệm các nhà ái quốc Hoàng Hoa Thám, Phan Đình Phùng, Phan Châu Trinh, Nguyễn Thái Học, Nguyễn An Ninh, Dương Bá Trạc. Hài cốt hỏa thiêu của Dương Bá Trạc đã được ông Trần Văn Ân gởi về từ Chiêu Nam (Singapore). Một bàn thờ Tổ Quốc với một đại kỳ màu vàng trên có khắc hai chữ Việt Nam đỏ chói được dựng lên giữa sân, khói trầm nghi ngút. Lần lượt lên diễn đàn có: Hồ Văn Ngà chủ tịch Việt Nam Quốc gia Độc lập Đảng, Trần Quang Vinh đại biểu Cao Đài, Nguyễn Vĩnh Thạnh đoàn trưởng Cận vệ quân và Nội ứng Nghĩa binh (đã cộng tác với quân đội Nhật trong ngày đảo chánh Pháp), luật sư Diệp Ba... Những lời kêu gọi dân chúng tham gia cùng đứng lên củng cố hàng ngũ quyết tâm xóa tan tàn tích thực dân Pháp, những lời tha thiết tưởng niệm các nhà ái quốc đã từng hy sinh cho đại cuộc chống ngoại xâm, đã được hùng hồn nói lên trong bầu không khí tự do, phấn khởi của một dân tộc không còn e dè, lo ngại kẻ thù như trước." [19]

(Translation:

"On March 18, 1945, i.e., more than one week after the Japanese military coup of March 9, for the first time in Sài Gòn, there was a huge public demonstration, with more than 50,000 people in the stadium of Vườn Ông Thượng. The Sài Gòn people have enthusiastically responded to the call of Mr. Hồ Văn Ngà to participate in the ceremony commemorating our patriots such as Hoàng Hoa Thám, Phan Đình Phùng, Phan Châu Trinh, Nguyễn Thái Học, Nguyễn An Ninh, Dương Bá Trạc. Mr. Dương Bá Trạc's ashes were sent back from Singapore by Mr. Trần Văn Ân. An altar for the Fatherland with a big yellow flag bearing the two bright red words Việt Nam was set up in the middle of the stadium, all in an ambience of burned sandal wooded-incense. The successive speakers were: Hồ Văn Ngà, President of Việt Nam Quốc gia Độc lập Đảng [Vietnamese Na-

tional Independence Party], *Trần Quang Vinh, Cao Đài Representative, Nguyễn Vĩnh Thanh, Leader of Cận vệ quân và Nội ứng Nghĩa binh* [Internal Support Volunteer Guards] *(having co-operated with the Japanese Army in the coup to overthrow the French), Lawyer Diệp Ba... The calls for the people to rise up, to strengthen the determination to wipe out all French colonialist relics, the fervent words in memory of all patriots having sacrificed in the fight against the invaders, all were pronounced in an atmosphere of freedom and enthusiasm of a nation that was no longer hesitant or afraid of the enemy like before..."*)

After the Japanese surrendered, when the British army arrived to disarm them, the French took advantage of the opportunity, and brought their troops back with the intention to recapture Việt Nam, the South Vietnamese people, from all walks of life, regardless of age, and with rudimentary weapons, like just bamboo sticks, once more, immediately organized their resistance from September 23, 1945, a long time before Hà Nội officially launched the national resistance on December 19, 1946. In Volume 2 of his memoir (1945-1954), the famous South Vietnamese reporter Nam Đình Nguyễn Kỳ Nam recounted that situation as follows:

> ***"Tức thì, hôm sau*** [tức là ngày 24-9-1945], ***súng nổ khắp nơi: Cầu Mac-Mahon*** [tức cầu Công Lý, trên đường dẫn ra phi trường Tân Sơn Nhứt] ***bị dân-quân giàn trận đánh quân Anh-Ấn giữ cầu rồi đến cầu Bông, cầu Thị Nghè, cầu Kiệu*** [cuối đường Hai Bà Trưng dẫn sang Phú Nhuận] ***đâu đâu cũng có trận đánh kịch-liệt. Dân-quân rút ra khỏi Saigon, tổ-chức lại: hể đêm đến, là đột-nhập châu thành đánh phá khắp nơi."*** [20]

(<u>Translation</u>:

"Right away, the next day [i.e., September 24, 1945], *firearms went off everywhere; the militia were deploying their forces, getting ready to attack the British-Indian troops that ware guarding the Mac-Mahon Bridge* [i.e., Công Lý Bridge on the road to Tân Sơn Nhứt airport]; *and along Bông Bridge, Thị Nghè Bridge, Kiệu Bridge* [at the end of Hai Bà Trưng Street

leading to Phú Nhuận] *fierce fighting was everywhere. The militia then withdrew out of Sài Gòn, and regrouped; at nights, they infiltrated back into the city and attacked everywhere.")*

From that moment on, Viet Minh, led by the VCP, have used all tricks to liquidate a fairly large number of the non-communist patriots in all groups, all political parties in order to have the monopoly of leading the national resistance against the French. Even right in Sài Gòn, the Communists were not hesitant in their killings of these patriots.

"Bà Nguyễn Ngọc Sương [Thủ Lãnh Phụ Nữ Tiền Phong], ***y khoa bác sĩ tốt nghiệp từ Pháp, và chồng là luật sư Hồ Vĩnh Ký, khoảng một tháng sau ngày mở màn Nam bộ Kháng chiến, đã bị bộ hạ của Trần Văn Giàu*** [cán bộ Cộng Sản, thủ lãnh Việt Minh] ***xử bắn ở Bến Súc cùng nhiều đồng chí khác, ngày 23 tháng 10-1945, khi quân đội Anh-Ấn tiến chiếm Thủ Dầu Một. Những người bị Trần Văn Giàu bắt ở Thủ Đức trong đó có Trần Văn Thạch (người đã hỏi Trần Văn Giàu trong buổi họp có báo chí tham dự ngày 30 tháng 8-1945, năm ngày sau khi Lâm ủy Hành chánh ra mắt: "Ai đã cử anh làm Chủ tịch Ủy Ban Hành Pháp?"), tất cả đã bị bọn cai ngục được lịnh phải thủ tiêu."*** [21]

(Translation:

"Mrs. Nguyễn Ngọc Sương [leader of the Vanguard Women Movement], *a medical doctor educated in France, and her husband Hồ Vĩnh Ký, a lawyer, were executed by subordinates of Trần Văn Giàu* [Communist cadre, Leader of Viet Minh] *in Bến Súc together with several other comrades on October 23, 1945 when the British-Indian troops attacked Thủ Dầu Một. All the people arrested by Trần Văn Giàu in Thủ Đức, including Trần Văn Thạch (the man who had asked Trần Văn Giàu at the meeting attended by the press on August 30, 1945, five days after the creation of the Provisional Administrative Committee: "Who nominated you to be Chairman of the Provisional Administrative Committee?") were liquidated by the prison guards ordered to do so.")*

During the first period of the Nam Bộ Kháng Chiến (Southern Resistance), Việt Minh, with the Quốc Gia Tự Vệ Cuộc (National Self-Defense Agency) under the leadership of Communist cadres such as Dương Bạch Mai, Nguyễn Văn Trấn (notorious as the Butcher of Chợ Đệm), have murdered numerous non-Communist patriots like Mr. Huỳnh Phú Sổ, Leader of Hòa Hảo Religious Sect, or even Communists, belonging to the Trotskyist Fourth International, like Phan Văn Hùm, Tạ Thu Thâu, Trần Văn Thạch, etc. Meanwhile, in North Vietnam, numerous members of nationalist political parties like the Việt Nam Quốc Dân Đảng (Viet Nam Nationalist Party) were also assassinated by the Communists. Khái Hưng, a famous author of Tự Lực Văn Đoàn (Self-Reliance Writers' Group), had the same fate[22] just because he was a member of Việt Nam Quốc Dân Đảng. Having discovered the true nature of the VCP, the non-Communist patriots began to leave the resistance, using all means to escape from the resistance zone and go back to the cities. In the North, ***"dinh tê,"*** (leave the resistance or leave for enemy-occupied zones) was the popular term for that movement, and in the South it was called ***"về thành."*** (go back to the city). Following are the two typical cases of two famous Southern politicians: 1) Professor Trần Văn Hương, when the Southern Resistance began, was Chairman of the Resistance's Administrative Committee of the Province of Tây Ninh; later he served as Mayor of Sài Gòn twice, Prime Minister also twice, Vice-President, and finally President of the Republic of Vietnam; 2) Dr. Nguyễn Lưu Viên, during the resistance time, was Chief Medical Officer of the 320 Division,[23] later he served as commissioner, minister, and deputy-prime minister in several governments of the RVN. The majority of these ***"về thành"*** persons did not collaborate with the French administration. For example: Mr. Trần Văn Hương joined the government in the position of Mayor of Sài Gòn only after Mr. Ngô Đình Diệm came back from France to form the government in July 1954. However, these efforts to leave and come back to the city were just some personal decisions. It was only after the VCP launched its program of land reform (Cải Cách Ruộng Đất) in 1953, killing hundreds of thousands of innocent people that the North Vietnamese people could see clearly its cruelty, brutality, and immorality,[24] and the ***"dinh tê"*** has really become a popular movement.

Another important political concept needs to be clarified: the legitimacy of the Government of North Vietnam. This issue was discussed by an author as follows:

"Phải thành thật mà nhận rằng, do hoàn cảnh lịch sử đưa đẩy, nhà nước Việt Nam Dân Chủ Cộng Hòa (VNDCCH) lúc mới thành lập đã hội đủ phần nào các điều kiện để mang tính chính thống và được hậu thuẫn của nhân dân. Điểm quan trọng cần ghi nhận ngay ở đây là sự hậu thuẫn này nhân dân Việt Nam dành cho một chính quyền đại diện cho toàn dân để tranh đấu cho độc lập và tự do của đất nước, chớ không phải dành cho một nhà nước Cộng sản để xây dựng chủ nghĩa xã hội. Cuộc kháng chiến thần thánh của nhân dân ta chống thực dân Pháp cũng đặt trên cơ sở này. Chính quyền VNDCCH đã tự động và đơn phương thay đổi điều kiện trong bản hợp đồng với nhân dân. Năm 1951, khi ĐCSVN tái sinh dưới danh hiệu Đảng Lao Động VN và trực tiếp nắm quyền lãnh đạo kháng chiến, đẩy nhân dân vào chỗ giết nhau trong các vụ đấu tố cải cách ruộng đất (trong khi miệng vẫn hô hào đoàn kết toàn dân) thì cũng chính năm đó phải được xem là thời điểm chấm dứt tính chính thống của nhà nước VNDCCH. Phân tích đến cùng, ta phải thấy rõ là thật ra chính ĐCSVN đã bức tử nhà nước chính thống VNDCCH. Và hành động bất hợp pháp này, ngay lập tức, đã bị nhân dân phản kháng và chống đối. Sự gia tăng rõ rệt của những vụ liều chết tìm cách rời bỏ chiến khu để trở về thành sau năm 1952 của nhiều phần tử yêu nước đã từng thực sự đóng góp cho kháng chiến và của đông đảo đồng bào nông thôn đã nói lên sự phản đối này. Tiếp theo đó, với sự chia cắt đất nước, trắng trợn phản bội quyền lợi của đất nước và với sự quyết liệt chối bỏ và xa lánh của hàng triệu người di cư vào Nam, sự chính thống của nhà nước VNDCCH vĩnh viễn chấm dứt." [25]

(<u>Translation</u>:

"Honestly, we have to recognize, by the special circumstances of the country, the Government of the Democratic Re-

public of Vietnam (DRV), at its creation, had partially fulfilled the conditions for legitimacy and the support of the people. The important point that needs to be emphasized here is that the support that the Vietnamese people had given to the DRV had been for a government representing the whole nation with the objective of fighting against the French for the country's independence and freedom, NOT for a Communist government to build socialism. The sacred Resistance of the Vietnamese people was also based on this foundation. The DRV had automatically and unilaterally changed these conditions in the contract with the Vietnamese people. In 1951, when the VCP changed its name to Vietnamese Labor Party (Đảng Lao Động Việt Nam) and directly led the Resistance, and pushed the people into the fratricide in the Land Reform Program (while still calling for national unity) then it is appropriate to take that year as the time the DRV's legitimacy officially ended. In final analysis, we have to admit that it was the VCP that sentenced the DRV to death and terminated its legitimacy. And this totally illegal action by the VCP was immediately opposed by the Vietnamese people. The huge surge of the ***"dinh tê"*** *movement after 1952, including the patriots who had contributed o the Resistance as well the rural people who had personally witnessed the atrocities of the Land Reform Program, was speaking loudly of this opposition to the DRV and to the VCP. After that, with the division of Vietnam in 1954 accepted by the DRV and the VCP, a blatant betrayal of the national interest, and with the strong determination of the Vietnamese people to reject the Communist regime in the great exodus of North Vietnamese people to the South in 1954-55, the legitimacy of the DRV was terminated for good.")*

In the meantime, the French Expeditionary Forces was gradually bogging down in the war, forcing the French government to find a political solution. The anti-Communist nationalist political parties have invited ex-Emperor Bảo Đại to come back to form a new government.

"Ngày 9-9-1947, 24 đại diện các đảng phái và đoàn thể sang Hong Kong gặp C.H. Bảo Dại."[26]

(<u>Translation</u>:

"On September 9, 1947, 24 representatives of political parties and organizations went to Hong Kong to meet ex-Emperor Bảo Đại.")

They presented their common aspiration:

"... yêu cầu Cựu hoàng Bảo Đại, người đại diện độc nhất, đủ tư cách của dân tộc Việt Nam ra chấp chính và mở cuộc đàm phán với nước Pháp, hầu tái lập hòa bình ở Việt Nam và thực hiện hòa bình và độc lập."[27]

(<u>Translation</u>:

"...demanded that ex-Emperor Bảo Đại, the only eligible representative of the Vietnamese people, form a government and open negotiations with France in order to re-establish peace and obtain independence for Vietnam.")

After the French Government has satisfied all of his demands, including the ***prerequisite of returning Cochinchina (i.e., Nam Kỳ) to Vietnam, the ex-Emperor accepted*** to come back to Vietnam, and formed the first Government of the State of Vietnam on July 1, 1949, of which he held the position of Prime Minister.[28] This State of Vietnam was the predecessor of the RVN that was created on October 26, 1955 with Mr. Ngô Đình Diệm as the first president.

All of these above-mentioned developments of the contemporary history of Vietnam show very clearly that the judgment by the "orthodox" authors regarding the DRV as the legitimate government of Vietnam and the RVN as a creation by the U.S. after the 1954 Geneva Accords ***was totally wrong***. Even the accusation that the RVN violated the 1954 Geneva Accords with its refusal to organize the general elections in 1956 (the main reason for which North Vietnam decided to launch the war in the south in order to reunify the country) was also legally baseless since the State of Vietnam (of which the RVN was the successor) ***did not sign and recognize the Accords***. Dr. Trần Văn Đỗ, Minister of Foreign Affairs and Head of the State of Vietnam Delegation at the Geneva Conference, has made the following announcement:

"Việc ký hiệp định giữa Pháp và Việt Minh có những điều khoản gây nguy hại nặng nề cho tương lai chính trị của Quốc gia Việt Nam. Hiệp định đã nhường cho Việt Minh những vùng mà quân đội quốc gia còn đóng quân và tước mất của (Quốc gia) Việt Nam quyền tổ chức phòng thủ. Bộ Tư lệnh Pháp đã tự ấn định ngày tổ chức tuyển cử mà không có sự thỏa thuận với phái đoàn quốc gia Việt Nam... chính phủ Quốc gia Việt Nam yêu cầu Hội nghị ghi nhận một cách chính thức rằng Việt Nam long trọng phản đối cách ký kết Hiệp định cùng những điều khoản không tôn trọng nguyện vọng sâu xa của dân Việt. Chính phủ Quốc gia Việt Nam yêu cầu Hội nghị ghi nhận rằng Chính phủ tự dành cho mình quyền hoàn toàn tự do hành động để bảo vệ quyền thiêng liêng của dân tộc Việt Nam trong công cuộc thực hiện Thống nhất, Độc lập, và Tự do cho xứ sở." [29]

(Translation:

"The signing of the accords between the French and Viet Minh has several clauses that will seriously harm the political future of the State of Vietnam. The accords have yielded to Viet Minh areas where the army of the State of Vietnam was still occupying, and deprived (the State of) Vietnam the rights to organize its defense. The French Command has unilaterally decided on the date to organize the general elections without the consensus of the State of Vietnam Delegation... The Government of the State of Vietnam demands that the Conference officially register Vietnam's opposition to the way the accords were signed and to the clauses that do not respect the deep aspiration of the Vietnamese people. The Government of the State of Vietnam demands the Conference register that it reserves the rights to act in order to protect the sacred rights of the Vietnamese people to achieve Unification, Independence, and Freedom for the country."

After the Geneva Accords were signed on July 20, 1954, there was a period of 300 days during which the people were free to move to where they wanted to live. And the result showed that during that time there were only 4,269 people who chose to go and live in the North, compared to a total of 892,876 people who chose to go and live in the South.[30]

Therefore, it is very clear that the Vietnam War was not a ***people's war*** like Dr. Schandler has determined. It must be seen as a ***war of invasion.*** The reasons were straightforward as follows:

• Both the RVN and the DRV were countries that possessed all factors regulated by international public laws according to the ***Montevideo Convention on Rights and Duties of States (1933)***:

o Having a defined territory
o Having a permanent population
o Having a government
o Having capacity to enter into relations with the other states

• ***"The act of using military forces to deprive another state of government, territory, according to the definition of Article 1, Resolution 3314 of 1974 of the General Assembly of the United Nations, is an act of invasion under international public laws."*** [31]

There is one additional point that needs to be cleared: this war of invasion was not an ordinary one but a very complex war of invasion mixed with ideology between people of the same blood, pretty much like the Korean War (1951-53), termed an invasion by the United Nations, which allowed many nations to send troops to fight against the invading North Koreans.

Arguments on U.S. Military Strategy in Vietnam

These arguments were based on the two following main points:

• The U.S. had used all its military forces and still failed to force North Vietnam abandon its intention to conquer South Vietnam

• If the escalation had continued a nuclear confrontation would not have been avoided

Let's take a close look at each of these points.

U.S. Had Used All Its Military Forces

This argument showed both the means and the objective of U.S. intervention in Vietnam: 1) means: using all military forces available; 2) objective: making North Vietnam know the price, and forcing it to abandon its intention to seize South Vietnam by force.

Let's discuss the objective. This argument showed very clearly the limit of the U.S. intervention: the U.S. only wanted North Vietnam to stop attacking South Vietnam, i.e., going back to the status quo of the two countries demarcated at the 17th parallel (just like the situations in Germany and Korea). Many people, therefore, have rightly criticized that the U.S. went to war but did not want a win, just a tie while the enemy was determined to win at all cost, and, thus, a U.S. loss was something in the making. Because of this limited objective, the U.S. Government, i.e., the civilian leaders, established numerous limitations called ***"rules of engagement,"*** for the military to observe. In the bombing of North Vietnam, i.e., Operation Rolling Thunder, the targets were very limited and were selected by the civilian leaders, with damaging results as can be seen in the following judgment by General Bruce Palmer, Jr. Commander of U.S. II Field Force in Vietnam during 1967-1968:

> ***"In the end, these limited strikes had little effect on the enemy build-up culminating in the massive Easter Offensive across the DMZ in late March 1972. This buildup, incidentally, should have warned the allies of the strong probability of an attack launched directly from the DMZ."*** [32]

It was also because of this limited objective that the U.S.

also applied the strategy of gradual escalation. This method of gradual escalation might bring good results in the political or diplomatic struggle, but, in a war, it was a big mistake, causing serious damages because it gave the enemy time to regroup, strengthen, and re-attack. To be more precise, however, the U.S. strategy was much worse: fight and stop, stop and fight, it was very clear that there was no intention to finish off the fight. Looking back at the proceeding of the war, we can see very clearly that the Communists had 3- or 4-year intervals to regroup for their general offensives: Tết Offensive (1968), Easter Offensive (1972), and the Hồ Chí Minh Campaign (1975). In their book "***The real lessons of the Vietnam War***", editors John Norton Moore and Robert F. Turner had the following criticism of this U.S. strategy:

> ***"In fact, our policy was not even gradual escalation; that is, progressive and increasing application of force to strangle the enemy. Instead, our policy was escalation and de-escalation, an "on again, off again" knee-jerk reaction that varied with the intuitive whims of President Johnson and his advisors."*** [33]

In summary, in terms of objective, it was no doubt the U.S. did not want to destroy the enemy, North Vietnam, i.e., they did not want an absolute, total victory in the Vietnam War. It was a war policy that was completely opposite to the military thoughts of generals from the ancient time to the modern time, reflected in General of the Army (5-star General) Douglas MacArthur's famous statement: ***"In war there is no substitute for victory."***

In term of the means, the judgment by the "orthodox" authors was that the U.S. had exhausted all its military means. Is it true?

Generally speaking, the U.S. military strategy in Vietnam included two components: 1) Introducing ground combat troops into the South in order to destroy units of the armed forces of the National Liberation Front (i.e., Viet Cong) and units of the armed forces of North Vietnam having infiltrated through the Ho Chi Minh Trail; and, 2) Using its Air Force to prevent the North Vietnamese troops from infiltrating through the Ho Chi Minh Trail and bombing North Vietnam to quench its intention of conquering the South.

Regarding the presence of the U.S. troops in the South, we have to admit that at the beginning of 1968, the U.S. was maintaining a very large army, almost half a million men (497, 498) of all services and combat-experienced units, including the following most significant units:

- U.S. Army:

  o 1St Cavalry Division - Airmobile
  o 3 infantry divisions: the 1st, the 9th, and the 25th
  o 23rd Infantry Division, named Americal Division
  o 101st Airborne Division
  o 3rd Brigade, 82nd Airborne Division

- U.S. Marine Corps:

  o 1st Marine Division, in Chu Lai, Quảng Ngãi Province
  o 3rd Marine Division, in Đà Nẵng, Quảng Nam Province
  o 5th Marine Division, in Khe Sanh, Quảng Trị Province

- U.S. Navy:

  o In the end, there was a total of 20 aircraft carriers deployed during the Vietnam War, such as Coral Sea, Enterprise, Hancock, Hornet, Midway, etc. Each aircraft carrier had hundreds of jet fighters, such as A-4 Skyhawk, A-6 Intruder, A-7 Corsair II, etc.

- U.S. Air Force:

  o Seventh Air Force, with its headquarters in Tân Sơn Nhứt và its squadrons deployed at 10 airbases scattered all over the RVN territory; most aircraft were the famous F-4 Phantom and F-105 Thunderchief jet fighters, etc.

What needs to be discussed here is how the U.S. had used these mighty, with what strategy and what results. The Command of all these forces was called MACV (Military Assistance Command, Vietnam) and the Commander was General (4-star general) William C. Westmoreland (1914-2005), nick-named Westy by the U.S. media. General Westmoreland graduated from Westpoint Military Academy in 1936, began his career as an artillery officer, saw action in World War II at various battlefields in North Africa, Italy, France, Germany, recorded numerous victories, and moved up very fast through the ranks to become a Colonel, Chief of Staff of the 9th Infantry Division. After World War II ended, he took a parachute jump training course offered by the Army, and was nominated Commander of the 504th Regiment of the 82nd Airborne Division, and then Chief of Staff of the Division. In 1952, at 38, he was promoted to Brigadier-General (one-star general) and became the youngest brigadier-general of the U.S. Army. In the Korean War, he was Commander of the 187th Airborne Regiment. After the Korean War, he successively assumed the positions of Commander of the 101st Airborne Division (1958-1960), Superintendent of the Westpoint Military Academy (1960-1963); he was then promoted to Lieutenant-General (3-star general) in July 1963, and nominated Commander of the XVIII Airborne Corps. In January 1964, he was sent to Vietnam as Deputy-Commander of MACV, and in June 1964 he was promoted to General (4-star general) and was nominated by President Johnson as Commander of MACV.

General Westmoreland put in place a strategy called ***Search and Destroy***, in fact a war of attrition with the objective of destroying enemy forces to the maximum in order to get to a ***"crossover point"*** defined as the point when the enemy re-supply of men could not make up their casualties. General Westmoreland, therefore, had decided to organize very expensive large-scale operations, using huge forces of regimental or divisional level, attacking important enemy bases and secret zones, e.g., Operation Attleboro in Dầu Tiếng, Bình Dương Province, from September 14 to November 25, 1966, Operation Cedar Falls in the Iron Triangle, from January 8 to January 26, 1967, and, Operation Junction City in War Zone C, from February 22 to May 14, 1967. In 3 years, with his army increasing from 184,300 (1965) up to 485,600 men (1967), General Westmoreland still could not reach the expected ***"crossover point,"*** even with the convenient way of calculating the order-of-battle (often referred to as OB) in his report by minimizing the numbers of the Communist guerillas and militia, resulting in a big controversy between MACV and the CIA (Central Intelligence Agency), reflected in the intelligence document called SNIE14.3-67. [34] In 1967, a number of people inside and outside of the U.S. government started to have some doubts, made critical comments of, and finally recommended that President Johnson drop General Westmoreland's ***"Search and Destroy"*** strategy. But President Johnson did not listen and continued to trust General Westmoreland. At the end of 1967, on November 21, at the National Press Club in Washington, D.C., General Westmoreland was still optimistic in his statement as follows:

> *"We have reached an important point where the end begins to come into view."* [35]

Only more than two months later, on January 31, 1968, the Tet Offensive was fiercely carried out by Communist forces in the capital city of Sài Gòn, in other large cities, and in almost all provincial downtowns of the RVN. General Westmoreland's "search and destroy" strategy was a total failure. His request for additional 200,000 men was bluntly rejected by President Johnson. He was called back to serve as U.S. Army Chief of Staff and his deputy, General Creighton Abrams (1914-1974) was nominated to replace him as Commander of MACV.

One important point needs to be kept in mind here. The Tet Offensive was a huge, unprecedented military defeat of the Communists. Following are casualty figures officially confirmed by the VCP:

" - 111306 cán bộ, chiến sĩ lực lượng vũ trang và chính trị ở miền Nam đã hy sinh và bị thương, hàng vạn quần chúng cách mạng đã ngã xuống" (dẫn theo Viện Nghiên cứu chủ nghĩa Mác - Lê-nin và Tư tưởng Hồ Chí Minh: Lịch sử Đảng Cộng sản Việt Nam, tập 2 - 1954-1975, Nhà xuất bản Chính trị quốc gia, Hà Nội, 1995, tr. 441).

- Trong đó, 44.824 cán bộ, chiến sĩ lực lượng vũ trang đã anh dũng hy sinh (Đường 9: 3.994, Trị Thiên: 4.862; Đồng bằng Khu 5: 10.732; Tây Nguyên: 3.436; Khu 6: 1.254; Khu 10: 440; Đông Nam Bộ: 14.121; Khu 8: 2.484; Khu 9: 3.501); 61.267 bị thương (Cục Tác chiến, số 124/TGi, hồ sơ 1.103 (11-2-1969))." [36]

(Translation:

"111,306 cadres, soldiers of the armed forces and political cadres in the south were sacrificed and wounded, tens of thousands of revolutionary people have fallen" (excerpt from Institute of Research of Marxist-Leninism and Ho Chi Minh's Thoughts: History of the Vietnamese Communist Party, volume 2 – 1954-1975, National Politics Publishing House, Hà Nội, 1995, p. 441).

- Including 44,824 cadres, soldiers of the armed forces were heroically sacrificed (Route 9: 3,994; Trị Thiên [i.e., Provinces of Quảng Trị and Thừa Thiên]: *4,862; Zone 5 Plains: 10,732; Western Highlands: 3,436; Zone 6: 1,254; Zone 19: 440; Eastern South Vietnam: 14,121; Zone 8: 2,484; Zone 9: 3,501; 61,267 wounded (Directorate for Combat Actions, no. 124/TGi, file 1,103 (February 11, 1969))."*

Ironically, however, the Americans saw it as a huge failure of the Free World, and, from that moment on, they decided to find ways to de-escalate the war, enter into negotiations with the Communists in order to withdraw. President Johnson ordered to stop the bombings of North Vietnam and announced that he would not seek re-election. After he was elected, President Nixon carried out the withdrawal of troops in his Vietnamization program.

The majority of the "orthodox" authors used the Tet Offensive in 1968 as the starting point when the U.S. Government definitely realized that a victory in Vietnam would be impossible. Three important books of the "orthodox" authors were: ***Vietnam: a history*** by Stanley Karnow, ***America's longest war*** *by* George Herring, and ***A Bright shining lie*** by Neil Sheehan all reserved a large number of pages to talk about the Vietnam War until 1968 (1965-1968), while the discussion of the remaining period of the Vietnam War (twice in length from 1968 to 1975) was very sketchy as can be seen below:

- ***Vietnam: a history***:
    - o For the period until 1968: 567 pages (pp.1-567)
    - o For the period 1968-1975: only 102 pages (pp. 568-670)
- ***America's longest war***:
    - o For the period until 1968: 221 pages (pp. 1-221)
    - o For the period 1968-1975: only 60 pages (pp. 222-282)
- ***A Bright shining lie***:
    - o For the period until 1968: 725 pages (pp. 1-725)
    - o For the period 1968-1975: only 65 pages (pp. 726-791)

In reality, it was very clear that since after the Tet Offensive the RVN and its Allies had won several big victories, sometimes having changed the course of the Vietnam War, and caused a lot of difficulties for the Communists.

In addition to the two big victories in 1968 and 1972 (Summer of Fire, Defending An Lộc, Recapture of Quảng Trị, and Safeguarding Kontum), the U.S. army, under the command of General Abrams, applied a new strategy called ***"Clear and Hold"*** with a focus on pacification. A high-ranking CIA agent, Mr. William Colby (formerly Chief CIA Station in Vietnam), was nominated to head CORDS (Civil Operations and Revolutionary Development Support), of which the main responsibility was to carry out a new pacification plan called APC (Accelerated Pacification Campaign). The core program of the APC was the Phoenix Program aimed at destroying the VCI (Viet Cong Infrastructure) in order to re-establish security for the hamlets and villages under the control of the RVN Government. The APC Plan had the initial objective for the first three months (90 days) of neutralizing the VCI and re-establishing security for 1,000 semi-controlled hamlets. This plan has achieved its initial objective very well in more than the planned 1,000 hamlets. In fact, in the beginning of January 1969, the RVN already had 1,320 hamlets under its total control.[37] The Phoenix Program caused great damages for the Communists as follows:

> ***"Between 1968 and 1972, Phoenix "neutralized" 81,740 people suspected of VC membership, of whom 26,369 were killed. A significant number of VC were killed, and between 1969 and 1971 the program was quite successful in destroying VC infrastructure in many important areas."*** [38]

Moreover, a number of limitations from the time of the Johnson administration were lifted. After General Lon Nol organized the successful coup overthrowing the pro-Communist government of Prince Sihanouk at the beginning of 1970, President Nixon, at the end of April 1970, ordered the U.S. troops, together with the ARVN, to cross the border, move into Cambodian territory, attack and destroy all Communist secured and secret zones located along the border, which had been authorized by Prince Sihanouk several years prior. This operation achieved the following important results as can be seen below:

> ***"Major General Nguyễn Duy Hinh, author of a postwar monograph, summed up results of the incursion overall, tabulating 9,300 tons of weapons, ammunition, and supplies seized, plus 7,000 tons of rice, altogether constituting enemy requirements for at least six months of operations in the COSVN area."*** [39]

Within the same spirit of abolishing the limitations imposed during the administration of President Johnson, on May 9, 1972, President Nixon ordered the aircraft carrier USS Coral Sea to implement the blockage of Hải Phòng port (where North Vietnam received 85% of its imported goods) by mining the Gulf of Tonkin. And when North Vietnam unilaterally and blatantly left the Paris Peace Talks at the end of 1972, President Nixon ordered USAF to use B-52 strategic bombers to carpet bomb Hà Nội for 13 days and nights during Christmas 1972 (Christmas Bombing) and forced Hà Nội to come back to the conference table.

All these above-mentioned points show very clearly that the strategy that the U.S. applied from 1965 (after bringing combat ground troops into South Vietnam) to 1968 (Tet Offensive) was a total mistake, and, thus, could not help achieve victory. We have also seen that with the new strategy, paying more attention to the issue of pacification, and, at the same time, all absurd barriers and limitations binding the hands of the military, and imposed by the American civilians, the U.S. army and the ARVN have achieved many clear-cut victories (during 1968, 1970, and 1972), that really changed the course of the Vietnam War in favor for the allies. All these points really helped to affirm that ***The Vietnam War definitely was not an unwinnable war and if the U.S. had applied a right strategy right from the beginning the U.S. and the RVN would have won the Vietnam War.***

If More Escalation Had Been Carried Out a Nuclear Confrontation Would Have Been Unavoidable

As previously mentioned, the possibility of using nuclear weapons was referred to in the memo of the JCS dated May 20, 1967 and caused some panic to Secretary of Defense Robert S. McNamara. Let's evaluate the value of this argument within the background of the Cold War and within the timeframe of 1965-1975.

As presented in details in the previous part of this Chapter, the probability for the U.S. and the RVN, with a different strategy and without those absurd barriers and limitations, to win the Vietnam War, without resorting to the use of nuclear weapons, would have been quite high.

Now, let's suppose that if even with a new strategy and without these barriers and limitations, the U.S. still could not win the war and had had to resort to the use of nuclear weapons then would a nuclear confrontation have occurred?

The answer is: ***very probably NOT***. Why NOT?

If the U.S. had used nuclear weapons in the Southern part of China, China would not be able to retaliate, and, thus, there would NOT have been any ***"nuclear confrontation"*** because, in fact, only China would get the nuclear bombs. China could not retaliate because, although they had already conducted some nuclear tests since October 1964, China did not yet develop the delivery system, i.e., intercontinental missiles with nuclear warheads. Moreover, during the 1960s, China was still suffering from the seriously chaotic and divisive Cultural Revolution. Only the Soviet Union had the means of retaliation against the U.S. But the probability for the Soviet Union to engage in a nuclear confrontation with the U.S. ***was almost certainly NIL***. There were two historical events, which could help us reach that conclusion.

First, during the 1962 Cuban Crisis, the Soviet Union had blinked in the showdown with the U.S. ready to accept a nuclear confrontation, and decided to dismantle all missiles already installed in Cuba. The Soviet Union had refused to sacrifice for Cuba, why should it sacrifice for China?

Second, the Soviet Union and China, during the 1960s, became enemies, and fought each other quite a few fierce battles in their border war in 1969 (from March 2 to September 1, 1969) in Zhenbao Island, on the Ussuri River, close to the border of Manchuria. It was exactly during the period of this border conflict that the Soviet Union has already explored the possibility to carry out a pre-emptive nuclear attack against the Chinese nuclear research and development facilities. The Soviet Union approached and sounded out the communist parties of Australia, Finland and Italy, and even the U.S. on that issue.[40]

Concluding Remarks

This Chapter has shown very clearly that the judgment ***"The Vietnam War was an unwinnable war"*** was totally wrong. If, right from the beginning, the U.S. had applied a different strategy, completely without the absurd barriers and limitations, it could have won the Vietnam War, and with a much lower price. In reality, the U.S. had not done it. Moreover, with the unscrupulous betrayal of the U.S. 93rd (1973-1975) and 94th (1975-1977) Congresses under the total control of the Democratic Party, abandoning its ally, cutting off all military aids, the U.S. Government had to witness the tragic result as its ally, the RVN, had to surrender and ceased to exist. (See details in Chapter Nine). An American author of the "revisionist" school has given a very correct judgment of the defeat of the RVN as follows:

> ***"The South Vietnamese regime did not fall in 1975 because it was uniquely corrupt and illegitimate. It fell to Soviet-equipped North Vietnamese tanks only because the United States, which had left troops in South Korea to defend a comparably corrupt and authoritarian dictatorship, had abandoned its allies in South Vietnam."***[41]

SEVEN CHAPTER

President Nguyễn Văn Thiệu and the Paris Peace Talks

The U.S. and North Vietnam officially began their open negotiations in Paris, France, on May 13, 1968. Because of the nature of open negotiations, both sides could not reach any compromise, and, thus, no result whatsoever. Both sides, therefore, decided to put an end to the open talks and began to have closed-door meetings. At the meeting of August 19, 1968, the Deputy Head of the American Delegation, Cyrus Vance, for the first time, suggested that the talks should be expanded to include both the RVN and the NFL (National Liberation Front, i.e., Viet Cong). The Deputy Head of the North Vietnamese Delegation, Hà Văn Lâu, agreed to consider this suggestion. President Nguyễn Văn Thiệu did not agree with this suggestion because he believed that doing so would be seen as a public and official recognition of the NFL as a political entity in the South, but, at that moment, he did not communicate his disagreement to the U.S. Government because he also believed that North Vietnam would not agree to this suggestion either since it never officially recognized the RVN.[1] It happened exactly like what President Thiệu had predicted: North Vietnam rejected that suggestion. Two months later, in October 1968, the U.S. presidential election entered its last phase (with the election day on November 5, which was very bitter and forceful between the two candidates, Mr. Hubert H. Humphrey of the Democratic Party, and Mr. Richard M. Nixon of the Republican Party. All polls showed that the distance between the two candidates was gradually narrowed with the popular support for Mr. Humphrey increased day by day and Mr. Humphrey could win the election. The Communists wanted Mr. Humphrey to win because his position on peace was beneficial to them. Turning 180 degrees, at the meeting of October 26, 1968, North Vietnamese Representative Xuân Thủy announced their acceptance of the U.S. suggestion for a four-party peace talks, considering that as a concession from them, and, of course, expecting a concession from the U.S. The Johnson government happily seized the opportunity. The U.S. Ambassador in the RVN, Mr. Ellsworth Bunker, received the order to do his best in persuading President Thiệu to sign the U.S. – Vietnam Joint Declaration on the bombing halt on North Vietnam (that President Johnson would announce in his speech in the evening of October 31, 1968) and to immediately send a South Vietnamese Delegation to Paris to participate in the peace talks. President Thiệu agreed with these suggestions from the U.S. On October 30, 1968, U.S. Representative Harriman informed Xuân Thủy in advance that, the next day, October 31, 1968, around 7 or 8 pm of Washington, D.C. time, President Johnson would announce the halt of all bombings in North Vietnam. With this event, it was certain that Mr. Humphrey would win the election in just 5 days. But, in the end, everything did not happen according to the plan that had been accepted by both the U.S. and RVN governments. It was also on October 30, 1968, President Thiệu turned 180 degrees, informed the U.S. that he refused to sign that Joint Declaration and also refused to send the RVN Delegation to Paris on November 6, 1968 as he had agreed upon. On October 31, 1968, having no other choice, President Johnson had to unilaterally announced the bombing halt. But because there would be no participation of the RVN Delegation, the Paris Peace Talks went nowhere and, thus, did not help the democratic candidate Humphrey at all. Five days later, Mr. Humphrey lost the election. Mr. Nixon won the election with an extremely narrow margin, under 1% of the popular votes. What happened that made President Thiệu change his mind at the last minute and help Mr. Nixon win the election? In his Memoir, Mr. Bùi Diễm, the RVN Ambassador in the U.S., has given the following reason:

"At about 4 A.M. on October 30, I was awakened by a phone call from Hoàng Đức Nhã, Thieu's cousin and personal secretary. Thieu had reconsidered his position and would not agree to the joint declaration after all. Subsequent to the agreement, Ambassador Lam cabled Thieu from Paris that he had just been told by Harriman and Vance that the United States was in fact not going to insist on some of the procedures that were included in the draft agreement. In particular, Harriman had told Lam it would be impossible for the United States to force the North Vietnamese into "serious and direct talks" with South Vietnam. Consequently, no such guarantee would be forthcoming. With this development, Thieu had decided to withdraw his commitment to send a delegation. Lam had already been recalled to Saigon for urgent consultations." [2]

That was the official reason that was given by the RVN to explain the last minute change of position regarding the Paris Peace Talks. From the U.S. side, the Johnson administration did not believe that story. President Johnson, in his memoir, recorded that story as follows:

"I believe Thiệu and his colleagues were eager to get on good terms with what they thought would be the new administration. I had reason to believe they had been urged to delay going to the Paris meetings and promised they would get a better deal from a Nixon administration than from Humphrey. I had no reason to think that the Republican candidate Nixon was himself involved in this maneuvering, but a few individuals active in his campaign were." [3].

When President Johnson said ***"I had reason to believe,"*** he was telling the truth in a courteous manner. Because, in fact, he had ordered the two U.S. security agencies, the CIA (Central

Intelligence Agency) and the FBI (Federal Bureau of Investigation) to tap Ambassador Bùi Diễm's telephone, and even intercept the cables from the Embassy to Vietnam. Everything began from the meeting of July 12, 1968 between Ambassador Bùi Diễm with the Republican candidate Richard Nixon at The Pierre Hotel through the introduction by Mrs. Anna Chennault. Mrs. Anna Chennault, a Chinese-American, widow of USAF General Claire Chennault, the famous Commander of the Flying Tigers Air Wing during World War II. She was an important member of Mr. Nixon's election campaign committee. After that July 12 meeting, she became the liaison person between Mr. Nixon's staff and Ambassador Bùi Diễm. The CIA and the FBI had secretly listened to all phone communications between her and Ambassador Bùi Diễm. In his memoir, Ambassador Bùi Diễm affirmed as follows:

"I did not know how many cables could have leaked to the American administration – or to Beverly Deepe, for that matter – but I had the uneasy feeling they knew everything." [4]

In spite of having obtained some evidence, President Johnson decided to let go the whole affair because such phone tapping and stealing secret cables of the embassy of an allied country were not only illegal but also damaging to the political and diplomatic prestige of the U.S. When everything was over, with Mr. Nixon as President-Elect, on December 7, 1968, President Thiệu officially sent a RVN Delegation headed by Vice-President Nguyễn Cao Kỳ to attend the Paris Peace Talks.[5]

Through this affair, we now have a good judgment of President Thiệu. He did not see the U.S. as a totally reliable ally in the Paris Peace Talks. He was a real patriot, daring to oppose actions of the Americans deemed harmful to the RVN's national interest, and he was definitely not a "yes-man" as expected by the Americans. Even Mr. Henry Kissinger had to recognize that character of President Thiệu. In his memoir, on pages 1324-1325, Mr. Kissinger has given the following judgments:

"Thiệu was a patriot and a highly intelligent man... But the imperatives on him were almost diametrically the opposite of ours... Our goal was honor; we could (as the phrase went) run a risk for peace. But Thiệu's problem was survival; he and his people would be left indefinitely after we departed; he had no margin for error." [6]

We will have more occasions to witness again this trait of character of President Thiệu, especially in his refusal to sign the Paris Accords in October 1972.

President Thiệu's lack of total trust of his American ally in the Paris Peace Talks had quite a few very legitimate reasons. Through regular reports from Ambassador Bùi Diễm, he came to know very well the U.S. Government's changes of policy and its determination to achieve at all cost a negotiated settlement in order to withdraw its troops. The U.S. has gradually and unilaterally de-escalated its basic conditions in the negotiations as follows:[7]

• In the letter sent to Hồ Chí Minh dated February 8, 1967: The U.S. would halt the bombing of North Vietnam if Hà Nội stopped the infiltration of troops into the South; and the U.S. would withdraw its troops if North Vietnam also withdrew its troops. Hồ Chí Minh rejected it.

• In the declaration of September 29, 1967 issued in San Antonio, Texas: the U.S. was ready to halt the bombing of North Vietnam if it would rapidly lead to serious discussions and if Hà Nội "not take advantage" of the bombing halt. Mai Văn Bộ, Hà Nội Representative in Paris still rejected it, and considered the bombing halt as "unconditional."

• In the declaration of March 31, 1968, President Johnson unilaterally and unconditionally halted the bombing of North Vietnam north of the 20th parallel. Hà Nội agreed to negotiate and both sides began to meet in Paris on May 13, 1968.

• In the declaration of October 31, 1968, President Johnson ordered the total halt of the bombing of North Vietnam, and agreed to expand the Paris Peace talks to include both the RVN and the NFL.

After Mr. Nixon was elected as U.S. President, replacing President Johnson, the U.S. government's way to implement its policy may have changed but its objective remained the same: it was disengagement, i.e., no matter what the RVN wanted, the U.S. would withdraw its troops and would conclude its negotiations with North Vietnam in order to finish off the troop withdrawal and to get back their prisoners. The most fundamental condition in the peace talks that the U.S. had set up right from the beginning, namely that ***North Vietnam must stop the infiltration of troops into the South and withdraw its troops,*** was dropped and would never be referred to again. In fact, the U.S. had already started its troop withdrawal right after the Midway Summit between President Nixon and President Thiệu on June 8, 1969, and by the end of 1971, the American troop level in the RVN went down from 536,100 (1968) to 156,800.[8] Because the Paris Peace Talks did not make any progress, President Nixon decided to have his National Security Advisor, Dr. Henri Kissinger, start secret talks with Lê Đức Thọ. After the one-on-one secret talks between Kissinger and Lê Đức Thọ began on February 21, 1970, the RVN government no more knew what was going on. In fact, Kissinger not only went from one concession to another in military matter (troop withdrawal), he also granted himself the right to discuss political issues of the RVN with North Vietnam. In principle, the U.S. must always consult and inform the RVN of progresses of the Paris Peace Talks, but, in reality, Kissinger only informed the RVN what he wanted to inform, and ignored all the rest, in particular his concessions in his secret talks with Lê Đức Thọ. North Vietnam, since they knew quite well that the U.S. wanted to withdraw its troops as soon as possible and to end the war, did not give any concession, prolonged the talks purposedly in order to have time to prepare their general offensive at the end of 1972, and, thus, would be able to negotiate from a position of strength. The Paris Peace Talks, therefore, did not make any progress for almost four years. Meanwhile, the U.S. actively tried to approach China. In July 1971, Kissinger secretly went to Beijing, preparing for President Nixon's official visit to China in February 1972. Then in May 1972, also by Kissinger's arrangement, Nixon went to Moscow to have a summit meeting with Brezhnev, Secretary-General of the Communist party of the Soviet Union. North Vietnam was worried by these events because they did not know if the U.S. had signed any secret pacts with China and the Soviet Union, especially with China (they still remembered having been stabbed in the back by China at the 1954 Geneva Conference). After their total failure in the 1972 General Offensive, and before the prospect of the re-election of President Nixon, i.e., they would have to deal with President Nixon for four more years, as well as the worries of the possible impact from the newly established U.S. – China diplomatic relations, North Vietnam was happy with what they had gained in the peace talks, and appeared to be willing to obtain a signed agreement with Kissinger before the U.S. presidential election in early November 1972. The result was that there were several positive meetings in the mid-1972, and the peace talks between the U.S. and North Vietnam were getting closer with a number of concessions from North Vietnam. In his memoir, Kissinger recorded on page 1318 the following statements:

"After three meetings, then, there had been significant movement, entirely by Hanoi; it was moving in the right direction but not at a pace that would keep it from reversing course later. Hanoi had given up the demand for Thieu's immediate removal. It had agreed to negotiating forums in which the Saigon government would participate, thus in a sense recognizing its legitimacy. It had abandoned the absurd demand for an unconditional deadline for the withdrawal of American forces. The proposed coalition government, heretofore a transparent front for a Communist takeover, had been reduced to a fifty-fifty split of power." [9]

On August 17, 1972, Kissinger arrived in Sài Gòn to present and discuss with the RVN government on these new developments. Now the focus of the negotiations was no longer on the military matter (U.S. troop withdrawal) because the U.S. had already withdrawn almost all of its troops (in August 1972, the U.S. had only 27,000 soldiers left in South Vietnam, just a little bit more than half of the 50,000 U.S. troops still stationed in South Korea since 1953), but on the political issues of the RVN. Kissinger presented to President Thiệu a number of proposals that he would announce and discuss with North Vietnam in the next meeting with Lê Đức Thọ on September 15, 1972. Militarily, the U.S. would change the time required to withdraw all of its remaining troops from four to three months. Politically, the U.S. would continue to reject North Vietnam's proposal to form a coalition government, but would suggest a tripartite committee to organize elections. During his presentation, Kissinger emphasized the need to do so in order to help President Nixon get re-elected in November. It was an untruthful reason because in fact President Nixon did not need it. In his memoir, President Nixon wrote the following statements:

> ***"The opinion polls confirmed my own intuition that, in terms of voter support, my handling of the war was generally viewed as a positive issue for me and a negative one for McGovern, who was perceived as weak and favoring surrender. Therefore, any settlement that was hastily completed in time for the election would look cynical and suspicious ... I am inclined to think that the better bargaining time for us would be immediately after the election rather than before."*** [10]

The next day, August 18, 1972, President Thiệu handed Kissinger a 4-page letter that included 20 proposed changes to the U.S. proposal, with the two following important points: 1) request to change the phrase "standstill cease-fire" by "general cease-fire"; and, 2) rejection of the proposed creation of the tripartite Committee of National Reconciliation, because such creation would create suspicion within the South Vietnamese people. President Thiệu also told Kissinger that he needed more time to reflect and prepare psychologically and politically on the U.S. proposal. In his memoir on the Paris Peace Talks, Mr. Nguyễn Phú Đức, Special Assistant of President Nguyễn Văn Thiệu, present at that meeting, gave the following account:

"In Saigon, at the end of the 18 August session, President Thieu told Kissinger: We need time to think about it. We are not prepared psychologically and politically on your proposal." [11]

After Kissinger left Sài Gòn, President Thiệu called a special meeting of the National Security Council, including Vice-President Trần Văn Hương, Prime Minister Trần Thiện Khiêm, Nguyễn Phú Đức and Hoàng Đức Nhã to review each point in Kissinger's proposal. After the meeting, the following guiding principles for negotiations at the Paris Peach Talks were established:

• The "Forum" between Washington and Hà Nội did not have authority to "resolve" the issues between the RVN and the NFL like Kissinger had proposed.

• Hà Nội did not have the right to intervenc into the political problems of the RVN. The 1954 Geneva Accords recognized that Vietnam was divided into two countries demarcated by the Demilitarized Zone. Pending reunification, the RVN Government did not intend to ask for changes of the political regime of North Vietnam. Consequentially, Hà Nội should not require a change of the political regime of South Vietnam.

• The Constitution of the RVN, legally approved by the popularly elected National Assembly of the South Vietnamese people, should be respected as President Thiệu had sworn to protect.

• A referendum could be organized in accordance with the Constitution. The organization of the referendum could be carried out by the Committee for National Reconciliation, instead by the Supreme Court according to the requirement of the Constitution, in order to guarantee fairness. But after the referendum, the Committee for National Reconciliation must be disbanded, and not allowed to stay on to make changes to the Constitution. After the referendum, the RVN Government could accept the participation in government of the members of the NFL based on the percentage of votes they obtained, with the condition they would have to recognize the Constitution.

• If President Thieu accepted to resign before the election to guarantee that the election would be fair, Vice-President Trần Văn Hương would not have any reason to resign because doing so would wipe out the Executive Branch of the RVN Government.

The RVN's official position on the Paris Peace Talks, based on the above-mentioned guiding principles, was presented in a letter given to Ambassador Bunker on August 28, 1972 so that it could be delivered to President Nixon and Kissinger before their meeting in Honolulu, Hawaii on August 30, 1972.[12] Kissinger, therefore, could not say that he did not know about the RVN's official position on the Paris Peace Talks. In his memoir, Kissinger stated as follows:

"I left Saigon with a false sense of having reached a meeting of the minds. Thieu and I had decided that we would settle the few remaining disagreements over our draft proposal by exchanging messages through Bunker. There were plenty of time – nearly four weeks until my next meeting on September 15. Instead, Thieu enveloped himself in silence; we heard absolutely nothing from the Palace." [13]

This account in the memoir was a blatant lie (just like other Kissinger's lies later revealed in declassified U.S. documents) because there was no reason to believe that Ambassador Bunker did not deliver the RVN letter dated August 28, 1972 to President Nixon and Mr. Kissinger at the Honolulu meeting on August 30, 1972. Following is a clear evidence showing that the U.S. Government had received the letter of August 28,

1972 on the RVN's official position on the Paris Peace Talks. In his memoir, Mr. Nguyễn Phú Đức recorded very clearly the meeting with Kissinger's Assistant, General Alexander Haig, on October 2, 1972 in Sài Gòn:

"PRESIDENT THIEU: The GVN has put down its views in its memo of August 28. Has the US transmitted these views to the North Vietnamese? HAIG: If we presented these views, this would break up the talks, and this would endanger our long-range possibility to support you."[14]

Thus, in fact, it was very clear that Mr. Kissinger had ignored the RVN Government's letter of August 28, 1972, and did continue his discussion with Lê Đức Thọ on the basis of his proposals. And that really confirmed President Nixon's judgment on Kissinger's mental state in his memoir as follows:

"... obsessed with the idea that there should be a negotiated settlement." [15]

Kissinger really wanted, and was ready to pay any price, to obtain a signed agreement with North Vietnam before the U.S. presidential election at the beginning of November 1972. And in fact he succeeded in obtaining an agreement with North Vietnam at the meeting of October 17, 1972. He immediately informed President Nixon his work schedule for the remainder of October 1972 as follows:[16]

• After October 17, in Sài Gòn for 3 days to present the agreement with North Vietnam, and to obtain the consensus from the RVN Government

• October 22: in Hà Nội to initial the Accords with North Vietnam

• October 26: arrive back in Washington to announce the Joint Communique on the Accords

• The cease-fire would be effective on October 30 when the Foreign Ministers of all sides signed the Paris Accords

In fact, Kissinger believed that, under his arrangement, everything was done. The RVN Government would agree easily and accept the Accords, which he had obtained with North Vietnam, because he believed that the Accords would be the best the RVN could obtain. The Accords included the following main points:

• An in-place cease-fire

• The U.S. troop withdrawal ended after 60 days

• North Vietnam agreed not to infiltrate more troops into the South

• Exchange of prisoners from both sides

• North Vietnam no longer demanded a coalition government; but instead, a tripartite Council of National Reconciliation would be established to organize elections

• North Vietnam no longer demanded President Thiệu's resignation

Kissinger came to Sài Gòn in that optimistic spirit. But everything did not happen -as he had expected. The two American and South Vietnamese delegations began their first meeting on October 19, 1972. At the beginning of the meeting, Kissinger delivered to President Thiệu President Nixon's personal letter, in which the main message was his advice to President Thiệu to accept the Accords with the following statement: ***"I believe we have no reasonable alternative but to accept this agreement."*** President Thiệu finished his reading of the letter without saying a word and the meeting began immediately.

The U.S. party included: Advisor Henry Kissinger, Ambassador Bunker and his assistant Charles Whitehouse, Mr. William Sullivan from State Department, Mr. Winston Lord of the National Security Council, and interpreter David Engel. The RVN Government party included: President Nguyễn Văn Thiệu, Vice-President Trần Văn Hương, Prime Minister Trần Thiện Khiêm, Minister of Foreign Affairs Trần Văn Lắm, Special Assistant Nguyễn Phú Đức, Mr. Trần Kim Phượng, RVN Ambassador in the U.S., Mr. Phạm Đăng Lâm, Head of the RVN Delegation at the Paris Peace Talks, and Mr. Hoàng Đức Nhã as interpreter. After Mr. Kissinger presented the agreement, the South Vietnamese officials asked a number of questions. At the end of the meeting, President Thiệu told Mr. Kissinger that the Vietnamese party needed to carefully study the agreement. In the morning of October 21, 1972, the RVN party demanded the U.S. make a total of 23 changes in the agreement. A meeting at the Independence Palace was scheduled at 2 p.m. to discuss these 23 changes. The meeting was then re-scheduled by the Vietnamese at 5 p.m. without any reason. There was no action whatsoever from the Vietnamese side at 5 p.m. Ambassador Bunker made a phone call to the Independence Palace and was informed that President was ~~being~~ busy in a meeting with the Cabinet. Half an hour later, Mr. Hoàng Đức Nhã phoned and informed the U.S. delegation that the meeting was again put off until 8 a.m. the next morning and then hung up without any explanation. On the next day, Sunday, October 22, 1972, at 8 a.m., there were only 4 people at the meeting: President Thiệu and Mr. Hoàng Đức Nhã on one side, and Kissinger with Ambassador Bunker on the other side. President Thiệu said he did not agree with several points in the agreement, especially on the following two most important points: 1) North Vietnam did not withdraw their troops; and, 2) Membership and activities of the Council of National Reconciliation. He also said that he needed to consult the National Assembly, and he was still waiting for the reports from his advisors on the U.S. reactions of the 23 points that the RVN side had demanded to be changed. He concluded the meeting by promising to see Kissinger again at 5 p.m. to give his final resolution regarding the agreement. At the 5 p.m. meeting, with the same people as in the morning meeting, President Thiệu, speaking in Vietnamese with translation provided by Mr. Hoàng Đức Nhã, ***definitively refused to sign the agreement.*** In his memoir, Kissinger wrote that during their presentation, both President Thiệu and Mr. Hoàng Đức Nhã, at some point, burst into tears.[18] In spite of his total failure in persuading President Thiệu, Kissinger still wanted to keep his intention to go to Hà Nội to initial the agreement with North Vietnam, but President Nixon did not agree [19] and ordered him to come back to the U.S. right away. Kissinger arrived back in the U.S. on October 23, 1972. Before he left Sài Gòn, Kissinger came to the Independence Palace to meet President Thiệu for the last time in the morning. This meeting proceeded more nicely, but President Thiệu was still very affirmative on three points: 1) North Vietnam would have to withdraw their troops; 2) The Demilitarized Zone should be respected, and 3) The membership of the Council of National Reconciliation must be determined based on the results of a referendum. Kissinger promised to try to re-negotiate these points with North Vietnam. In the afternoon, President Thiệu gave a speech at a bicameral plenary special session of the National Assembly, which was televised live for the whole country to watch. He told everything to the National Assembly, which applauded him and gave him a very strong support. Special Assistant Nguyễn Phú Đức made a proposal and got President Thiệu's approval: sending his advisors to friendly and allied countries in the region to present and explain the RVN Government's decision on the peace talks in order to obtain their consensus and support, with Assitant Nguyễn Phú Đức going to Cambodia, Laos, Thailand, Ambassador Trần Kim Phượng to Singapore, Malaysia, Australia, New Zealand, and Ambassador Phạm Đăng Lâm to the Philippines, South Korea, and Japan.[20]

North Vietnam, angry because Kissinger did not come to Hà Nội to sign the agreement as agreed upon, on October 25, 1972, unilaterally made public the whole agreement that both sides had agreed upon before Kissinger came to Sài Gòn with the intention to cause the U.S. loosing face and embarrassed. Kissinger had to call a press conference the next day, October 26, 1972, to respond to Hà Nội that the U.S. still respected the signed agreement, and at that occasion he spoke the famous phrase ***"Peace is at hand."*** He also suggested that both sides come back to the conference table to discuss the RVN's proposed changes. On November 4, 1972, three days before the U.S. presidential election, North Vietnam agreed to come back to the conference table on November 14, 1972.

On November 7, 1972, President Nixon was re-elected for a second term by a ***landslide victory***. In terms of popular votes, Nixon received 47,168,710 votes (60.7%) against McGovern's 29,173,222 (37.5%); in terms of electoral votes, Nixon received 520 votes while McGovern received only 17 votes. Nixon won in 49 states, McGovern won only one state, Massachusetts, backyard of the pacifist antiwar people, and the District of Columbia, where blacks were the majority.[21]). Thus, Nixon decidedly defeated George McGovern, the Democratic candidate, whose election campaign had been based on a policy of peace at all cost and an immediate cut of all military and economic aids to the RVN. The election result showed that President Nixon's judgment that the signing of the agreement with North Vietnam ***before*** *the* election was completely unnecessary, totally different than Kissinger's beliefs. It also showed that the American people did not agree with the policy of peace at any cost and abandon of the RVN. The glorious victory of President Nixon, however, did not help the Republican Party obtain the majority in Congress: in the House, the Democrats occupied 242 seats, the Republican had only 192; in the Senate, there were 56 Democrats against 42 Republicans. Because the opposition party still held the majority, President Nixon thought he needed to sign the agreement with North Vietnam the sooner the better.

The next day, November 8, 1972, North Vietnam demanded that the meeting be put off until November 20, 1972 because Mr. Lê Đức Thọ was sick. The U.S. agreed and the Paris Peace Talks resumed on November 20, 1972.

In preparing for the November 20, 1972 meeting, General Haig was sent to Sài Gòn. On November 10, 1972, at the beginning of the meeting at the Independence Palace, General Haig presented to President Thiệu a letter from President Nixon dated November 8. The 4-page letter promised that the U.S. would change the agreement to include the changes proposed by the RVN in order to have President Thiệu accept the agreement, but, at the same time, it also contained some implied threats in case President Thiệu still opposed the agreement. On page 3 of the letter there was a very clear paragraph as follows:

"The other alternative would be for you to pursue what appears to be your present course. In my view this would play into the hands of the enemy and would have extremely grave consequences for both our peoples and it would be disaster for yours." [22]

After President Thiệu finished his reading of the letter, General Haig presented the following work schedule of the U.S. Delegation at the Paris Peace Talks:

- From the 12th to the end of November 1972, meetings and talks between Kissinger and Lê Đức Thọ in Paris
- On the 1st and 2nd of December 1972, Kissinger would arrive in Sài Gòn to work with the RVN Government
- On December 3, 1972, Kissinger would go to Hà Nội to initial the agreement
- The cease-fire would become effective from December 10, 1972
- The agreement would be officially signed by the Ministers of Foreign Affairs of all sides in Paris on December 13, 1972

And he added as follows:

"If you go your separate way, we can manage the difficulty, but for you it will be fatal." [23]

The situation of the peace talks, therefore, was almost still the same, no big difference from the situation in the past October. The U.S. had already decided to sign the agreement, even before the peace talks resumed. The promises of changes made to the agreement based on the demands of the RVN would be just promises, which even the U.S. did not believe that they could be done. More than anyone else, President Thiệu saw that reality very clearly, but, as far as there was still any possibility, especially when it was very clear that Kissinger could no longer be trusted, he decided to dispatch Special Assistant Nguyễn Phú Đức to represent him and negotiate directly with President Nixon. It was a calculated move by President Thiệu but, coincidentally, was a right one at the right time. This action by President Thiệu was at the right time because right at that time the intimate relationship between President Nixon and Advisor Kissinger started having some cracks. Before that, Nixon had almost given Kissinger carte blanche in the Paris Peace Talks. Occasionally, he did not agree with Kissinger on certain matters, he let it go and did not say anything, for example, he disagreed with Kissinger to sign the agreement with North Vietnam before the election (November 7, 1972). But then he saw that Kissinger had gone too far when he answered Italian lady correspondent Oriana Fallaci in an interview with the following statement:

> ***"Americans like the cowboy ... who rides all alone into the town, the village, with his horse and nothing else ... This amazing, romantic character suits me precisely because to be alone has always been part of my style or, if you like, my technique."*** [24]

This statement implied that Kissinger was the real person at the center of everything, not President Nixon. Nixon felt badly insulted. On November 19, 1972, when Kissinger left for Paris to have secret talks with Lê Đức Thọ, Nixon did not see him leave, just gave him a call from his office. When President Thiệu revealed his intention to send Special Assistant Nguyễn Phú Đức to see him, he accepted immediately. Mr. Đức came to Paris first to meet with the RVN Delegation and the U.S. Delegation as well in order to have a firm grasp of the situation. While Mr. Đức was still in Paris, President Thiệu sent Mr. Hoàng Đức Nhã there to deliver to him a long letter carrying new instructions. The English version of that letter was 24-page long. On November 28, 1972, Mr. Đức left Paris for Washington, D.C. During that time, Kissinger had two more meetings with Lê Đức Thọ, on November 20 and November 25, 1972, without any progress because North Vietnam rejected all important changes to the agreement proposed by the RVN. Nixon ordered Kissinger to come back to the U.S.

On November 29, 1972, Mr. Đức together with Ambassador Trần Kim Phượng were received by President Nixon at the White House in the Oval Office, with the presence of Kissinger and General Haig. Advisor Đức presented to President Nixon the 24-page letter by President Thiệu, and then gave explanations to each and every point in the letter, with the focus on the two main points: 1) The demand for North Vietnam's troop withdrawal; and, 2) The issue of the Council of National Reconciliation and its membership. President Nixon appeared to agree and immediately ordered Kissinger that he, by all means, should try to improve the agreement on these two points. After that, he said clearly his point of view regarding the agreement as follows:

"The agreement is just a piece of paper. What counts is our determination to support you." [25]

And he also mentioned clearly his commitments as follows:

• Continue to provide military and economic aids to the RVN after the signing of the agreement

• The USAF stationed in Thailand and on the aircraft carriers would re-start the bombings if the U.S. intelligence discovered that North Vietnam violated the agreement

• Firmly keep the position of support for President Thiệu

• The U.S. already had agreements with the Soviet Union and China on limitations of aids to North Vietnam

The next day, November 30, 1972, in the meeting with Mr. Nguyễn Phú Đức, when Mr. Đức asked him about the withdrawal of North Vietnamese troops, Kissinger blatantly answered that such condition would never be in the agreement.[26] Confronted with almost an impasse, Special Assistant Đức suggested to Kissinger that the U.S. could sign a separate agreement with North Vietnam to withdraw and bring back the prisoners. The RVN would commit the release of 10,000 Communist prisoners in exchange for the release by North Vietnam of all American prisoners. After that, the RVN would continue to negotiate with North Vietnam and the NFL on the political issues of the South. Kissinger reported Mr. Đức's suggestions to President Nixon and President Nixon subsequently held another meeting with Mr. Đức in the same day. After he listened to Mr. Đức's presentation of his suggestions, President Nixon informed that he had consulted the hawkish Representatives and Senators (i.e., the supporters of the RVN), members of the Armed Forces Committees of both the House and the Senate, and all of them have agreed on the agreement. If the RVN refused to co-sign with the U.S., Congress would cut off all aids. He said very clearly as follows:

> ***"I hope that we shall go forward together, then you will have economic and military assistance. Please convey this to President Thiệu, what counts is U.S. alliance. I can make that commitment."*** [27]

After that, President Nixon asked Mr. Đức to let him know of the priorities that the RVN wanted the U.S. to discuss with North Vietnam in the next up-coming meetings of the peace talks. Mr. Đức said that in addition to the withdrawal of North Vietnamese troops, the RVN opposed the existence of two governments in South Vietnam, and, therefore, could not accept the use of the PRG as replacement for the NFL, and the RVN also opposed the point of considering the Council of National Reconciliation as having three equal partners. On the next day, December 1, 1972, Mr. Đức met with Kissinger to work on details of some concrete issues in the agreement, such as the in-place cease-fire, the problems of Laos and Cambodia, etc. On December 2, 1972, Mr. Đức left Washington, D.C. for Sài Gòn.

On December 3, 1972, in the meeting of the National Security Council at the Independence Palace presided by President Thiệu, Special Assistant Đức reported everything from his meetings in Washington with President Nixon and Advisor Kissinger. At the end of the meeting, when President Thiệu asked him for his personal opinion, Mr. Đức answered immediately that signing the agreement with these clauses would lead to the loss of the South. In his memoir, he recorded as follows:

"President Thieu asked me this basic question: Do you think that we should sign this Agreement? I replied: In my judgment, if we sign the Agreement, as it is, South Vietnam will be lost." [28]

President Thiệu and all members of the National Security Council agreed with this point of view.

In the meantime, the U.S. and North Vietnam returned to the conference table starting from December 4, 1972 but they made no progress because North Vietnam rejected all Kissinger's demands of changes based on requests from the RVN. On December 17, 1972, President Nixon ordered the blockage of Hải Phòng port again as well as the resumption of the bombings of North Vietnam, and, this time, for the first time in the Vietnam War, with B-52s carpet bombing Hà Nội. This operation was code-named Linebacker II, carried out from the 18th to the 29th of December 1972, and was referred to as ***"The Christmas Bombing"*** in the U.S. media and the Vietnam War literature.

On December 19, 1972, President Nixon sent General Haig to Sài Gòn, with his letter dated December 17, 1972 to President Thiệu containing very strong words, almost like an ultimatum. In his memoir, President Nixon wrote very clearly as follows:

"Haig arrived in Saigon on December 19, carrying the strongest letter I had yet written to Thieu. In it I stated: "General Haig's mission now represents my final effort to point out to you the necessity for joint action and to convey my irrevocable intention to proceed, preferably with your cooperation but, if necessary, alone… I have asked General Haig to obtain

your answer to this absolutely final offer on my part for us to work together in seeking a settlement along the lines I have approved or to go our separate ways."" [29]

Facing a serious situation caused by this "ultimatum," President Thiệu convened right away a meeting of the National Security Council, this time expanded to include the leaders of the Legislative and Judiciary Branches: Mr. Nguyễn Văn Huyền, President of the Senate, Mr. Nguyễn Bá Cẩn, Speaker of the House, and Chief Justice Trần Văn Linh of the Supreme Court. [30]

Although President Nixon's letter was almost an ultimatum, President Thiệu still did not believe that President Nixon could proceed with signing the agreement with North Vietnam. After the meeting, therefore, he ordered Mr. Đức to prepare a letter, dated December 20, to reply President Nixon's letter of December 17. This letter began with a summary of the three basic demands by the RVN: 1) North Vietnam must withdraw its troops; 2) No recognition for the PRG; and, 3) The membership and responsibility of the Council of National Reconciliation indicated that it was a disguised coalition government. The letter then suggested that the RVN was ready to accept the agreement of December 12, 1972 if the two following demands were resolved: 1) The PRG should not be seen as the government in parallel with the RVN Government in South Vietnam, and, 2) North Vietnam must withdraw all of its troops concurrently with the troop withdrawals by the RVN's allied countries. Finally, the letter concluded:

"I must say the South Vietnamese Government and people absolutely cannot go beyond these new important concessions, because otherwise it would be tantamount to surrender." [31]

In the meantime, Operation Linebacker II, although having caused some surprised damages to the U.S. by the loss of 15 B-52s being shot down, something that had never happened before to the USAF, caused very serious damages to North Vietnam, both in terms of physical facilities and in terms of mental state of the population of the capital city of Hà Nội. In a very short time, only 11 days (except for only one day, Christmas of 1972), the U.S. carried out 741 sorties of B-52s and 1,274 sorties of all types of USAF and Navy jet fighters (including the F-111 being the most advanced jet fighter at that time), and dropped a total of 20,237 tons of bombs, causing great panic to Hà Nội people.[32] From the North Vietnamese side, the air defense forces fired off a total of 1,000 SAM (**S**urface-to-**A**ir **M**issiles), and, thus, was able to down a significant number of B-52s that always flew at very high altitude (during the years of providing tactical ground supports in the South –and causing horrible fears to North Vietnamese and VC soldiers -- not a single B-52 had ever been shot down). On December 28, 1972, North Vietnam agreed to resume peace talks on January 2 and January 8, 1973. Operation Linebacker II officially ended at 7 p.m. of December 29, 1972.

On January 2, 1973, one day before the U.S. Congress resumed, the Democratic Representatives in the House voted 154/75 to cut off all military aids to the RVN immediately after the agreement was signed to help the U.S. withdraw all its troops and get back all prisoners. On January 4, 1973, one day after the U.S. Congress resumed, Senator Edward Kennedy proposed a similar resolution to the Democratic caucus in the Senate and the resolution was passed with a score of 36/12. Facing such a serious situation, both President Nixon and Advisor Kissinger thought that the agreement needed to be signed with North Vietnam before the support for the RVN in Congress was completely wiped out.

In preparing for the resumption of the Paris Peace Talks on January 8, 1973, on January 5, 1973, President Nixon again sent another letter to President Thiệu with the promise to re-table the issue of North Vietnam's troop withdrawal but he believed that

North Vietnam would reject it again, and he also promised that, if the RVN agreed to sign the agreement with North Vietnam then, later, if North Vietnam violated the agreement, he would fiercely retaliate with all U.S. military strength. Following is the original statement in his letter:

> ***"With respect to the question of North Vietnamese troops, we will again present your views to the Communists as we have done vigorously at every other opportunity in the negotiations. The result is certain to be once more the rejection of our position… Should you decide, as I trust you will, to go with us, you have my assurance of continued assistance in the post-settlement period and that we will respond with full force should the settlement be violated by North Vietnam."*** [33]

After he received this letter, President Thiệu responded immediately with his letter dated January 7, 1973, in which he still maintained his position in his letter of December 20, 1972, and emphasized that those conditions were vital for the survival of South Vietnam.

On January 8, 1973, the Paris Peace Talks resumed. The first day ended without any progress. On the second day, January 9, 1973, both sides agreed to use the draft of December 23, 1972 as basis for the discussions of additional details. The issue of North Vietnamese troop withdrawal was discarded for good, never to be tabled again. Only two following main issues were discussed and ended in consensus: 1) The issue of the DMZ along both sides of the 17th parallel; and, 2) The issue of the PRG. Regarding the DMZ, North Vietnam agreed with the formula that Kissinger had proposed in December 1972: both North and South Vietnam continued to respect the DMZ but would negotiate for the civilian travel across that zone. The issue of the PRG, in order to satisfy the RVN's demand, would be resolved in two ways: 1) The name of the PRG would be used only in the preamble but would be completely absent in the main text of the agreement; 2) In the section for signatures, the Communist side, i.e., North Vietnam and the PRG, would sign in one page, and the Free World side, i.e., the U.S. and the RVN, would sign in a different page. On January 13, 1973, both sides completely agreed on all clauses of the accords, and on the accords signing procedures as well.

On January 14, 1973, President Nixon sent an additional letter to President Thiệu and this time it was again delivered by General Haig. In the letter, President Nixon said very clearly that he had decided to sign the agreement on January 27, 1973, and, if necessary, he would sign it alone; in that case he would officially announce that the RVN had obstructed peace. And in order to help the RVN easily accept to co-sign the agreement, he again promised to continue providing military and economic aids to the RVN, and, if North Vietnam violated the accords, he would strongly retaliate. The original statement in his letter reads as follows:

"I have therefore irrevocably decided to proceed to initial the Agreement on January 23, 1973 and to sign it on January 27 in Paris. I will do so, if necessary, alone. In that case I shall have to explain publicly that your Government obstructs peace." [34]

President Thiệu still did not yield; he sent another letter to President Nixon, dated January 17, 1973, requesting some adjustments to the clauses regarding the DMZ, the presence of North Vietnam's troops in the South, and the role of the cease-fire control commission. This time, President Nixon did not yield either. He responded immediately, in the same day, repeating all the points in his letter of January 14, and demanded that President Thiệu answer this letter in the morning of January 20, 1973 at the latest (the day of his inauguration to begin his second term as U.S. President). President Thiệu did not accept the demand, and again sent another letter, dated January 20, 1973, in which he suggested some ways to resolve the issue of the presence of North Vietnamese troops in the South. The next day, January 21, 1973, President Nixon sent to President Thiệu a ***cable***, in which he said clearly that there was no more time to consider whatever proposal from the RVN, and demanded President Thiệu, if he agreed to co-sign with the U.S., respond before 12 p.m. of January 21, 1973, Washington, D.C. time, i.e., in the early morning of January 22, 1973, Sài Gòn time.[35] This time, President Thiệu knew very well that he had no option but to agree to sign the Paris Accords, i.e., he had to do something that he had not wanted to do when he said to General Haig, on December 19, 1972, after he finished reading President Nixon's letter of December 17, 1972, that the U.S. wanted him to sign not for peace but for continued U.S. aids. In his memoir, President Nixon recounted this event in the following words:

"After Thieu had read the letter through twice, he looked up and said that it was obvious that he was not being asked to sign an agreement for peace but rather an agreement for continued American support. Haig replied that as a soldier and as someone completely familiar with Communist treachery, he agreed with Thieu's assessment." [36]

Concluding Remarks

It is safe to say that the Paris Peace Talks (from May 13, 1968 to January 27, 1973) was the biggest political concern of President Nguyễn Văn Thiệu during most of his first term and almost half of his second term. Right from the beginning, it was quite certain that he had already seen the big and almost irreversible change in the U.S. policy on the Vietnam War: de-escalation, troop withdrawal, and negotiations in order to end the war and get back their prisoners. Although the method of action of the two successive presidents (Johnson then Nixon) was different but their objective remained the same. The survival of the RVN, although not completely ignored by the U.S., could not be placed above that objective. President Thiệu understood this point very well and did his best in that extremely difficult political–diplomatic background. He had enough courage to challenge and confront these two successive U.S. presidents. Although he could not achieve the expected objective (forcing

North Vietnam to withdraw its troops), he was able to obtain from President Nixon written promises to continue U.S. military and economic aids to the RVN and to strongly retaliate if North Vietnam violated the Paris Accords, before he agreed, at the last minute, to co-sign that Accords with the U.S. In order to obtain President Nixon's public confirmation of these two promises, he visited the U.S. at the beginning of April 1973, in spite of the fact that he knew in advance that he would not be welcomed in Washington, D.C. as a Chief of State. The Joint Communique of the two Presidents after the meeting of April 3, 1973 in San Clemente, California re-affirmed these promises. Unfortunately, President Nixon had to resign on August 9, 1974 because of the Watergate affair. His successor, President Gerald Ford, was the first president in the U.S. history that was not elected by the American people, was neutralized by the U.S. Congress totally controlled by the majority of Representatives and Senators of the Democratic Party. All military aids to the RVN, promised by President Nixon, were blatantly cut off, and the retaliations against the violations of the Paris Accords by North Vietnam (attacks and captures of Phước Long in January 1975, and of Ban Mê Thuột in March 1975), committed by President Nixon, did not materialize. The collapse of the RVN on April 30, 1975 was the unavoidable consequence of the American abandoning of its ally.

CHAPTER EIGHT

Autopsy of the Disastrous Retreat from II Corps In March 1975

It can be safely said that the military forces of the Republic of Vietnam (RVN) have grown the fastest under the Second Republic. Created in 1950, with only about 60,000 men, these forces were called the Army of the State of Vietnam. During the First Republic (1955-1963), it was renamed Army of the Republic of Vietnam. From 1965 onward, these military forces were officially called the Armed Forces of the Republic of Vietnam (ARVN), and in 1970, with a very strong support from the U.S., grew to more than one million men, having all modern and well-equipped services, exactly like the American army, in order to confront the invasion carried out by North Vietnam, and greatly supported by the Communist bloc, of which the two most important countries were the Soviet Union and the People's Republic of China. The ARVN became the pride of South Vietnam, but it also became a double-edged sword vis-à-vis the security of the South. It was able to help the RVN effectively confront the combat-experienced and well-equipped Communist divisions infiltrating from the North during the two General Offensives of 1968 and 1972, but, without sufficient military aids from the U.S. for its activities, it rapidly and tragically collapsed in the record shortest time of only 44 days.

President Nguyễn Văn Thiệu was the most qualified president to assume the constitutional role of the supreme Commander-in-Chief of the ARVN (Article 60, 1967 Constitution), for the following reasons:

• He was a high-ranking, three-star Lieutenant-General of the ARVN

• Compared to other generals of his time, not only had he more seniority (even the Chairman of the General Staff, four-star General Cao Văn Viên, who was only promoted to Major-General on March 3, 1964 while Mr. Thiệu had been promoted to Major-General since November 2, 1963), but also, in some cases, he had been their direct superior (e.g., Lieutenant-Generals Đặng Văn Quang, Nguyễn Bảo Trị, and Vĩnh Lộc)

• He had been commanders of all military unit levels, including Division Commander (5th Infantry Division), and Corps Commander (IV Corps)

From 1969 onward, President Thiệu, abusing his constitutional role as the supreme Commander-in-Chief, seized all military powers, giving orders directly to the commanders of all Corps and big units, bypassing the General Staff.[1] Therefore, he should be responsible for the military collapse of the RVN in 1975.

First of all, in order to understand President Thiệu's motives in his important decisions of military affairs from the end of 1974 to the beginning of 1975 leading to the defeat of the South, we need to have a good understanding of the nature of the war, its limitations, and the strategy that the RVN used to fight the war.

In terms of nature of the war, for the RVN, this war was an invasion carried out by the Democratic Republic of Vietnam (DRV, or North Vietnam). The RVN, or South Vietnam, was the victim with its territory invaded. For the RVN, this war, therefore, was for self-defense. The U.S. and the allied countries (South Korea, Thailand, The Philippines, Australia, and New Zealand) brought their troops to Vietnam to help the RVN in its self-defense war against the invasion by the DRV. In terms of the limitations of the war, in order not to expand the war and give China a good reason to bring its troops into North Vietnam (just like what happened in Korea at the beginning of the 1950s), the U.S. did not support the RVN's "Marching North" policy. Therefore, strategically, throughout almost 20 years of the war, the RVN was always passively in the defense. The ARVN had to stretch its forces all over the country, from the 17th parallel to the South, to protect its territory, which was divided into 4 Military Regions each defended by a Corps:

• Region I: including the five northernmost provinces of Quảng Trị, Thừa Thiên (including Huế), Quảng Nam (including Special District of Đà Nẵng), Quảng Tín, and Quảng Ngãi, defended by I Corps with three infantry divisions (the 1st, the 2nd, and the 3rd), all local units of the Air Force and Navy, of the Regional Forces and Militia belonging to each Sub-District (each province is a Sub-District).

• Region II: including the seven highland provinces of Kontum, Pleiku, Phú Bổn, Darlac, Quảng Đức, Lâm Đồng, Tuyên Đức, and the five coastal provinces of Bình Định, Phú Yên, Khánh Hòa, Ninh Thuận and Bình Thuận, defended by II Corps with two infantry divisions (the 22nd and the 23rd), all local units of the Air Force and Navy, of the Regional Forces and Militia of each Sub-District.

• Region III: including the eleven eastern South Vietnam provinces of Phước Long, Bình Long, Phước Tuy, Bình Tuy, Bình Dương, Tây Ninh, Hậu Nghĩa, Long An, Long Khánh, Biên Hòa, Gia Định, and the Special District of Vũng Tàu, defended by III Corps with three infantry divisions (the 5th, the 18th, and the 25th), all local units of the Air Force and Navy, of the Regional Forces and Militia of each Sub-District.

• Region IV: including the sixteen western South Vietnam provinces of Gò Công, Kiến Tường, Định Tường, Kiến Hòa, Kiến Phong, Sa Đéc, Vĩnh Long, Vĩnh Bình, Châu Đốc, An Giang, Phong Dinh, Ba Xuyên, Kiên Giang, Chương Thiện, Bạc Liệu, An Xuyên, defended by IV corps with three infantry divisions (the 7th, the 9th, and the 21st), all local units of the Air Force and Navy, of the Regional Forces and Militia of each Sub-District.

In addition to these fixed territory-defending units, the General Staff of the ARVN also created a number of mobile units called General Reserve Forces, which could be deployed anywhere when needed. They included the Airborne Division, the Marine Division, five Rangers Brigades, and the 81st Commando Airborne Brigade.

In addition to the Army with the above-mentioned units and together with other branches like Armored Cavalry, Artillery, Signals, and Engineers, etc., the ARVN had two more services, the Air Force and the Navy, which also had developed very rapidly into modern forces with all kinds of aircraft and battle ships. The Air Force (AFVN) had a total of six Air Divisions located all over the RVN's territory as follows:

- Air Division 1: located in Đà Nẵng
- Air Division 2: located in Nha Trang
- Air Division 3: located in Biên Hòa
- Air Division 4: located in Cần Thơ
- Air Division 5: located in Sài Gòn
- Air Division 6: located in Pleiku

The Navy also had its sea and river fleets everywhere, and in each Region there was a naval command headed by a Rear Admiral (one-star general; same rank as a Brigadier-General in Army and Air Force).

Definitely, the RVN did not have the economic capability to feed and keep such strong and modern military armed forces without the U.S. aids.

At the end of 1973, after the U.S. Senate did not ratify the Paris Accords, Congress passed the War Powers Act on November 7, 1973, limiting to the maximum the presidential right to send troops overseas. Before that, from October 1973, the U.S. had gone through a series of serious political scandals, which almost paralyzed the Executive Branch. First of all, it was the resignation of Vice-President Spiro Agnew because of his involvement in some corruption. President Nixon had to nominate Mr. Gerald Ford, a Republican Congressman from Michigan, Minority Leader of the House, as Vice-President on December 6, 1973. In the early months of 1974, the Watergate scandal exploded uncontrollably, and, in order to avoid impeachment, President Nixon had to resign on August 9, 1974. Based on the U.S. Constitution, Vice-President Gerald Ford automatically became President. On December 19, 1974, Present Ford nominated Mr. Nelson Rockefeller, former Governor of New York (1959-1973), as Vice-President. The U.S. was falling into an unprecedented situation in its history: both the President and the Vice-President ***were not elected by the people.*** The U.S. Executive was totally inferior before the Legislative, i.e., Congress, which, at that time, was under the absolute control of the Democratic opposition holding the majority of seats in both chambers. (This issue will be discussed in details in Chapter Nine).

At the beginning of 1975, before such a disadvantageous situation, certainly, President Thiệu must have thought that he could no longer rely on sufficient U.S. military aids for the war with a Congress under the control of the anti-war and anti-RVN Representatives and Senators, as well as on the U.S. retaliations against North Vietnam's violations of the Paris Accords by a weak and un-elected president.

Following are a number of important events that led President Thiệu to think that he was right. First, the U.S. Congress had cut off military aids to the RVN very severely. The number went down from 2.8 billion\s dollars in 1973 to just one billion dollars in 1974, and, only three days after President Nixon's resignation, on August 11, 1974, Congress cut 300 million more to only 700 million dollars.[2] Secondly, the U.S. had no reaction whatsoever after the Communists had seriously violated the Paris Accords in their attack of the Province of Phước Long in mid-December 1974 and capture of that province on January 6, 1975. Thirdly, ***"One day before General Phú announced the loss of Ban Mê Thuột, the U.S. House of Representatives had voted to deny the supplementary 300-million-dollars military aids to the RVN previously proposed by President Ford."*** [3]

President Thiệu was led to think the RVN no longer had the capability and the means to protect its whole territory. On March 11, 1975, one day after the fall of Ban Mê Thuột, he convened a very important meeting at the Independence Palace. Present at the meeting with him were: General Trần Thiện Khiêm, Prime Minister, General Cao Văn Viên, Chairman of the Joint General Staff, and Lieutenant-General Đặng Văn Quang, Security and Military Advisor of the President. It was at this meeting, for the first time, President Thiệu presented his idea that the ARVN was now able to keep only the III and IV Corps, i.e., the I and II Corps in the Northern part of the RVN's territory should be cut and abandoned for the Communists. In hindsight, that action was not completely right. President Thiệu should have presented such an extremely important strategy in a meeting of the National Security Council. Three days later, on March 14, 1975, again with these same three generals, President Thiệu again had another important meeting in Cam Ranh, this time with the presence of Major-General Phạm Văn Phú, Commander of II Corps. It was at this fateful meeting that President Thiệu, as President and supreme Commander-in-Chief of the ARVN, ***turned his thinking into action, and gave a direct order to General Phú to retreat and abandon Pleiku-Kontum.*** Years later, in a conversation with Dr. Nguyễn Tiến Hưng, he tried to justify his action by saying:

"Tôi ra lệnh tái phối trí tức là rút quân khỏi Pleiku và Kontum để tái chiếm Ban Mê Thuột, chứ không phải rút lui hoàn toàn khỏi Quân Đoàn II." [4]

(Translation:

"I ordered the re-deployment of troops from Pleiku and Kontum in order to counter-attack and re-capture Ban Mê Thuột, not to retreat completely from II Corps.")

But, even if this justification was correct, the historical truth was still that it was him who ordered General Phú to retreat from Pleiku where the II Corps was headquartered. Besides, in that conversation with Dr. Hưng, he added:

"Tôi ra hai chứ không phải một lệnh: đó là thứ nhất, rút quân khỏi Pleiku để tái chiếm Ban Mê Thuột; và thứ hai, Bộ Tổng Tham Mưu 'theo dõi và giám sát' (suivre et surveiller) cuộc triệt thoái này." [5]

(Translation:

"I gave two orders, not just one: the first, withdraw the troops from Pleiku to re-capture Ban Mê Thuột; and the second, the General Staff 'follow and watch' this retreat.")

Regarding that second order, General Cao Văn Viên, Chairman of the General Staff, informed that it did not exist. Even if it did exist, General Viên would have executed it reluctantly because he had stopped doing his job actively several years prior for the following reason: he did not agree with President Thiệu's giving direct orders to Corps commanders, bypassing the Gene ral Staff. In fact, he had submitted his resignation many times but President Thiêu did not accept it. His reaction was not to fully carry out his duty as Chief of the General Staff. Going back to this second order, there was some basis to believe that Gene ral Viên did not tell the whole truth. In his memoir, ***Đôi dòng ghi nhớ*** (meaning *A few lines of memories*), Colonel Phạm Bá Hoa (former Head of Office of the Chief of the General Staff, 1965-1966), recorded that in the afternoon of March 15, 1975

General Viên phoned him, who was at the time Chief of Staff of the Directorate General of Supplies of the General Staff, and ordered him to send all available and operable C-130 cargo planes to the II Corps, without giving any reason but at the same time telling him to keep it as a secret.[6] Through this story, it is safe to conclude that President Thiệu had in fact given that second order since, without it, with his negative behavior, General Viên would not have phoned Colonel Hoa as reported. And General Viên's action completely fitted to his negative way of carrying out his duty.

Going back to the order of retreating from Pleiku-Kontum, there are several issues that need to be analyzed in order to understand and evaluate President Thiệu's action: the background and timing of the order, the characteristics of the order, the contents of the order, the execution of the order, and the end results of the order.

Background and Timing of the Order

In terms of background and timing, President Thiệu directly gave this order to Major-General Phạm Văn Phú, Commander of II Corps, at the meeting in Cam Ranh, on March 14, 1975. At this point in time, the RVN was going through the most difficult period of the war that had lasted for almost 20 years:

• U.S. military aids had been cut seriously, and, probably, would be completely gone in FY 1976, and the ARVN would not be able to fight effectively like before;

• no more General Reserve Forces could be deployed to battlefronts that need them; all of them had already been deployed;

• the two provinces of Phước Long and Ban Mê Thuột had been captured by the Communists but the ARVN did not have the capability to re-capture them;

• and facing with such a serious situation, the supreme Commander-in-Chief of the ARVN, President Nguyễn Văn

Thiệu, had made the decision to abandon the two Regions I and II, and keep only Regions III and IV.

When he gave General Phú the order to retreat from Pleiku-Kontum, President Thiệu, for the first time, officially put his decision to cut off the RVN's territory into effect. Although he had met with the senior generals on March 11, 1975, as mentioned above, he alone was responsible for this decision because it was his own idea and because the other generals did not make any contributions in the meeting; they were simply playing the roles of witnesses. It was the same thing at the meeting of March 14, 1975 in Cam Ranh because all the generals present did not have any counter arguments. General Phú was the lowest ranking general at the meeting, and, thus, he did not have any opinion since he could see very clearly that President Thiệu had decided with the consensus of the three other senior generals. It was really something very unfortunate about the meeting since it was extremely important for the political and military future of the RVN.

Characteristics of the Order

In terms of the characteristics of the order, it was a top secret one, and only the high-ranking officers at II Corps Headquarters knew about it; even high-ranking officers at the General Staff in Saigon were not notified. In his memoir, Colonel Hoa also said that when he contacted Colonel Lê Khắc Lý, II Corps Chief of Staff, to let him know that he was sending C-130 cargo planes to Pleiku for the II Corps, Colonel Lý did not tell him what II Corps would use these planes for.[7] American officials in Vietnam were also left completely in the dark about this order. Author Đỗ Sơn, in his book entitled ***Chuẩn Tướng Phạm Duy Tất và sự thật cuộc triệt thoái Quân Đoàn II*** (meaning: *Brigadier-General Phạm Duy Tất and the truth of the retreat from II Corps*), has recorded his interview with Brigadier-General Phạm Duy Tất on this retreat. When asked how General Phú relayed President Thiệu's order at the meeting of the II Corps in the evening of March 14, 1975, General Tất answered as follows:

"Lệnh Tổng Thống là giữ bí mật tuyệt đối, chỉ rút quân chủ lực, còn bỏ lại tất cả. Có nghĩa là bỏ Tiểu Khu, bỏ Địa Phương Quân, Nghĩa Quân, và dân chúng. Có người đã hỏi tại sao vậy? Tướng Phú trả lời: Tổng Thống đã có nói nếu họ muốn theo thì họ sẽ biết cách đi theo, các anh không phải lo. Phải rút nhanh, gọn để bảo toàn sự bất ngờ." [8]

(Translation:

"The President's order was to keep it as an absolute secret, withdraw only the main forces, abandon all the rest. That meant abandoning sub-districts, abandoning Regional Forces, Militia, and people. Someone asked why? General Phú answered: The President said if they wanted to follow, they would know how to follow, you guys don't have to worry. Withdraw fast, neat in order to keep it a surprise.")

This characteristic of absolute secret could not be kept for long because, in fact, it was ***impossible*** to keep secret the move of a whole military corps. Colonel Hoa's memoir revealed that when the first C-130 cargo plane, which he sent to Pleiku in the morning of March 16, 1975, arrived at Cù Hanh airfield, it just:

"không thể nào đáp xuống phi trường được, vì người ta đông không thể tưởng tượng nổi." [9]

(Translation:

"could not land in the airfield, because it was unbelievably crowded there.")

Contents of the Order

In terms of the contents, President Thiệu's order included two parts: 1) Abandon Pleilu-Kontum, withdraw all II Corps' main forces to the coastal area; and, 2) Regroup all forces in order to re-capture Ban Mê Thuột. The II Corps carried out only part 1 of the order; part 2 of the order could never be carried out because, in reality, after the retreat, the II Corps no longer existed. President Thiệu's order, as previously mentioned, was: ***"withdraw fast, neat in order to keep the surprise,"*** but did not say anything about the time frame, and, thus, could be interpreted as giving General Phú complete authority to make his decision on this matter. And General Phú, in his meeting with the senior officers at the II Corps Headquarters in the evening of March 14, 1975, decided to begin the retreat in the morning of March 16, 1975, i.e., ***after only one day of preparations,*** i.e., in reality, ***no preparations at all***, something unimaginable for an operation at corps level. One more thing that was also very irregular: no operation order whatsoever was issued to the II Corps' subordinate units.

Feasibility of the Order

In terms of the feasibility of this order, issued by President Thiệu in such an extremely serious political – military situation, there were several issues that needed to be considered and evaluated sufficiently and objectively. The first issue was the way of issuing the order by President Thiệu: when he felt that he could not persuade General Phú on his decision to abandon Region II (because General Phú asked him for permission to stay and fight to the death with his troops), he had to use the worst method: threatening to relieve General Phú of his command and put him in jail.[10] As previously mentioned, the order to retreat included two parts: 1) Withdraw II Corps' main forces from Pleiku-Kontum, and 2) Regroup all forces in order to counter-attack and re-capture Ban Mê Thuột. The second part, therefore, was the objective used to justify the first part, which was only the means. ***This argument was totally baseless.*** Ban Mê Thuột had been lost; and the II Corps, with existing forces (without any more expected General Reserve Forces units), could not mount a counter-attack to re-capture it after the retreat. That was just a consideration based purely on fighting forces. What about the soldiers' fighting spirit? Certainly, it was seriously affected by the two big losses of the ARVN in Phước

Long and Ban Mê Thuột, leading to the withdrawal of the whole II Corps. The President could have thought that by abandoning Pleiku-Kontum the II Corps would no longer have to defend these areas, and, therefore, would be able to concentrate more troops to attack Ban Mê Thuột. If, indeed, that was the way he thought then he had forgotten that North Vietnam also would no longer need their divisions to surround Pleiku and Kontum, and would be able to concentrate more troops to defend Ban Mê Thuột. Besides, in terms of fighting spirit, it was quite certain that the North Vietnamese troops' spirit was much higher than the one of the ARVN soldiers because they had already had two big victories and had forced the ARVN to withdraw a whole corps, something that had never happened during almost twenty years of the war. ***The idea of re-capturing Ban Mê Thuột, main objective of this order to retreat, was clearly utopian.*** The question that needs to be answer is: Is it possible that President Thiệu, a high-ranking general having a lot of experiences, and a person who had always thought out carefully before acting, could have thought so shallowly like that? My answer is: **NO**. President Thiệu used it only as a pretext to implement his decision to cut off Military Region II that he had at the meeting of Mach 11, 1975 at the Independence Palace with generals Khiêm, Viên, and Quang. A little bit more thinking would reveal that he had never referred to the re-capture of Pleiku-Kontum, i.e., the counter-attack would be to re-capture Ban Mê Thuột only, not the whole Military Region II. In brief, the feasibility of the order was very much in doubt.

Execution of the Order

In terms of the execution of the order, it can be summarized in the following phrase: ***It was not carefully prepared, if we don't want to say that there was no preparation at all.*** It was a mistake, a huge one, by General Phú. Although President Thiệu's order was to carry out the retreat fast, General Phú would not and should not carry it out that fast. Certainly, he should have known the people in Military Region II, in particular people in Pleiku, where the II Corps was headquartered, would know about the retreat, and they would follow the troops. Therefore, he should not just consider the factor of his troops and their equipment, but should also anticipate the factor of the people, especially the people becoming panic before this great and unprecedented retreat. In addition, a number of General Phú's other actions during that time should be evaluated too. First, his request, almost a trade-off for his obligation to carry out this very difficult order, that President Thiệu promote Colonel Pham Duy Tất, Commander of II Corps Rangers, to Brigadier-General. The military situation at that time was not appropriate for giving promotion; the ARVN was losing heavily, not winning gloriously. Second, the promotion was only for one colonel, Colonel Tất, (without any reason, but, certainly, not for any extraordinary action in the battlefield at that time) would definitely cause backbiting or denigration (Colonel Tất was known as a close friend of General Phú for years) or jealousy and dissatisfaction by other colonels at II Corps' headquarters, when there was a need for unity and close co-operation of everyone in this extremely important operation. Third, General Phú was almost completely absent in this retreat. In the morning of March 15, 1975, with a number of staff officers, he flew to Nha Trang with the reason of establishing the new headquarters for II Corps, and gave the general command of the retreat to General Tất.[11] This could be seen as his prime motive in his effort to obtain from President Thiệu the promotion to Brigadier-General for Colonel Tất.

According to the "plan," only Air Division 6 would take care of itself in its move to Phan Rang airbase, all remaining forces of II Corps would go together, each day in a convoy of 200-250 vehicles carrying soldiers and equipment. The whole main forces of II Corps in the Pleiku-Kontum area at that time included the following units:

- 1 battalion of the 44th Regiment, 23rd Infantry Division

• 6 Ranger Brigades: the 4th, 7th, 21st, 22nd, 24th, and 25th

• The 21st Squadron (M-48 tanks), of the 2nd Armored Cavalry Brigade

• 2 Artillery Battalions of 155-mm Howitzers

• 1 Artillery Battalion of 175-mm long-range canons

• 20th Combat Engineers Brigade

• 231st Support and Supply Brigade

According to the plan that General Phú had proposed at the meeting of March 14, 1975 in Cam Ranh and subsequently unanimously approved by President Thiệu and the other senior generals, the local inter-provincial route 7B (LTL-7B), branching from National Route 14 (Pleiku – Ban Mê Thuột) at Mỹ Thạch and going southeast to Tuy Hòa, was selected for the retreat. Reason: both essential national routes linking the highlands to the coastal areas, National Route 19 (Pleiku – Qui Nhơn) and National Route 21 (Ban Mê Thuột – Ninh Hòa) were blocked and cut off by North Vietnamese units. LTL-7B was a gravel road, 182-km long, unused for a long time, and therefore, almost abandoned with many badly broken sections. It included 3 sections as follows:

• from Mỹ Thạch Intersection to Cheo Reo: 84 km, relatively in good shape

• from Cheo Reo to Củng Sơn: 48 km, through Tuna Pass (about 4 km south of Cheo Reo; today called Tô Na Pass), through Ba River Bridge (under French administration, called Le Bac Bridge; Ba River at this point was quite large, and the bridge was up to 600-m long but already broken), and finally through Cà Lúi Bridge (a tributary of Ba River) before reaching Củng Sơn

• from Củng Sơn to Tuy Hòa: 50 km, this section was heavily mined by the South Korean allied troops before 1973

Generally speaking, LTL-7B was not a good road for the retreat, but it was the only one available and it could provide the surprise factor needed for the retreat.

The timetable of the retreat was set as follows:

• March 16: the 20th Combat Engineers Brigade took the lead, cleared the road, built / repaired road / bridges as needed; the 7th Ranger Brigade going together and providing support for the Engineers; going also in this wave would be supply units, all in a convoy of 200 vehicles, together with some units of artillery, and some units of M-48 tanks belonging to the 21st Squadron for the protection of the whole convoy.

• March 17: the remaining units of supply, artillery, and medical medicine, in a convoy of about 250 vehicles with some units of M-48 tanks for the protection of the convoy.

• March 18: units of the II Corps Headquarters, some units of the 23rd Infantry Division Headquarters, units of Military Police, the Battalion belonging to the 44th Regiment, 23rd Infantry Division, all in a convoy of 250 vehicles with some units of tanks for the protection of the convoy.

• March 19: the remaining Ranger Brigades and the last armored cavalry units formed the rear of the retreating forces to fight back the enemy pursuit.

The first day of the retreat proceeded quite smoothly, as planned and on schedule because the people as well as the North Vietnamese were still not aware of the retreat. But at the end of the day, the people of Pleiku were already aware of the retreat, and they started to follow the retreating force in great number. It was in the evening of that day, North Vietnamese General Văn Tiến Dũng was also aware of the retreat of II Corps, and ordered the 320th Division to immediately and rapidly launch the pursuit and attack the retreating forces in the move on LTL-7B.

The next day, March 17, the people began to merge into the retreating column by all means of transportation that they had, including a large number of them walking, and prevented the column from moving fast.

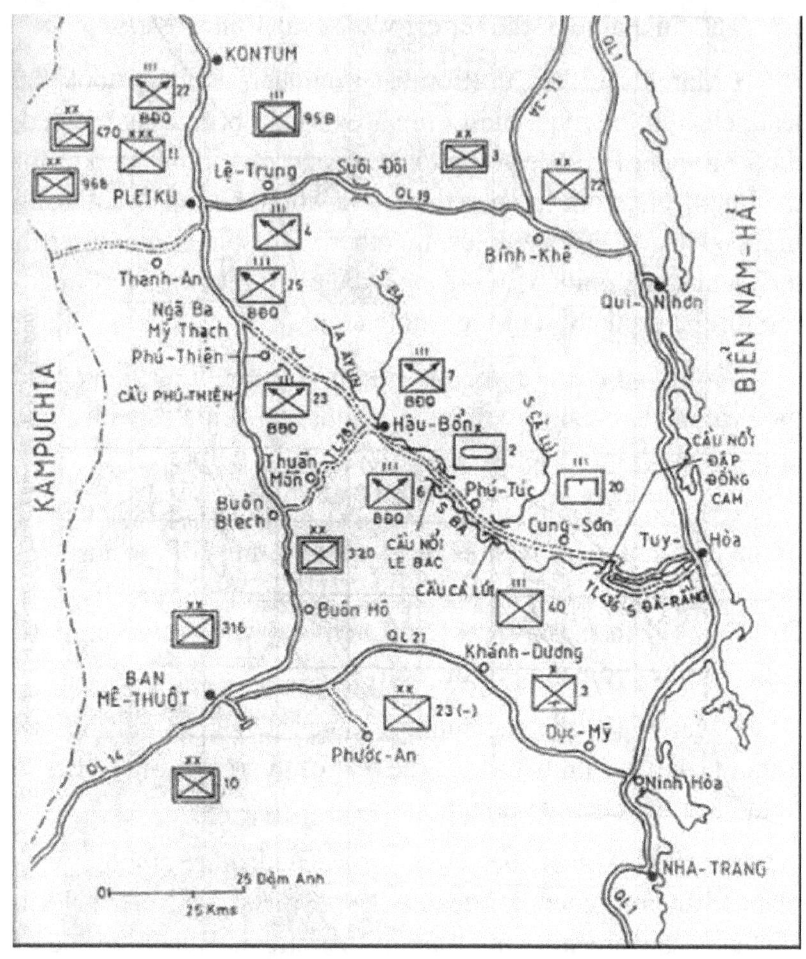

Figure 8.1. Map of the Inter-Provincial Route 7B

Figure 8.2. One scene of the retreating troops on LTL-7B

On March 18, the column reached Cheo Reo (Hậu Bổn) and stopped because the Engineers had not finished building the bridge across the Ba River south of Cheo Reo. On the same day, seeing the retreat going quite well with the surprise factor, General Phú changed his mind. In his book, author Nguyễn Đức Phương recorded as follows:

"... do yếu tố bất ngờ và mặt lộ còn sử-dụng được, cuộc lui binh không gặp trở-ngại nào đáng kể. Yếu tố nhanh chóng và dễ dàng này khiến Tướng Phú thay đổi ý-kiến. Ông ra lệnh ngưng cuộc lui binh và thay vào đó là lệnh lập tuyến phòng-thủ tại Hậu-Bổn." [12]

(Translation:

"... with the factor of surprise and the road surface still usable, the retreat did not meet any significant obstacles. These two factors of fastness and easiness led General Phú to change his mind. He ordered to stop the retreat and establish the defense line at Hậu Bổn."

The Advanced Headquarters of II Corps, under the command of Brigadier-General Trần Văn Cẩm, was positioned right at a school in the town of Hậu Bổn. But in the evening of the same day, units of the North Vietnamese 320th Division caught up the retreating forces in Cheo Reo, and began their attacks with all kinds of fire powers they had, causing heavy damages and casualties to the retreating forces and the people as well, with a lot of vehicles and tanks destroyed, and bodies of civilians scattered everywhere on the LTL-7B and in the town. The 22nd Ranger Brigade was ordered to move up seizing the Ban Bleik Pass west of the town of Cheo Reo in order to stop the North Vietnamese attack, buying time for the Engineers to complete the bridge across the Ba River.

On March 19, the fierce fighting was still on in Cheo Reo between the Ranger Brigades and the units of the North Vietnamese 320th Division in pursuit. On the same day, a number of units of Montagnard Regional Forces revolted, deserted, ransacking and causing some chaos within the retreating troops. While the fierce fighting was still raging, unfortunately, an AFVN flight of A-37 jet fighters mistakenly dropped their bombs on friendly troops, causing heavy casualties to one battalion of the 7th Ranger Brigade, and made the already bad situation much worse. Order and discipline almost no longer existed. A number of commanding officers of the armored cavalry and ranger units having the responsibilities of providing support and protection for the retreating forces could no longer command their men. Confronted with this chaotic, uncontrollable situation in Hậu Bổn, General Phú once more changed his mind, gave order to abandon the defense line in Hậu Bổn, and continue the retreat to Tuy Hòa. In his book, author Đỗ Sơn recorded what General Tất had said in the previously-mentioned interview as follows:

"Tướng Phú cho trực thăng tới bốc Bộ Tư Lệnh Tiền Phương của Quân Đoàn đưa về Tuy Hòa, riêng Tướng Cẩm là người ở lại sau cùng nên chính trực thăng của tôi [tôi = Chuẩn Tướng Phạm Duy Tất] ***bốc ông."*** [13]

(Translation:

"General Phú sent his helicopter to pick up all staff of the Advanced Headquarters of the Corps and bring them to Tuy Hòa, General Cẩm was the last person to leave and was picked up by my helicopter.") [my helicopter = General Tất's helicopter]

From that moment on, ***there was no more general in the retreating forces.*** The unified command no longer existed, the troops were like a headless snake, the soldiers felt abandoned, the commanding officers and the units were left to worry with saving their own skins. In the meantime, the AFVN was ordered to bomb and destroy all heavy equipment so that they could not be utilized by the enemy. In the morning of March 20, the retreating forces tried to break the siege imposed by units of the North Vietnamese 320th Division, got out of Hậu Bổn, and moved toward Củng Sơn, but were stopped halfway because Phú Túc had already been captured by the Communists. The 7th Ranger Brigade was ordered to move up, succeeded in its fierce assault, and re-captured Phú Túc in the same day. The next day, March 21, the retreating forces continued to move toward Củng Sơn despite the enemy's continued attack. After leaving Phú Túc, the situation of no discipline within the retreating forces was getting much worse; many soldiers competed with each other, even shooting each other, to move to the front… In his book, author Hoàng Khởi Phong gave the following statement:

"… Súng bắt đầu nổ từ một phe, bạo lực lan nhanh như lửa cháy đồng, trong chốc lát nó bao trùm đoàn xe, súng nổ khắp nơi, người ta bắn để cướp đường giành đi trước…

Bấy giờ súng không nổ phát một, người ta bắn hàng tràng đại liên, không bắn chỉ thiên, mà bắn xả trên đầu." [14]

(Translation:

"Guns began to fire off from one side, violence was spreading fast like a bushfire, in a short moment it engulfed the whole convoy, guns firing off everywhere, people were shooting to

steal way in order to move to the front... Now guns no longer fired off by single rounds, people were shooting with machine guns, not warning shots to the sky, but indiscriminately over people's heads...")

The convoy, finally, reached the bank of the Ba River. At that moment, the 20th Combat Engineers Brigade was still working on the bridge. In his book, ***The Final Collapse***, General Cao Văn Viên, then Chief of the General Staff of the ARVN, reported as follows:

> ***"A pontoon bridge had been brought to Tuy Hoa from Nha Trang, but it was impossible to move the bridge to Cung Son by road because of several enemy blocking positions. Finally, the bridge was carried to Cung Son piece by piece by CH-47 helicopters.".***[15]

The 6th Ranger Brigade, at the defense line west of Củng Sơn, fought fiercely to stop several enemy attacks by the 64th Regiment of the 320th Division, in order to help the Engineers finish off their work on the bridge across the Ba River. On March 22, the pontoon bridge was completed, and the convoy began to cross the Ba River. At the start, because of the competition to cross the bridge as fast as possible, a number of vehicles ran too fast and caused the collapse of one section of the pontoon bridge with some casualties. The Engineers rapidly repaired the section, and the convoy continued to cross the Ba River, and moved toward Tuy Hòa. The 35th and 51st Battalions of the 6th Ranger Brigade continued to safeguard the defense line in Củng Sơn to protect the rear of the convoy. The 34th Battalion of the 7th Ranger Brigade advanced in front of the convoy, removed each and every enemy blockage, and opened the road for the convoy to move toward Tuy Hòa. On March 27, at 9 pm, the first military vehicles of the convoy reached Tuy Hòa.

End Results of the Order

In terms of end results of the order, this retreat was the first step of the unbelievably fast collapsing process of the ARVN: if counting from March 16, 1975, the starting day of the retreat, to April 30, 1975, the day General Dương Văn Minh, the last President of the RVN surrendered to the North Vietnamese troops at the Independence Palace, the period was only 44 days.

The first and direct result of this unprecedented retreat in the history of the ARVN was the fact that the II Corps was wiped out, meaning that the RVN lost one quarter of its military forces in the span of only more than 10 days. Again, author Nguyễn Đức Phương provided some statistics as follows:

"Khoảng 60 ngàn quân chủ lực khi về đến Tuy Hòa chỉ còn lại khoảng 20 ngàn. Năm liên đoàn BĐQ với quân số khoảng 7 ngàn chỉ còn lại 900 người. Lữ Đoàn 2 Kỵ Binh với hơn 100 thiết-xa các loại chỉ còn đúng 13 thiết-vận-xa M-113." [16]

(Translation:

"The main forces of about 60,000 men were reduced to around 20,000 at their arrival in Tuy Hòa. The five Ranger brigades totaling around 7,000 soldiers had only 900 left. The 2nd Armored Cavalry Brigade with more than 100 armored vehicles had only 13 of the M-113 personnel carriers left.")

General Cao Văn Viên, then Chief of the General Staff of the ARVN, again, in his book, ***The Final collapse***, summarized the total loss of the II Corps as follows:

"At least 75 percent of II Corps combat strength, to include the 23rd Infantry Division as well as Ranger, armor, artillery, engineer, and signal units, had been tragically expended within ten days." [17]

In terms of territory, the II Corps lost most of its highland provinces, i.e., the provinces of Pleiku, Kontum, Darlac, and Phú Bổn, with the remaining provinces of Lâm Đồng, Tuyên Đức, and all the coastal provinces being under serious enemy threats.

The subsequent chain result was the fact that the ARVN had to withdraw from all territories of I and II Corps under heavy pressure from many North Vietnamese divisions. During that time, a number of high-ranking commanding officers of II Corps, such as Brigadier-General Trần Văn Cẩm, Commander of the Advanced Headquarters, and Colonel Nguyễn Văn Đồng, Commander of the 2nd Armored Cavalry Brigade, were taken as prisoners by the enemy. Lieutenant-General Ngô Quang Trưởng, Commander of I Corps, had to withdraw and abandon Huế and Đà Nẵng. All territories of these two Military Regions I and II were successively lost to the Communists. The III Corps had to establish its Advanced Headquarters in Phan Rang, but not for long, this defense line was also broken on April 15, 1975, and Lieutenant-General Nguyễn Vĩnh Nghi, Commander of the Advanced Headquarters, and Brigadier-General Phạm Ngọc Sang, Commander of the Air Division 6 (relocated from Pleiku) were also taken as prisoners by the enemy. Five North Vietnamese divisions concentrated their forces to attack Xuân Lộc but were stopped by Major-General Lê Minh Đảo's 18th Infantry Division. The Communists decided to bypass Xuân Lộc and advanced directly to Saigon, and the RVN surrendered at noon of April 30, 1975.

Concluding Remarks

The ARVN had been able to safeguard South Vietnam for 20 years, defeated all general offensives of the North Vietnamese armed forces, but disintegrated and defeated in the span of only 44 days from March 16, 1975, the starting day of the retreat of the II Corps from Pleiku following President Nguyễn Văn Thiệu's order, to April 30, 1975, the day President Dương Văn Minh surrendered. The "running away" and abandoning its ally, the RVN, by the U.S. Government through its reduction and, finally, complete cut-off of military aids to the RVN, ironically, were the "guarantee" for the RVN's defeat. General Fred C. Weyand, U.S. Army Chief of Staff, in his report of April 4, 1975, submitted to President Gerald Ford, after his fact-finding mission on the military situation of the RVN from March 28,

1975 to April 4, 1975, gave the following judgment:

> ***"The present level of U.S. support guarantees GVN defeat."*** [18]

President Nguyễn Văn Thiệu's order to retreat from the II Corps, leading to the RVN's surrender on April 30, 1975, in final analysis, was indeed a catalyst for the quick collapse of the RVN.

CHAPTER NINE

Abandoning of the Republic of Vietnam by the US: Who was to Blame?

The Republic of Vietnam (RVN) was declared dead at noon of April 30, 1975. Every South Vietnamese knew that fact. And they knew that the RVN lost the war because it had been abandoned by the U.S. For several years, most South Vietnamese people hated President Richard M. Nixon and National Security Advisor (and later Secretary of State) Henry A. Kissinger, believing that they had sold out the RVN and stabbed it in the back with the Paris Accords signed on January 27, 1973. This Chapter tries to analyze the abandoning of the RVN by the U.S. and find out who was to blame.

The War Between U.S. Executive and Legislative Branches 1973-1975

After the presidential and congress election of November 7, 1972, at the beginning of 1973, following President Richard M. Nixon's inauguration for his second term on January 20, 1973, the U.S. politics was divided with the President from one party while the House and the Senate were controlled by the other party; more precisely:

• Executive: President Nixon, a Republican, won a big landslide, defeating his Democratic opponent, South Dakota's Senator George McGovern, as follows:

o In terms of popular votes: Nixon received 47.1 million votes (60.7%); McGovern got only 29.1 million votes (37.5%)

o In terms of electoral votes: Nixon received 520 votes (Nixon won in 49 states, including South Dakota, the home state of McGovern); McGovern got only 17 votes (McGovern won only one state, Massachusetts, and Washington, DC.[1]

• Legislative: On the contrary, U.S. Congress (93rd, from 3-Jan-1973 to 3-Jan-1975) was under total control of the Democratic Party with the following details:

o In the House of Representatives: The Democrats had the majority of 241 seats while the Republicans had the minority of 192 seats.

o In the Senate: The Democrats held the majority with 56 senators while the Republicans had the minority with only 42 senators.[2]

Under the seriously divisive and highly tense U.S. political atmosphere created by the Vietnam War, the results of the 1972 elections showed very clearly that the American people wanted the following two goals:

• The Republican administration, led by President Nixon, would be successful in its negotiations to end the war.

• The Democratic Congress, with an absolute majority in both chambers, would be successful in guaranteeing that the U.S. would not be drawn into a similar war.

In such situation, both the Executive Branch and the Legislative Branch believed they had a very solid base for their "mandate" to achieve what the people had wanted. But at the same time, they also understood very clearly the limitation of their "mandate" because the other side had their "mandate" too.

On the Executive side, President Nixon, in his memoir, had

the following judgment in the evening of November 7, 1972 while the votes were still being counted:

"In state after state we were winning big. Texas, for example, was going to be ours by more than a million votes. But there was also bad news: we were not picking up enough congressional seats to provide the legislative support my own New Majority mandate would need." [3]

In order to persuade President Thiệu to co-sign the Paris Accords, President Nixon, in his secret letters to President Thiệu, promised, not only one time but many times, that the U.S. would retaliate if North Vietnam violated the Accords. That promise was again repeated in President Nixon's secret letter of January 5, 1973 to President Thiệu:

"... we will respond with full force should the settlement be violated by North Vietnam." [4]

All of these secret letters were drafted by National Security Advisor Dr. Henry A. Kissinger, and signed by President Nixon. Mr. Kissinger, however, never said a word about them. Moreover, since he knew clearly that the Legislative Branch would oppose a repetition of the Vietnam War, after the Paris Accords was signed, he always avoided to give direct answers to the American correspondents' questions whether the U.S. would send its troops back to Vietnam in case North Vietnam violated the Accords. In his book, ***"Kissinger: a biography,"*** author Walter Isaacson recorded as follows:

"Asked at a news conference in early 1973 if the U.S. "would ever again send troops into Vietnam" if the accord was violated, he responded: "I don't want to comment on a hypothetical situation that we don't expect to arise." [5]

From the Legislative Branch, the Democratic Congressmen and Senators saw very clearly President Nixon's and Kissinger's policy through the Vietnamization of the War with the continued military aids for the RVN, the transfer of military bases and equipment to the ARVN from 1969 synchronously with the withdrawal of U.S. troops. The strengthening of the ARVN's fighting capability reached its peak through the two aid programs called ***Enhance*** (May 1972) and ***Enhance Plus*** (October 1972). These two programs transferred to the ARVN, within a very short time, an unprecedented huge amount of equipment as follows:

- ***Enhance*** transferred:
    - o 69 helicopters
    - o 55 jet fighters
    - o 100 aircraft of other kinds
    - o 7 patrol boats
    - o 2 battalions of air defense artillery
    - o 3 battalions of 175-mm big canons
    - o 2 battalions of M-48A3 tanks
    - o 141 TOW missile launchers
- ***Enhance Plus*** transferred:
    - o 234 F-5A and A-37 jet fighters
    - o 32 C-130 cargo planes
    - o 177 UH-1H helicopters
    - o 72 armored vehicles
    - o 177 personnel carriers
    - o 1,726 transport vehicles [6]

After these two waves of equipment transfer, the AFVN became the 4th largest air force in the world in terms of the number of aircraft (only behind the U.S., the Soviet Union, and China).

The U.S. Congress under the Democratic Party's control, therefore, did everything to prevent a repetition of the Vietnam War from happening. In order to achieve this objective, the Democratic Congressmen and Senators believed that they had to pass a legislation to limit the president's power to deploy U.S. troops overseas. That was the reason for Congressman Clement J. Zablocki (Democratic - Wisconsin) to submit to the House the bill for the ***War Powers Act*** on May 3, 1973. The bill was passed in the House on July 10, 1973, and in the Senate on July 20, 1973, but it was vetoed by President Nixon on October 24, 1973. The U.S. Congress re-tabled the bill and this time defeated President Nixon's veto, on November 7, 1973, with an absolute majority vote of 284/135 in the House, and 75/18 in the Senate.[7] The ***War Powers Act*** required that the president notify Congress within 48 hours the deployment of U.S. troops overseas, and forbade the use of troops more than 60 days unless there was a permission from Congress or a declaration of war by Congress.

Meanings and Roles of the Paris Accords

The two opposing sides within the U.S. government, President Nixon and National Security Advisor Kissinger (later, from September 22, 1973, Secretary of State) on one side, the Democratic congressmen and senators on the other, were fighting each other continuously in the issue of policy for the RVN after the signing of the Paris Accords on January 27, 1973. After all, what were the real meanings of the Paris Accords?

Right from the beginning of the negotiations with North Vietnam, Nixon and Kissinger had the three following clear objectives: 1) A cease-fire must be achieved at all cost, i.e., the war must be resolved militarily so that the U.S. could complete its troop withdrawal from Vietnam, and bring home all prisoners held by North Vietnam in Hà Nội; 2) The political resolution of the war would be left to the Vietnamese parties; 3) American aids would continue to help the RVN survive.

It was precisely for the above-mentioned objective no.1, the U.S. accepted even to allow the North Vietnamese troops to stay in the South while the U.S. withdrew its troops from South Vietnam. It was also to achieve this objective, President Nixon, despite the fierce opposition by Congress and the American people, ordered the Christmas Bombing in 1972 to force North

Vietnam to come back to the conference table and sign the Paris Accords. Also, for this objective no. 1, President Nixon, in his secret letter of January 20, 1973 to President Thiệu, blatantly said that even if the RVN refused to sign, the U.S. would go ahead, unilaterally sign the Accords:

"I must meet with key Congressional leaders Sunday evening, January 21, to inform them in general terms of our course. If you cannot give me a positive answer by then, I shall inform them that I am authorizing Dr. Kissinger to initial the Agreement even without the concurrence of your Government. In that case, even if you should decide to join us later, the possibility of continued Congressional assistance will be severely reduced." [8]

Why did Nixon and Kissinger give the signing of the Paris Accords such high priority? This was one of the most important points in Nixon' and Kissinger's strategy of resolving the Vietnam War that we need to understand clearly. When he ran for the U.S. presidential election in 1968, Mr. Nixon saw clearly that the Vietnam War had become the cause of the very serious division within the American people and that it would have to be ended as soon as possible. He ran with the promise to negotiate for ending the war, and he won, defeating his opponent, Democratic candidate and current Vice-President Hubert H. Humphrey, but he won with a very narrow margin (Nixon: 31,783,783 votes or 43.4%; Humphrey: 31,271,839 votes or 42.7%) [9] He also realized that the American people were opposing the Vietnam War because the war did not have any legal basis. In World War II, in 4 years (1941-1945), the U.S. lost almost half a million soldiers killed in action (416,800), but its commitment was supported 100% by the people without any opposition. Why? Because it was a war declared by U.S. Congress on December 8, 1941, one day after the Japanese attack of Pearl Harbor. Both Mr. Nixon and Mr. Kissinger did not have any illusion that North Vietnam would respect and comply with the Paris Accords. Both of them thought and believed that North Vietnam would violate the Accords, attack the RVN to achieve its objective of unifying

Vietnam. And because of that firm belief, both of them needed some solid legal basis to retaliate these violations without facing any opposition. The Paris Accords would be that needed solid legal basis. Mr. Kissinger presented this strategy very clearly at the meeting at the beginning of January 1973 with Mr. Bùi Diễm, President Thiệu's Roving Ambassador, and Mr. Trần Kim Phượng, South Vietnamese Ambassador in the U.S. as follows:

"We thought that if we could end the war honorably, with your government in office and with clear obligations in the agreement, that we would have so much authority afterwards that if we said that North Vietnam was violating the agreement, we could bomb them and no one would challenge us. ... Who knows today about the armistice was all about in Korea? If Korea is attacked, we would defend it. Why should we do this in Korea and not in Vietnam? There is no reason. ... With an army of over a million and controlling a large part of the territory, we think you can handle a ceasefire, at least for a long enough period until there are violations of the agreement. ... We thought in that the name of an agreement we would be better able to help than in the name of war. That is our cold-blooded appraisal. ... The only use of provisions is to give us a pretext to act. ... The agreement buys time." [10]

This judgment was completely in line with President Nixon's commitment in his previously mentioned secret letter of January 5, 1973 to President Thiệu.

After the Paris Accords was signed on January 27, 1973, the U.S. continued to lobby the international community to support the Accords. The result was that an international conference was convened in Paris on March 2, 1973 with the participation of nine countries, the U.S., the United Kingdom, France, Canada, China, the Soviet Union, Indonesia, Hungary, Poland, and the three parties involved in the Vietnam War, the RVN, the DRV, and the PRG, and with the presence of the Secretary-General of the United Nations; all participants signed the joint communique recognizing the Paris Accords and guaranteeing the peace in Indochina.[11]

In order to fulfill President Nixon's commitments to forcefully retaliate North Vietnamese violations of the Paris Accords, the U.S. had several concrete preparations. Since they had known for certain in advance that the sending of combat ground troops back to Vietnam was completely infeasible, Nixon and Kissinger could only retaliate these violations against the Paris Accords by Air Force with B-52 strategic bombers to minimize possible damages by the air defense network of North Vietnam. Among these preparations, the establishment of a special Air Force unit in Thailand was very important. It was the Command of the United States Support Activities Group / Seventh Air Force (USSAG/7AF) located in Nakhon Phanom, northeast of Thailand, with the following mission:

"USSAG/7AF, Thailand, will plan for resumption of an effective air campaign in Laos, Cambodia, RVN and NVN as directed by CINCPAC; …" [12]

Another document of the Office of Air Force History of the USAF Headquarters confirmed the existence of that unit:

"… The U.S. Support Activities Group / Seventh Air Force (USSAG / 7AF) command allowed the United States to retain a full military position, not in South Vietnam, but in Thailand. Its considerable forces, in conjunction with Strategic Air Command (SAC) forces and the U.S. Seventh Fleet, were intended primarily as a deterrent and warning to North Vietnam not to overrun South Vietnam. There is no doubt that President Nixon believed he would be able to use American air power in Thailand to keep his promises to protect South Vietnam against North Vietnamese cease-fire violations." [13]

In fact, facing with serious violations by North Vietnam, such as the continued infiltration of troops into South Vietnam through the Ho Chi Minh Trail, the U.S. had very clear warnings. Following are the details of these warnings mentioned in the same previously mentioned document:

"On April 1, on the <u>Meet The Press</u> television program, Defense Secretary Richardson warned Hanoi that failure to comply with the cease-

fire agreement could result in a resumption of US mining and bombing of North Vietnamese heartland. A few days later, Deputy Secretary of Defense William P. Clements said the President had asked for and received a list of possible military actions to back up his warning. Clements said he didn't think "the President has any intention of letting this situation go down the drain." [14]

At the conference ***"The Paris Agreement on Vietnam: twenty-five years later"*** held at The Nixon Center, in Washington, D.C., in April 1998, Mr. Kissinger said clearly:

> ***"President Nixon had decided to resume bombing in March '73, when the infiltration started. And he and I had a little debate whether to do it while we still had prisoners there, or whether to wait until all the prisoners were out, and he decided to do it after the last prisoner was out, early in April."*** [15]

Unfortunately, right at that time, April 1973, the ***Watergate*** affair [16] exploded, and President Nixon no longer had time to implement the bombings of North Vietnam as warned by the U.S. Author Dr. Larry Berman, in his book, ***"No peace, no honor: Nixon, Kissinger, and betrayal in Vietnam,"*** cited an article by William F. Buckley, Jr., printed in ***The Wall Street Journal***, issue of April 27, 1975, with the following information:

> ***"... that Watergate had derailed the president's plan to pulverize Hanoi... My own information is that it was planned, sometime in April, to pulverize Hanoi and Haiphong."*** [17]

President Nguyễn Văn Thiệu officially visited the U.S. from April 2 to April 4, 1973. President Nixon received him in San Clemente, California (President Nixon decided not to receive President Thiệu in Washington, D.C. for fear of creating a new anti-war demonstration), and repeated his commitments to support the RVN as well as his promises to retaliate forcefully if North Vietnam violated the Paris Accords. After their talks, a Joint Communique was issued on April 3, 1973, which included the following very clear and strong statement:

"Both Presidents, while acknowledging that progress was being made toward military and political settlements in South Vietnam, nevertheless viewed with great concern infiltrations of men and weapons in sizable numbers from North Vietnam into South Vietnam in violation of the agreement on ending the war, and considered that actions which would threaten the basis of the agreement would call for appropriate vigorous reactions." [18]

Betraying RVN: US Congress Controlled by Democratic Party

While President Nixon and his associates actively tried to force Hà Nội to comply with the Paris Accords, the U.S. Congress actively worked in the opposite direction.

First of all, as previously mentioned, the 93rd Congress, under total control of the Democratic Party in both chambers, passed the ***War Powers Act*** aimed at tying the hands of the Nixon administration in the use of military forces. Within this disadvantageous internal political turmoil, President Nixon and Mr. Kissinger committed a grave mistake in their decision not to submit the Paris Accords for ratification by Congress because they thought it would not pass the Senate.

At the previously mentioned conference,***"The Paris Agreement on Vietnam: twenty-five years later,"*** one participant, USAF retired General Charles Graham Boyd (General Boyd was the unique among the American prisoners held at Hỏa Lò prison in Hà Nội; he later became a four-star general of the USAF) made the following judgment:

"I believe that had the Paris Peace Accords been brought back and presented to the Congress of the United States for ratification that we would have been able to sustain the support necessary to honor the commitment to the government of South Vietnam. ... it seems to me that it would have been very difficult for the Congress of the United States to have refused at that point to support a document knowing that it would not lead to withdrawal of troops and a repatriation of the prisoners if they did not do so. It would have made them stakeholders in that process, making

it impossible to pull the rug out from under the Paris Peace Accords the following year. ..." [19]

General Boyd might have been right. The U.S. Senate, although under control by the Democrats (that made President Nixon and Kissinger worry), might still have ratified the Paris Accords because a poll taken at the end of January 1973, immediately after the signing of the Accords, showed that a very high percentage of the American people supported the Accords:

"Gallup polls in January 1973 showed that 80 percent were satisfied with the Paris Agreement, 58 percent believed that it was indeed a "peace with honor," [20]

Realizing Nixon administration's intention to retaliate against the violations of the Paris Accords by resuming the bombings of North Vietnam, which could revive the Vietnam War, the U.S. Congress tried to prevent it from happening by cutting down military aids for the RVN.

Right at that point in time, the Watergate exploded. The U.S. internationally respected newspapers, such as ***Time, New York Times***, and especially the ***Washington Post***, with the two reporters Bob Woodward and Carl Bernstein, began to expose the affair, showing high-ranking officials of the Department of Justice, the two security agencies CIA, FBI, and even the White House were involved in the break-in of the Democratic Party Campaign Committee at the Watergate building, and later in the cover-up of the affair. The confidence in President Nixon plummeted dramatically:[21]

• In January 1973: after his re-election and the signing of the Paris Accords, a Gallup poll showed that he got 68% support of the people

• In April 1973: the support went down to 48%

• In August 1973: the support was only 31%

From mid-April 1973, knowing that North Vietnam continued the infiltration of troops into the South, a clear violation of the Paris Accords, Kissinger recommended President Nixon many times to implement the retaliation but Nixon took it lightly and let it go because he was very much busy dealing with the Watergate affair. Author Johannes Kadura, in his book, ***The War after the War***, described it very clearly as follows:

"Kissinger reasoned, "Whatever the cost may be, in my judgment it will be far less than the cost which we will have to pay if, because of our inaction now, the Agreement completely fails as a result of major North Vietnamese actions in the coming months." Nixon, however, did not make the hard decision, favored by Haig and Kissinger, to extensively bomb the Ho Chi Minh Trail and (possibly) infiltration routes across the Demilitarized Zone. … Confronted with the increasingly unsettling domestic crisis, Nixon did not have the nerve to raise the stakes in Indochina." [22]

Having seen clearly Nixon's reluctance and even lack of fighting spirit, the U.S. Congress, under the absolute control of the Democratic Party, started to strongly push forward its anti-war policy. As already mentioned, Congressman Zablocki submitted the bill for the ***War Powers Act*** in the House on May 3, 1973. Next, it tried to limit the U.S. intervention in Cambodia. For a long time, Cambodia, under the leadership of Prince Norodom Sihanouk, allowed the Communists (i.e., North Vietnam and the Viet Cong) to establish their bases on its territory. In March 1970, while Sihanouk was in France for an official visit, Prime Minister Lon Nol staged a successful coup, eliminating Sihanouk. Cambodia re-established diplomatic relations with the U.S. In April 1970, the ARVN, in co-ordination with the American troops, crossed the Cambodian border, attacked and destroyed the Communist bases. The Vietnam War was expanded to Cambodia. After the Paris Accords was signed on January 27, 1973, Lon Nol also unilaterally declared a cease-fire in Cambodia. The Khmer Rouge (Cambodian Communists) did not agree with the cease-fire, continued the war, and in April 1973, they were closing in and surrounded the capital city of Phnom Penh. President Nixon ordered the 7th Air Division of the

USAF to bomb all Khmer Rouge positions and broke the siege of Phnom Penh. On June 25, 1973, the U.S. House passed a bill, which was originated from and was already passed by the Senate, to cut off all funds reserved for the bombings of the USAF in Cambodia, effective on June 30, 1973. Of course, President Nixon immediately vetoed this bill. Right at that point in time, the testimony by John Dean [23] before the Senate's investigation committee [24] revealed that Nixon himself had been involved in the Watergate affair, leading to the further decline of the popular confidence in Nixon. Although it did not have enough votes to beat President Nixon's veto, the U.S. Congress still continued to table the bill, and Senator Mike Mansfield, Senate Majority Leader, announced that the bill would be tabled again and again until it was passed. Following is what he said verbatim:

"again, again and again until the will of the people prevails." [25]

President Nixon realized that he could not win, he accepted a compromise with the Congress: let the bill pass with two changes: 1) extending the last day of bombing in Cambodia from June 30, 1973 (as in the bill) to August 15, 1973, and 2) making the bill applicable to North and South Vietnam too. This legislation was called Supplemental Appropriations Act for FY 1973, it included the following clause:

"None of the funds herein appropriated under this act may be expended to support directly or indirectly combat activities in or over Cambodia, Laos, North Vietnam, and South Vietnam by United States forces, and after August 15, 1973, no other funds heretofore appropriated under any other act may be expended for such purpose." [26]

After this legislation was signed into law by President Nixon, Mr. Kissinger lamented as follows:

"It is getting impossible to do anything in Indochina. ... That finishes us." [27]

After June 1973, for the U.S. officials in Washington, D.C., the collapse of the RVN was considered only as a matter of time.

It was highly probable that from that time, even Mr. Kissinger also thought about a "decent interval," just like what author Frank Snepp, the CIA Intelligence Analyst at the U.S. Embassy in Saigon, until April 29, 1975, coined it in his famous book, ***Decent interval: an insider's account of Saigon's indecent end***, published by Random House in 1977. According to this point of view, the U.S. must find some way to help the RVN extend its survival for a decent period of time, two or three years, so that the U.S. could avoid being seen as abandoning its ally. This could be true because Mr. Kissinger, in one of his books, revealed his thinking as follows:

> ***"As for Indochina, I observed it with the melancholy shown toward a terminally ill relative, hoping for a long respite and a miracle cure I was unable to describe."*** [28]

During 1973-1974, in terms of U.S. internal politics, the Watergate affair was getting more serious, and President Nixon had to spend a lot of his time to deal with it. In the meantime, in terms of international politics, there were many important crises happening, such as the military coup against President Allende in Chile (September 11, 1973), the Yom Kippur War in the Middle East (from October 6 to October 25, 1973) between Israel and an Arab alliance led by Egypt and Syria, and the oil crisis of summer 1973. In such circumstances, the Vietnam issue became much less important. Before that, during his first term, President Nixon always gave more weight to the foreign affairs and acted as if he were the Secretary of State (the role of Mr. William P. Rogers as Secretary of State was very obscure; President Nixon almost always discussed issues in foreign affairs only with National Security Advisor Kissinger). Now, confronting with the increasing seriousness of the internal affairs caused by the Watergate, President Nixon felt that he could no longer spend more time in foreign affairs, and decided, on September 22, 1973, to nominate Mr. Kissinger to replace Mr. Rogers as Secretary of State.

Right at the moment the Nixon administration was troubled with the political storm created by the Watergate crisis, another bad luck struck: Vice-president Spiro Agnew, former Governor of Maryland, was exposed by the media that he had been involved in a corruption scandal during his time in Maryland. At the trial, he pleaded guilty, and had to resign on October 10, 1973. President Nixon had to find someone to replace him and Mr. Gerald Ford, Republican House Minority Leader, was chosen. At the end of October 1973, the Watergate crisis entered a new period, much more serious when President Nixon decided to fire Special Prosecutor Archibald Cox because Mr. Cox demanded many times that the White House deliver the tapes recording the conversations of President Nixon with his important associates in his office. President Nixon ordered Attorney General Elliot Richardson to fire Cox, but Richardson refused, and resigned. Nixon had to fire Cox himself and dissolved the Office of the Special Prosecutor. His actions caused a huge political storm of protests from the American people and the U.S. Congress. President Nixon had to take a step back, he nominated a new Special Prosecutor, and announced that he would deliver the tapes.

Having witnessed the collapse of President's political prestige, the U.S. Congress re-tabled the bill for ***War Powers Act***, previously vetoed by President Nixon on October 24, 1973, and this time, on November 7, 1973, it succeeded in defeating Nixon's veto by an absolute majority vote in both chambers: 284/135 in the House, and 75/18 in the Senate. The Nixon administration had its hands tied vis-à-vis the direct use of the USAF special unit USSAG / 7AF (located in Thailand, as previously mentioned) to retaliate against North Vietnamese violations of the Paris Accords. Nixon and Kissinger, however, still had other means to stop North Vietnam's attack to conquer the South.

Right from the beginning of the Paris Peace Talks, Nixon and Kissinger already had in mind the two following plans: 1) Plan A, known as Equilibrium Strategy, was to provide all means of support to help the RVN fight back any attack from North Vietnam, and, on that basis, would proceed to negotiate a cease-fire, allowing the U.S. to withdraw its troops and to bring home all their prisoners; and, 2) Plan B, acting as an Insurance Policy, would be used when the U.S. could no longer support the RVN, including two parts: 1) Using the tripartite relationship US – Soviet Union – China in its effort to prevent North Vietnam from conquering the South; and, 2) In case of failure of Part 1, i.e., the collapse of South Vietnam could not be avoided, trying to minimize the damage to the U.S. prestige within the international community.[29]

Immediately after the U.S. Congress passed the Appropriations Act for FY 1973, cutting off all funds appropriated for Indochina at the end of June 1973, showing clearly that Plan A would not be feasible, Nixon and Kissinger moved into the implementation of Part 1 of Plan B. Kissinger had a meeting with Anatoly Dobrynin, Russian Ambassador in the U.S., to remind him of the "détente" policy between the U.S. and the Soviet Union, and let him know that the U.S. would withdraw from Cambodia, with the intention to encourage the Soviet Union making some influence on North Vietnam in the same "détente" direction. In November 1973, Kissinger went to Beijing to meet Zhou Enlai, Prime Minister of the People's Republic of China. Both actions, aimed at utilizing the tripartite relationship U.S. – Soviet Union – China, did not bring about any result. Nixon and Kissinger did not have any choice but turn to the implementation of Part 2 of Plan B, making any effort to show that the U.S. had done everything it could in helping the RVN. At the end of June 1973, Nixon agreed when Kissinger said to him:

"I think if we have to go down, the record must show that we did everything." [30]

Their effort to implement Part 2 of Plan B also had the secondary objective, which was to show the whole world that the responsibility of losing South Vietnam to the Communists did not belong to the U.S. Executive Branch (i.e., first the Nixon Administration, and then the Ford Administration) but did belong completely to the U.S. Congress.

And, later, history did show that that judgment was exactly accurate. The U.S. Congress did not hesitate but actively played the role of a traitor in its abandoning of the RVN, by first cutting off and then terminating military aids to the RVN while North Vietnam blatantly violated the Paris Accords, renewed the war, attacked South Vietnam with huge aids from the Soviet Union and China, leading to the extremely fast collapse of the RVN, even faster than North Vietnam's expectation. The U.S. Congress, under the absolute control of the Democratic Party, did the following cuts to the aids to the RVN:

• For FY 1974 (from 1-July-1973 to 30-June-1974): Nixon Administration proposed 1.6 billion dollars in aids to the RVN but Congress cut it to 1.126 billion dollars [31]

• For FY 1975 (from 1-July-1974 to 30-June-1975): Nixon Administration, on April 24, 1974, proposed 1.45 billion dollars in aids to the RVN, and Congress cut it to only 700 million dollars [32]

When Congress was still debating on the FY 1975, in June and July 1974, the Nixon administration submitted a report of the military situation in the RVN prepared by a joint U.S. – RVN committee. The report stated clearly that if the aid funding went down below the level of 1.126 billion dollars it would have serious effect on the spirit as well the fighting capability of the ARVN. During his testimony before Congress, in response to the question "what would happen if the ammunition level supplied to the ARVN were cut down because of the decrease of military aids"), Secretary of Defense James Schlesinger gave the following answer:

"The ability of the [South Vietnamese] ***government to survive would be severely compromised. As you recall, at the time of the cut off of the tactical air support last summer, there was some question whether the government could survive. It pulled itself together, but it is dependent upon its own forces and the munitions that are supplied to these forces. Without such munitions, it is hard to see how it could survive."*** [33]

In his monograph, ***The Final collapse***,[34] General Cao Văn Viên, Chair, General Staff of the ARVN, presented clearly and undeniably that the cut off of the aid funding to the RVN by the U.S. Congress led to the following serious consequences to the ARVN:

• The total appropriated funding of 700 million dollars included 46 million dollars for DAO [35]; therefore, in reality, the direct support for the ARVN was only 654 million dollars: [36]

Services	Minimum Requirement	Allotted	Percentage
Air Force	414	183	44%
Army	841	458	54%
Total	1,283	654	51%

• With the appropriated funding being seriously cut, the VNAF had to implement the following measures:

o Suspended more than 200 aircraft of all kinds (including all A-1 Skyraider fighters of Squadrons 514th, 518th in Biên Hòa, and Squadron 530th in Pleiku) [37]

o Ended the replacement program of jet fighters F-5A with F-5E

o Recalled all 400 pilot cadets, who were learning to fly helicopters and jet fighters in the U.S.

o Cancelled training programs of about 1,000 specialists for the AFVN, and transferred them to the Army

o Reduced the numbers of flights in training and support; the AFVN then provided only 50% of fire-support flights, and 58% of observation and reconnaissance flights o Reduced up to 70% transport flights of helicopters, seriously affecting the medical evacuations of wounded soldiers

o Reduced up to 50% transport flights by propeller-powered aircraft; among the 32 giant 4-engine Lockheed Hercules C-130 only 4-8 of them were operable on the daily basis

• Activities of the Navy were also reduced up to 50%; the River Groups were only 28% active, leading to a very serious reduction of the naval control over the rivers, especially in the IV Military Region

• The ARVN then had only 33% of its capacity of replacement of weapons; the maintenance and repair of weapons and equipment were seriously affected: [38]

Item	Percentage of requirement
o M-113 armored personnel carrier	80-85
o M-48 tank	75-80
o 105- and 155-mm. howitzers	90-95
o 175 mm. howitzers	60-75
o M-79 grenade launcher	80
o 2.5-ton truck	80-85
o 5-ton wreckers	70-75
o Signal equipment	90

• The ARVN also suffered from very serious shortages of fuels and ammunitions:

o Fuels: right from 1974, the fuel supply level was down 30% compared to 1973; with this level of funding cut, the ARVN would not have sufficient fuels for use starting from May 1975

o Ammunitions: among the 458 million dollars reserved for the Army, 239 million were for ammunitions, which would satisfy only 56% of the Army's real needs for ammunitions; according to the calculations by the General Staff of the ARVN, in February 1975, the ammunitions available in its depots would be enough for use only for: [39]

Munition	Balance on Hand (Days)
o 5.56 mm. rifle	31
o 40-mm. grenade	29
o 60-mm. mortar	27
o 81-mm. mortar	30
o 105-mm. howitzer	34
o 155-mm. howitzer	31
o Fragmentation grenade	25

During the ensuing period of eight months, the Nixon Administration had submitted a series of proposals for supplementary military aids for the RVN but all were voted down by the U.S. Congress. On August 9, 1974, after realizing that he would not have any chance avoiding impeachment, President Nixon resigned, and Vice-President Gerald Ford automatically became President. Within the background of the tense opposition between the Executive and Legislative Branches of the U.S. government, the political situation of the Executive Branch was getting much worse for two reasons: 1) Mr. Ford was the first U.S. President who was ***not elected by the American people***, i.e., he did not have any mandate from the people; 2) Personally, Mr. Ford did not have a large power base since he was only a Representative, not a Senator, or a former Governor. Therefore, he was very much inferior ranked before Congress. Moreover, after the elections in the Fall of 1974, the Democrats won more seats, and their majority became much more strengthened at 291/144 in the House, and 61/39 in the Senate.[40]

After the disastrous retreat from II Corps, and then with the serious situation in I Corps, at the end of March 1975, President Ford sent General Frederick C. Weyand, U.S. Army Chief of Staff, to Vietnam for a fact-finding mission. After his return to the U.S, on April 2, 1975, General Weyand submitted his report to President Ford, in which he proposed an immediate military funding of 722 million dollars to provide the ARVN with the following weapons and equipment:

- 744 big guns
- 446 armored vehicles
- 100,000 rifles
- 5,000 machine guns
- 11,000 grenade launchers
- 120,000 tons of bombs and ammunitions
- 2,000 transport vehicles

General Weyand believed that this armament would be sufficient to re-equip 8 infantry divisions and rangers, and 28 independent regiments created from the existing regional forces, to replace the losses in I and II Cors.[41] President Ford forwarded this proposal to Congress. On April 17, 1975, the Senate Armed Forces Committee voted to reject this proposal completely.[42]

Concluding Remarks

About two weeks later, on April 30, 1975, the ARVN surrendered and the RVN ceased to exist. The U.S. has gone through the ***Vietnam Syndrome*** for many decades. The U.S. Congress (93rd for 1973-75, and 94th for 1975-77), under the absolute control of the Democratic Party, was totally responsible for the betrayal of the RVN, a U.S. ally for years. ***The Democrats during these two sessions of the U.S. Congress have acted unscrupulously, totally ignoring the sacrifices of 55,000 U.S. and 200,000 South Vietnamese soldiers who had fallen during the Vietnam War.*** President Ford, in a press conference after he submitted his request to the U.S. Congress for urgent aid for the RVN in April 1975, reminded of the sacrifices of 55,000 U.S. soldiers, and concluded with the following statement:

"I think it is up to the American people to pass judgment on who was at fault and where the blame may rest."[43]

EPILOGUE

All military textbooks, from the ancient time to the present day, recognize that in wars winning or losing should be considered as a fact of life and acceptable by the military. In addition, our ancestors have said: ***"We do not discuss heroism based on winning or losing."*** This judgment is very accurate when we evaluate the defeat of the ARVN, an undeniable historical truth. But at the same time, we also have another undeniable historical truth: ***The ARVN was a strong, brave, heroic army, with uncountable glorious victories but, because of its ally's betrayal, abandoning, and stripping of its fighting means, it was left for dead, defeated, and surrendered. It was then humiliated by its underserving enemy's despicable revenge, with the cemetery of its fallen comrades-in-arms being immorally mutilated.*** The ARVN was also an army with a number of generals, who, upon being defeated, committed suicides, choosing the death with their soldiers rather than surrendering to the enemy. The ARVN was also an army respected by the people, who always remember its sacrifices for the Fatherland through the following famous poem:

An Lộc Địa Sử Ghi Chiến Tích
Biệt Cách Dù Vị Quốc Vong Thân

Meaning:

History Recorded Victory in the Land of An Lộc
Commando Airborne Soldiers Fell for Fatherland

Due to its undeserved death, the ARVN deserves to be recognized as a ***Heroic-Ready-To-Sacrifice-For-The-Fatherland Army.***

This book was written with the hope that the young Vietnamese, inside and outside of Vietnam, will have a document containing important, and reliable information, to help them recognize the following historical truth: ***The ARVN Was a Heroic Army Unjustly Abandoned and Left for Dead.***

NOTES

Chapter One

1. Quân sử Không Quân Việt Nam Cộng Hòa (History of the Air Force of the Republic of Vietnam). Melbourne: Lý Tưởng Úc Châu (Ideals, Australia), 2005. General information of the history of the different branches of the AFVN (observation, fighters, helicopters, etc.), as well as detailed information of various units (divisions, wings, squadrons, etc.; dates of creation, names and ranks of commanding officers, etc.) have been taken from this document.

2. Trần Ngọc Thống, Hồ Đắc Huân, Lê Đình Thụy. ***Lược sử Quân Lực Việt Nam Cộng Hòa*** (Brief history of the Armed Forces of the Republic of Vietnam). San Jose, Calif.: Hương Quê, 2011. pp. 391-392.

3. Nguyễn Hữu Thiện. ***Ngành khu trục trong Không Lực Việt Nam Cộng Hòa*** (The Fighter branch in the Air Force of the Republic of Vietnam), online document, accessible in full-text at this URL: ***http://hoiquanphidung.com/content.php?4149-Ng%C3%A0nh-Khu-Tr%E1%BB%A5c-trong-Kh%C3%B4ng-L%E1%BB%B1c-Vi%E1%BB%87t-Nam-C%E1%BB%99ng-H%C3%B2a.*** This document stated that upon his return to Vietnam after his graduation in 1957, joining the Fighter and Observation Squadron, predecessor of the 514th Fighter Squadron, Mr. Nguyễn Đức Khánh was only a Warrant Officer.

4. Trần Mạnh Khôi. ***Sơ lược về sự thành lập các đơn vị Không Quân*** (A Summary of the creation of the Vietnamese air force units), online document, accessible in full-text at this URL: http://hoiquanphidung.com/showthread.php?9293-S%C6%A1-l%C6%B0%E1%BB%A3c-v%E1%BB%81-s%E1%BB%B1-th%C3%A0nh-l%E1%BA%ADp-c%C3%A1c-%C4%91%C6%A1n-v%E1%BB%8B-Kh%C3%B4ng-Qu%C3%A2n This document provides numerous rare and precious details on the dates of creation as well as the names and ranks of the commanding officers of various Vietnamese air force units, and was used extensively in this article.

5. Trần Ngọc Thống, Hồ Đắc Huân, Lê Đình Thụy, op. cit., p. 529. According to this document, Mr. Phạm Long Sửu was born in November 1925, graduated from the pilot training program at the Nha Trang Air Force Training Center, and his highest rank was Colonel. After April 30, 1975, he was incarcerated in re-education camps in Vietnam for 13 years. After being admitted to the U.S. in the H.O. Program, he settled down in the city of Glandale, California, and passed away in 2011 at the age of 86.

6. Nguyễn Hữu Thiện. ***Ngành khu trục trong Không Lực Việt Nam Cộng Hòa*** (The Fighter branch in the Air Force of the Republic of Vietnam), op. cit.

This document provides additional information on Mr. Phạm Long Sửu, as follows: he graduated top of his class of observation pilots at the Nha Trang Air Force Training Center, he was then sent to France to attend training courses for fighter and jet fighter pilot at the Air Academy of Salon-de-Provence, and Mecknès, in Morocco, North Africa. Later, at the rank of Captain, he was made the first Commander of the Second Squadron of Fighter Aircrafts headquartered in Nha Trang (this squadron was later relocated in Đà Nẵng, and renamed 516 Squadron or Squadron of Flying Tigers). This document will be used extensively in this article in providing data on other squadrons of fighter aircrafts.

7. Nguyễn Hữu Thiện. *"Phiên hiệu của các Phi Đoàn Trong KQVN"* (Registration numbers of the squadrons in the AFVN), in ***Quân sử Không Quân Việt Nam Cộng Hòa*** (History of the Air Force of the Republic of Vietnam), op. cit., pp. 352-353.

8. Võ Ý. ***Ngành quan sát không lực VNCH*** (The Observation branch of the Air Force of the Republic of Vietnam), online document, accessible in full-text at this URL: https://hoiquanphidung.com/showthread.php?9282-Ng%C3%A0nh-Quan-S%C3%A1t-Kh%C3%B4ng-L%E1%BB%B1c-VNCH&s=cfaed16e0f4ddef9f7e5c62fb3a85ee2 This document, authored by the former Commander of the North Star Observation Squadron 118, provides adequate information on the observation branch of the AFVN, based on reference materials as well as contributions from other senior officers of the ARVN. It is used extensively in this article for information regarding the observation squadrons.

9. Cessna O-1 Bird Dog, online document, accessible in full-text at this URL: https://en.wikipedia.org/wiki/Cessna_O-1_Bird_Dog

10. Cessna 185 Skywagon, online document, accessible in full-text at this URL: https://www.skybrary.aero/index.php/C185

11. Phạm Văn Cần. ***Phi Đoàn 427 – C-7A- Caribou: không vận chiến thuật*** (Squadron 427 – C-7A – Caribou: tactical air transport), online document, accessible in full-text at this URL: http://hoiquanphidung.com/showthread.php?9466-Phi-%C4%91o%C3%A0n-427-c-7a-caribou

12. De Havilland Canada DHC-4 / C-7 Caribou, online document, accessible in full-text at this URL: http://nhungdoicanh.blogspot.ca/2008/08/de-havilland-canada-dhc-4-c-7-caribou.html

13. Đỗ Văn Hiếu. ***Ngành trực thăng trong Không Lực Việt Nam Cộng Hòa*** (The Helicopter branch in the Air Force of the Republic of Vietnam), online document, accessible in full-text at this URL: http://hoiquanphidung.com/showthread.php?9287-Ng%C3%A0nh-Tr%E1%BB%B1c-Th%C4%83ng-Trong-Kh%C3%B4ng-L%E1%BB%B1c-Vi%E1%BB%87t-Nam-C%E1%B-

B%99ng-H%C3%B2a This document will be used extensively in this article in describing the helicopter squadrons.

14. Sikorsky H-34, online document, accessible in full-text at this URL: https://en.wikipedia.org/wiki/Sikorsky_H-34#Specifications_.28H-34_Choctaw.29

15. Boeing CH-47 Chinook, online document, accessible in full-text at this URL: http://vietnamwar.wikia.com/wiki/Boeing_CH-47_Chinook

16. Frankum, Ronald B. ***Historical dictionary of the War in Vietnam***. Lanham, Md.: ScarecrowPress, 2011. pp. 196-200.

17. Nguyễn Kỳ Phong. ***Từ điển Chiến Tranh Việt Nam, 1954-1975*** (Dictionary of the Vietnam War, 1954-1975). Garden Grove, Calif.: Tự Lực, 2009. pp. 421-423

18. Bell UH-1 Iroquois, online document, accessible in full-text at this URL: https://en.wikipedia.org/wiki/Bell_UH-1_Iroquois

19. Cessna A-37 Dragonfly, online document, accessible in full-text at this URL: https://en.wikipedia.org/wiki/Cessna_A-37_Dragonfly

20. Northrop F-5A Freedom Fighter, online document, accessible in full-text at this URL: http://www.wmof.com/f5a.htm

21. Trần Ngọc Thống, Hồ Đắc Huân, Lê Đình Thụy, op. cit., ***p***. 403.

22. Trần Ngọc Thống, Hồ Đắc Huân, Lê Đình Thụy, op. cit., pp. 179-180.

23. Douglas AC-47 Spooky, online document, accessible in full-text at this URL: https://en.wikipedia.org/wiki/Douglas_AC-47_Spooky#Specifications_.28AC-47.29

24. Bùi Tá Khánh. *"Chuyến bay tử thần vào Đồi 31 Hạ Lào"* (The Deadly flight into Hill 31 in Lower Laos), in ***Quân sử Không Quân Việt Nam Cộng Hòa*** (History of the Air Force of the Republic of Vietnam), op. cit., pp. 281-284.

25. Trần Ngọc Thống, Hồ Đắc Huân, Lê Đình Thụy, op. cit., ***p***. 450.

26. Trần Ngọc Thống, Hồ Đắc Huân, Lê Đình Thụy, op. cit., pp. 363-365.

27. Douglas A-1 Skyraider, online document, accessible in full-text at this URL: https://en.wikipedia.org/wiki/Douglas_A-1_Skyraider#Specifications_.28A-1H_Skyraider.29

28. Nguyễn Văn Ức. ***Phi Đoàn 221 trực thăng*** (Helicopter Squadron 221), online document, accessible in full-text at this URL: http://hoiquanphidung.com/showthread.php?18598-Phi-%C4%90o%C3%A0n-221-Tr%E1%BB%B1c-Th%C4%83ng

29. Trần Ngọc Thống, Hồ Đắc Huân, Lê Đình Thụy, op. cit., pp. 247-248.

30. Trần Ngọc Thống, Hồ Đắc Huân, Lê Đình Thụy, op. cit., pp. 428-429.

31. Trần Phước Hội. ***Thành lập Phi Đoàn 217: giai đoạn H-34*** (Creation of Squadron 217: H-34 phase), online document, accessible in full-text at this URL: http://hoiquanphidung.com/showthread.php?9448-Th%C3%A0nh-l%E1%BA%ADp-Phi-%C4%90o%C3%A0n-217

32. Cố Trung Tá Phạm Văn Trung PĐT PĐ 249 (Late Lieutenant-Colonel Pham Văn Trung, Commander of Squadron 249), online document, accessible in full-text at this URL: https://hoiquanphidung.com/showthread.php?2061

33. Trần Ngọc Thống, Hồ Đắc Huân, Lê Đình Thụy, op. cit., pp. 449.

34. Thành-Giang. ***Hoa không gian 1: những chị Hằng của Phi Đoàn 314*** (Space flowers 1: the pretty ladies of Squadron 314), online document, accessible in full-text at this URL: https://hoiquanphidung.com/showthread.php?21896-Hoa-Kh%C3%B4ng-Gian-1-Nh%E1%BB%AFng-ch%E1%BB%8B-H%E1%BA%B1ng-c%E1%BB%A7a-Phi-%C4%90o%C3%A0n-314

35. Thành-Giang. ***Phi Đoàn 431 Phượng Long*** (Squadron 431 Phoenix Dragon), online document, accessible in full-text at this URL: http://lhccshtd.org/LHCCSHTD_SH/kq/thanhgiang/2015/pd431/LSCCSHTD_SH_kq_thanhgiang_2015_pd431_hashPD431PhuongLong_2015AUG09.htm

36. Lâm Vĩnh Thế. ***Tình báo trong Chiến Tranh Việt Nam*** (Intelligence in the Vietnam War), online document, accessible in full-text at this URL: https://sites.google.com/site/namkyluctinhorg/tac-gia-tac-pham/i-j-k-l-m/lam-vinh-the/tinh-bao-trong-chien-tranh-viet-nam

37. Phi Đoàn 716 Hoàng Long và Phi Đoàn 718 Thiên Long (Squadron 716 Hoàng Long (Royal Dragon) and Squadron 718 Thiên Long (Divine Dragon)), online document, accessible in full-text at this URL: http://phong7bttm.blogspot.ca/2016/02/phi-oan-thien-long-718.html

38. Douglas EC-47D Dakota, online document, accessible in full-text at this URL: http://dc3dakotahistory.org/c-47dakota-military/ec-47/

39. Quân sử Không Quân Việt Nam Cộng Hòa (History of the Air Force of the Republic of Vietnam), op. cit., p. 148.

40. Fairchild C-119 Flying Boxcar, online document, accessible in full-text at this URL: https://en.wikipedia.org/wiki/Fairchild_C-119_Flying_Boxcar#Specifications_.28C-119C.29

41. Fairchild C-123 Provider, online document, accessible in full-text at this URL: https://en.wikipedia.org/wiki/Fairchild_C-123_Provider

42. Lockheed C-130 Hercules, online document, accessible in full-text at this URL: https://en.wikipedia.org/wiki/Lockheed_C-130_Hercules#Specifications_.28C-130H.29

43. Phi hành đoàn cuối cùng của Không Quân VNCH hy sinh cho Tổ Quốc (Sacrifice for the Fatherland of the last aircrew of the Air Force of the Republic of Vietnam), online document, accessible in full-text at this URL: https://thntsaigon.forumvi.com/t175-topic

44. Trần Lý. Những phi vụ hành quân cuối cùng của Không Quân VNCH trên không phận Sàigòn (The Last sorties of the AFVN above Saigon area), online document, accessible in full-text at this URL: http://www.luanhoan.net/Bai%20Moi%20Trong%20Ngay/html/bm%2015-6-24.htm

45. Fairchild AC-119, online document, accessible in full-text at this URL: https://aerocorner.com/aircraft/fairchild-ac-119/#aircraft-specifications

46. Trần Lý, op. cit.

47. Trần Ngọc Thống, Hồ Đắc Huân, Lê Đình Thụy, op. cit., pp. 425-427.

48. Phạm Ngọc Sang. *"Trận Phan Rang: hồi ức của Chuẩn Tướng Phạm Ngọc Sang,"* (The Battle of Phan Rang: memoir of Brigadier-General Phạm Ngọc Sang), in ***Quân sử Không Quân Việt Nam Cộng Hòa*** (History of the Air Force of the Republic of Vietnam), *op. cit.,* p. 297. The people referred to in this article were: 1) Colonel Lương was Colonel Nguyễn Thu Lương, Commander of the 2nd Airborne Brigade; 2) Lt.-General Nghi was Lieutenant-General Nguyễn Vĩnh Nghi, former Commander of IV Corps, and at that point in time, Commander of the Advanced Headquarter of III Corps; Mr. Lewis was an American, a Communications Specialist sent by the US Embassy in Saigon to maintain communication with the Embassy.

Chapter Two

1. Trần Ngọc Thống, Hồ Đắc Huân, Lê Đình Thụy, op. cit., pp. 203-204.

2. ***Những Giai Thoại Sạch của Tướng Thắng*** (Anecdotes of General Thắng's incorruptibility), online document, accessible in full-text at this URL: http://www.generalhieu.com/ndthang-u.htm

3. Clarke, Jeffrey J. ***United States Army in Vietnam: advice and support: the final years, 1965-1973***. Washington, D.C.: U.S. Army Center of Military History, 1988, p. 256.

4. *"CIA report on the Situation in South Vietnam as of 10/24/66,"* CIA classified document, dated 24-Oct-1966, declassified 4-Mar-1994, 15 pages, accessible in full-text in the database called ***Declassified Documents Reference System (DDRS)***, pp. II-1 và II-2.

5. *"CIA report on the Siituation in South Vietnam covering period 10/31-11/6/66,"* CIA classified document, dated 7-Nov-1966, declassified 16-Dec-1993, 24 pages, accessible in full-text in ***DDRS***, pp. II-1 và II-2.

6. Lâm Vĩnh Thế. ***Republic of Vietnam, 1963-1967: Years of Political Chaos.*** Hamilton, Ont.: Hoài Việt, 2010, p. 158.

7. Trần Ngọc Thống, Hồ Đắc Huân, Lê Đình Thụy, op. cit., pp. 127-128.

8. ***Nguyễn Đức Thắng, Phan Trọng Chinh, Lê Minh Đảo, Lý Tòng Bá***, online document, accessible in full-text at this URL: http://vanghe.blogspot.ca/2011/09/nguyen-uc-thang-phan-trong-chinh-le.html

9. ***Tưởng nhớ Trung Tướng Phan Trọng Chinh*** (In remembrance of Lieutenant-General Phan Trọng Chinh), online document, accessible in full-text at this URL: http://vietnamcuongthinh.blogspot.ca/2015/03/tuong-nho-trung-tuong-phan-trong-chinh.html

10. *Intelligence report on the situation in South Vietnam," CIA classified document, dated 19-Dec-1966, declassified 16-June-1998, accessible in full-text in **DDRS**, p. II-4.*

11. Ahern, Thomas L., Jr. ***CIA and the generals: covert support to military government in South Vietnam.*** Langley, Va.: CIA, 2009, p. 113.

12. Trần Ngọc Thống, Hồ Đắc Huân, Lê Đình Thụy, op. cit., pp. 199-202.

13. Nguyễn Mậu Quý. ***Trung Tướng Nguyễn Viết Thanh*** (Lieutenant-General Nguyễn Viết Thanh), online document, accessible in full-text at this URL: http://www.generalhieu.com/nvthanh-u.htm

14. Fulghum, David, Terrence Maitland. ***South Vietnam on trial: mid-1970 to 1972***. Boston: Boston Publishing Company, 1984, (The Vietnam experience), Section: ***Two fighting generals***, pp. 60-61

15. Trần Ngọc Thống, Hồ Đắc Hu, Lê Đình Thụy, op. cit., pp. *235-237.*

16. Lê Xuân Nhuận. ***Biến-loạn Miền Trung: hồi ký*** (Revolt in Central Vietnam: memoir). Alameda, Calif.: Xây Dựng (Construction Publishing House), 2012, p. 285.

17. Minh Dũng. ***Trung Tướng Ngô Quang Trưởng: Tư Lệnh Quân Đoàn I và Vùng I Chiến Thuật*** (Lieutenant-General Ngô Quang Trưởng: Commander of I Corps and Miltary Region I), online document, accessible in full-text at this URL: *http://www.luanhoan.net/danang/htm/danang10_12.htm*

18. ***Trận Hắc Dịch: ngày 9 & 10/2/1965*** (The Battle of Hắc Dịch: 9 & 10 February 1965), online document, accessible in full-text at this URL: http://nhaydu.com/index_83hg_files/left_files/T-Chien/1965-TranHacDich.pdf

19. Ngô Quang Trưởng. ***The Easter Offensive of 1972***. Washington, D.C.: U.S. Army Center of Military History, 1980, (*Indochina Monographs),* pp. 15-77.

20. Giang Văn Nhân. *"Tiểu đoàn 3/TQLC dựng cờ trên Cổ Thành Quảng Trị 15/9/1972,"* (The 3rd Marines Battalion raised the flad on the Quảng Trị Citadel

on September 15, 1972) in ***Tuyển tập 2: hai mươi mốt năm chiến trận của binh chủng Thủy Quân Lục Chiến Việt Nam (1954-1975)*** (Selected Works no. 2: twenty-one years of fighting of the Vietnamese Marines Corps (1954-1975)). Santa Ana, Calif.: Tổng hội TQLC/VN tại Hoa Kỳ (General Association of the Vietnamese Marines Corps, 2005, pp. 438-450.

21. James H. Willbanks. ***"The most brilliant commander: Ngo Quang Truong"***, online document, accessible in full-text at this URL: http://www.historynet.com/the-most-brilliant-commander-ngo-quang-truong.htm

22. Hà Giang. ***Cố Trung Tướng VNCH Ngô Quang Trưởng đã về nhà*** (The Late Lieutenant-General Ngô Quang Trưởng of the RVN has come home), online document, accessible in full-text at this URL: http://aihuubienhoa.com/a1532/co-trung-tuong-vnch-ngo-quang-truong-da-ve-nha-ha-giang

Chapter Three

1. Trần Ngọc Thống, Hồ Đắc Huân, Lê Đình Thụy, op. cit., pp. 175-176. Lieutenant-General Nguyễn Văn Minh was born in February 1929 in Sài Gòn, and graduated from the 4th Class of the Đà Lạt Inter-Arm Military Academy as a Second-Lieutenant on December 1, 1951. He was nicknamed *"Minh Guitar"* because he had played music in Sài Gòn night-clubs before his military service. (The ARVN has a total of 4 generals named Minh with the following nicknames: 1) General Dương Văn Minh was "Big Minh" because of his great body size; 2) Lieutenant-General Trần Văn Minh was "Little Minh"; 3) The second and younger Lieutenant-General Trần Văn Minh, Commander of the Air Force, was *"Minh Fuck"* because of his bad habit of swearing; and 4) Lieutenant-General Nguyễn Văn Minh was *"Minh Guitar."*) Under the First Republic, he usually held administrative functions, such as District Chief of Đức Hòa (1956-1958), Province Chief of An Giang (1959-1963). On March 21, 1965, as a Colonel, he was appointed Commander of the 21st Infantry Division; on November 1 of the same year, he was promoted to Brigadier-General. In 1968, as a Major-General he was appointed Commander of the Special District of the Capital City of Sài Gòn. On February 23, 1971, he was appointed Commander of III Corps, replacing General Đỗ Cao Trí killed in a helicopter accident. In general, he has been a political appointee for most of his military service. He was, definitely, not a general with a lot of combat experience.

2. Trần Ngọc Thống, Hồ Đắc Huân, Lê Đình Thụy, op. cit., pp. 384-388. Brigadier-General Lê Văn Hưng, born on March 27, 1933 in Hóc Môn, Province of Gia Định, graduated from the 5th Class of the Thủ Đức Reserve Officer Training School as a Second-Lieutenant on February 1, 1955. Unlike Lieutenant-General Nguyễn Văn Minh, he was a combat officer, and had assumed many combat positions like Platoon Commander, Company Commander, Battalion Commander, and had been specially promoted several times at the

battlefields. On June 14, 1971, as a Colonel, he was appointed Commander of the 5th Infantry Division. And then on the occasion of the 17th anniversary of the Division, March 9, 1972, he was promoted to Brigadier-General and his star was pinned by President Nguyễn Văn Thiệu (the President himself was also a former Commander of the Division). On April 30, 1975, as Deputy-Commander of the IV Corps, he killed himself with his handgun at 8:45 pm at his residence in Cần Thơ.

3. Trần Ngọc Thống, Hồ Đắc Huân, Lê Đình Thụy, op. cit., pp. 463-465. Brigadier-General Lê Nguyên Vỹ, born on August 22, 1933 in the Province of Sơn Tây, North Vietnam, graduated from the 2nd Class (Class of Lê Lợi) of the Huế Local Military School as a Warrant Officer on October 1, 1951. He began his military service in the Airborne, was transferred to the Infantry, and successively held positions as Battalion Commander and then 8th Regiment Commander of the 5th Infantry Division. From mid-1971, he was Deputy-Commander of the 5th Infantry Division. On November 7, 1973, he was appointed Commander of the 5th Infantry Division, and was promoted to Brigadier-General on November 1, 1974. In the afternoon of April 30, 1975, he killed himself with his handgun at the Headquarters of the 5th Infanty Division.

4. Trần Ngọc Thống, Hồ Đắc Huân, Lê Đình Thụy, op. cit., pp. 454-456. Brigadier-General Mạch Văn Trường, born in March 1936 in the Province of Bạc Liêu, graduated from the 12th Class of the Đà Lạt Inter-Arm Military Academy as a Second-Lieutenant on December 2, 1956. On March 1, 1972, as Commander of the 8th Regiment of the 5th Infantry Division, he was promoted to Colonel. In November 1974, he was appointed Commander of the 21st Infantry Division. On April 26, 1975 he was promoted to Brigadier-General (being the last high-ranking ARVN officer to be promoted to this rank). After 1975, he was incarcerated in a re-education camp in North Vietnam for 17 years. After his release from the camp, he was allowed to go to the U.S. in the HO Program and lived in Houston, Texas. He passed away on June 30, 2021 at the age of 85.

5. Trần Ngọc Thống, Hồ Đắc Huân, Lê Đình Thụy, op. cit., pp. 417-419. Brigadier-General Trần Văn Nhựt, born on December 17, 1935 in Sài Gòn, graduated from the 10th Class of the Đà Lạt Inter-Arm Military Academy as a Second-Lieutenant on June 1, 1954. He had been Commander of the 1st Marines Battalion, Deputy-Commander and Chief of Staff of the Marines Brigade, and Commander of the 48th Regiment of the 18th Infantry Division before he was appointed Province Chief and Sub-District Chief of the Province of Binh Long in January 1970. On July 7, 1972, after the Battle of An Lo65cf, he was promoted to Colonel. On August 27, 1972, he was appointed Commander of the 2nd Infantry Division, and on November 1, 1972, he was promoted to Brigadier-General. After 1975, he lived in Houston, Texas, USA.

6. Mạch Văn Trường. ***Trung Đoàn 8 Bộ Binh và trận chiến An Lộc (Mùa Hè 1972): hồi ký của Chuẩn Tướng Mạch Văn Trường*** (The 8 th Infanty Regiment and the Battle of An Lộc: memoir of Brigadier-General Mạch Văn Trường), online document, accessible in full-text at this URL: https://dong-songcu.wordpress.com/2021/07/04/trung-doan-8-bo-binh-va-tran-chien-an-loc-mua-he-1972-hoi-ky-cua-chuan-tuong-mach-van-truong/

7. Willbanks, James H. ***The Battle of An Loc***. Bloomington: Indiana University Press, 2005. The author wrote on p. 17: *"A subset of Giap's strategy called for a Communist Provisional Revolutionary Government to be established in An Loc as a precursor for the assault on Saigon."*

8. Andradé, Dale. ***America's last Vietnam battle: halting Hanoi's 1972 Easter Offensive***. Lawrence: University Press of Kansas, 2001. On p. 344, the author wrote: *"Beginning in February 1972, U.S. intelligence stressed that Tay Ninh was the most likely target of a North Vietnamese offensive on the region."*

9. Mạch Văn Trường, op.cit.

10. Willbanks, op. cit., pp. 44-45.

11. Willbanks, op. cit., pp. 55-61.

12. Mạch Văn Trường, op. cit.

13. Mạch Văn Trường, op. cit. The two above-mentioned books by the American authors both recorded that Colonel Nguyễn Công Vĩnh surrendered to the enemy. This should have been based on recounts of the U.S. Advisors, who have survived after the Battle of An Lộc (they were held as prisoners-of-war and returned to the U.S. after the Paris Accords were signed on January 27, 1973). But this is hard to believe because of the following reasons: 1) Colonel Nguyễn Công Vĩnh was also returned to the ARVN after the signing of the Paris Accords; 2) After a very thorough investigation by the Military Security Services, he was reinstalled to his former rank and appointed Commander of the Military Affairs Agency in Sài Gòn until April 30, 1975; 3) After 1975, he was incarcerated in re-education camps until 1988; 4) He was allowed to go to the US in the HO Program in 1993, lived in Southern California until he passed away on February 23, 2017 at the age of 90. More information is available online at this URL: https://www.nguoi-viet.com/tuong-nho/tuong-nho-co-dai-ta-nguyen-cong-vinh/

14. Willbanks, op. cit., p. 54.

15. Nguyễn Quốc Khuê. ***Liên Đoàn 3 Biệt Động Quân với trận chiến An Lộc – Bình Long*** (The 3rd Rangers Brigade with the Battle of An Lộc – Bình Long), online document, accessible in full-text at this URL: https://www.nguoi-viet.com/cuu-chien-binh/ccb-t4-lien-doan-3-biet-dong-quan-voi-tran-

chien-loc-binh-long/ The 3rd Rangers Brigade was under the command of Lieutenant-Colonel Nguyễn Văn Biết, and included 3 battalions: 1) The 31st Battalion with Major Trương Khánh as Commander; 2) The 36th Battalion with Major Tống Viết Lạc as Commander; and, 3) The 52nd Battalion with Major Lê Quý Dậu as Commander.

16. Ngô Quang Trưởng. ***The Easter Offensive of 1972***. Washington, D.C.: US Army Center of Military History, 1979, (Indochina monograhs), pp.116-117.

17. Mạch Văn Trường, op. cit..

18. Willbanks, op. cit., p. 79.

19. Nguyễn Văn Dướng. ***Tướng Lê Văn Hưng tuyên bố "tử thủ An Lộc,"*** (General Lê Văn Hưng announced: "fight to the death to keep An Lộc"), online document, accessible in full-text at this URL: https://dongsongcu.wordpress.com/2017/09/06/tuong-le-van-hung-tuyen-bo-tủ-thủ-an-loc/

20. Vũ Văn Bảo. ***QLVNCH: Phi Đoàn 237 CH-47A Chinook*** (ARVN: Squadron 237 CH-47A Chinook), online document, accessible in full-text at this URL: http://chauxuannguyen.org/2016/03/18/qlvnch-phi-doan-237-ch-47a-chinook-vu-van-bao/

21. Nguyễn Văn Dướng. ***Inside An Lộc: the battle to save Saigon, April – May 1972*** / Van Nguyen Duong with Nghia M. Vo. Jefferson, N.C.: McFarland, 2016, pp. 98-99. During the time of the Battle of An Lộc, the principal author, Nguyễn Văn Dướng, was a Major, J-2 (Intelligence Chief) of the 5th Infantry Division. When the battle was over, he was promoted to Lieutenant-Colonel. He had been also a classmate of General Hưng of Class 5 at the Thủ Đức Reserve Officer Training School.

22. ***Kỷ niệm 40 năm chiến thắng "Hà Nội – Điện Biên Phủ trên không": những điều chưa biết về "pháo đài chiến lược" B-52 của Không Quân Mỹ*** (40th Anniversary of the Victory "Hà Nội – Điện Biên Phủ in the air": unknown stories about the "stratofortress" B-52 of the American air force), online document, accessible in full-text at this URL: https://thethaovanhoa.vn/the-gioi/nhung-dieu-chua-biet-ve-phao-dai-chien-luoc-b52-cua-khong-quan-my-n20121218112605556.htm

23. Andradé, op. cit., pp. 396-397.

24. Trần Ngọc Thống, Hồ Đắc Huân, Lê Đình Thụy, op. cit., pp. 404-407. Brigadier-General Lê Quang Lưỡng, born in August 1932 in Bình Dương Province, graduated as a Second-Lieutenant from the 4th Class of the Thủ Đức Reserve Officer Training School. He volunteered to join the Airborne, and had been appointed commanders of platoon, company, battalion, and brigade, before he was promoted to Brigadier-General and became Commander of the Airborne Division on November 1, 1972. After April 1975, he

lived in Bakerfield, California, USA. He passed away on September 21, 2005 at the age of 73.

25. Nguyễn Văn Dưỡng, op. cit., pp. 107-111.

26. Nguyễn Văn Ức. ***Phi Đoàn 221 trực thăng*** (The Helicopter Squadron 221), online document, accessible in full-text at this URL: https://hung-viet.org/a21141/phi-doan-221-truc-thang Major Nguyễn Văn Ức was later promoted to Lieutenant-Colonel and was appointed Deputy-Commander of Tactical Air Wing 64, Air Division 4 in Cần Thơ.

27. Vương Hồng Anh. ***Lữ Đoàn 1 Nhảy Dù ở Bình Long 1972*** (The 1st Airborne Brigade in Bình Long 1972), online document, accessible in full-text at this URL: https://ongvove.wordpress.com/2012/03/05/l%E1%BB%AF-do-an-1-nh%E1%BA%A3y-du-%E1%BB%9F-binh-long-1972/

28. Đại Tá Phan Văn Huấn / Liên Đoàn 81 Biệt Cách Nhảy Dù (Colonel Phan Văn Huấn / 81st Commando Airborne Brigade), online document, accessible in full-text at this URL: http://conhungnguoianh.blogspot.ca/2012/03/ai-ta-phan-van-huan-lien-oan-81-biet.html

29. Ngô Quang Trưởng, op. cit., p. 123.

30. Vương Hồng Anh, op. cit.

31. Willbanks, op. cit., p. 99.

32. Mạch Văn Trường, op. cit.

33. Willbanks, op. cit., p. 98.

34. Nguyễn Quốc Khuê, op.cit.

35. Willbanks, op. cit., p. 104.

36. Mạch Văn Trường, op. cit..

37. Andradé, op. cit., p. 432.

38. Mạch Văn Trường, op. cit.

39. Andradé, op. cit., p. 432.

40. Andradé, op. cit., p. 434.

41. Lê Đắc Lực. ***An Lộc Địa*** (The Land of An Lộc), online document, accessible in full-text at this URL: https://dongsongcu.wordpress.com/2016/08/12/an-loc-dia/

42.Trần Ngọc Thống, Hồ Đắc Huân, Lê Đình Thụy, op. cit., pp. 181-182. Lieutenant-General Nguyễn Vĩnh Nghi, born in October 1932 in Gia Định Province, graduated from the 5th Class of the Đà Lạt Inter-Arm Military Academy as a Second-Lieutenant on April 24, 1952. He was promoted to Major on

January 1, 1955, and was appointed Chief of Staff of the 21st Infantry Division. He was promoted to Colonel in February 1966, and on March 16, 1968 he was appointed Commander of the 21st Infantry Division. He was promoted to Brigadier-General on September 16, 1969 and Major-General on September 16, 1970. On May 3, 1972, he passed the command of the 21st Infantry Division to Brigadier-General Hồ Trung Hậu, Deputy-Commander of the Airborne Division, and on the next day, May 4, 1974, he was appointed Commander of IV Corps, replacing Lieutenant-General Ngô Quang Trưởng, who had just left for Đà Nẵng to assume the command of I Corps. On March 1, 1974, he was promoted to Lieutenant-General. On November 1, 1974, he passed the command of IV Corps to Major-General Nguyễn Khoa Nam, and assumed the command of the Thủ Đức Reserve Officer Training School. At the end of March 1975, he was appointed Deputy-Commander and Commander of the Advanced Headquarters of III Corps in Phan Rang. He was captured by the Communists there in the evening of April 16, 1975 together with Brigadier-General Pham Ngọc Sang, Commander of Air Division 6. He was incarcerated in re-education camps until 1988. After his release from the camp, he went to the U.S. in the H.O Program in 1992, and has lived there since then.

43. Willbanks, op. cit., p. 134.

44. ***Hồ Ngọc Cẩn (đại tá)*** (Hồ Ngọc Cẩn (Colonel)), online document, accessible in full-text at this URL: https://vi.wikipedia.org/wiki/H%E1%BB%93_Ng%E1%BB%8Dc_C%E1%BA%A9n_(%C4%91%E1%BA%A1i_t%C3%A1)#Qu%C3%A2n_l%E1%BB%B1c_Vi%E1%BB%87t_Nam_C%E1%BB%99ng_h%C3%B2a Colonel Hồ Ngọc Cẩn was one among a very small number of high-ranking officers of the ARVN, who rose through the ranks from a private to a colonel. His last position was Province Chief of Chương Thiện Province. After April 30, 1975, he still kept fighting until he was captured by the Communists. He was executed by a firing squad on August 14, 1975 in the Cần Thơ stadium. He was then only 37 years old.

45. ***Tiểu Đoàn 6 Nhảy Dù*** (The 6th Airborne Battalion), online document, accessible in full-text at this URL: http://nhaydu.com/index_83hg_files/main_files/TieuSu-TDND/TS-TD6ND.pdf

46. Willbanks, op. cit., p. 142.

47. Lê Đắc Lực, op. cit.

Chapter Four

1. Lieutenant-General Ngô Quang Trưởng was the best general of the ARVN. Born on December 13, 1929 in Bến Tre Province (later called Kiến Hòa Province), he graduated from the 4th Class of the Thủ Đức Reserve Officer Train-

ing School as a Second-Lieutenant on June 1, 1954. He volunteered to join the Airborne, and was given command of a platoon of the 5th Airborne Battalion. He moved up the ranks as follows: First-Lieutenant on December 1, 1955; Captain in 1961; Major in 1964; Lieutenant-Colonel in April 1965; In-service Colonel on June 19, 1966; In-service Brigadier-General on February 4, 1967; In-service Major-General on June 3, 1968; and, In-service Lieutenant-General on November 1, 1971. He had the reputation as an exemplary general in terms of behavior and discipline, totally dedicated to his duties, and always present at hot spots within his area of responsibility. He was also known as an incorruptible general, who did not tolerate his subordinates' bad actions, especially corruption and/or stealing people's properties. He was also one among a very small number of generals, who did not have any political ambition and did not get involved in political intrigues or events. He reserved all his time for military activities. General Trưởng was also one of a few ARVN generals, who had assumed command from the lowest to the highest levels: Platoon Commander in July 1954 (one platoon of the 5th Airborne Battalion); Company Commander at the beginning of 1955 (1st Company of 5th Airborne Battalion); Battalion Commander in 1961 (5th Airborne Battalion); Division Commander in 1966 (1st Infantry Division); Corps Commander (IV Corps, 1970-1972 and I Corps, 1972-1975). After April 30, 1975, he lived in Springfield, Virginia, USA. He passed away there on January 22, 2007 at the age of 78. Based on his will, his ashes were brought back by his family to Vietnam and spread over Hải Vân Pass.

2. Lavalle, A.J.C., editor. ***Airpower and the 1972 spring invasion***. Washington, D.C.: United States Air Force, Office of Air Force History, 1985. (U.S.A.F. Southeast Asia monograph series; v. 2, monograph 3), p. 58.

3. Brand, Matthew C. ***Airpower and the 1972 Easter Offensive***. Fort Leavenworth, Kansas: U.S. Army Command and General Staff College, 2007. (Thesis of Master of Military Art and Science submitted by U.S. Air Force Lieutenant-Colonel Matthew C. Brand), p. 83.

4. Major-General Bùi Thế Lân was one of the most senior officers of the South Vietnamese Marine Corps. Born in November 1932 in Hà Nội, he graduated from the 4th Class of the Thủ Đức Reserve Officer Training School as a Second-Lieutenant on June 1, 1954. He immediately volunteered to join the Marine Corps and was appointed commander of one company of the 1st Marine Battalion. In 1960, he was promoted to First-Lieutenant and appointed Chief of Staff of the Marine Brigade. On June 1, 1961, he was promoted to Captain and appointed Commander of the 4th Marine Battalion. In 1963, he attended the U.S. Marine Corps Command and Staff Training Course in Quantico, Virginia. After his graduation, he came back, was promoted to Major, and, again, was appointed Chief of Staff of the Marine Brigade. He was successively promoted to Lieutenant-Colonel (in 1963), Colonel (in 1964), and, in 1971, he

was appointed Deputy-Commander of the Marine Corps. On May, 4, 1972, he was appointed Commander of the Marine Corps, and, on May 24, 1974, he was promoted to Brigadier-General. At the beginning of April 1975, he was promoted to Major-General. After 1975, he lived in the U.S., and passed away on January 14, 2014 in San Jose, California, at the age of 82.

5. Major-General Phạm Văn Phú, born on October 16, 1928, in Hà Đông Province, North Vietnam, graduated from the 8 th Class of the Đà Lạt Inter-Arm Military Academy as a Second-Lieutenant in 1953. He volunteered to the Airborne, and was appointed commander of a platoon of the 5th Airborne Battalion. In 1954, he was promoted to First-Lieutenant, commander of a company of the same battalion. His battalion participated in the Battle of Điện Biên Phủ where he was promoted "at the battlefield" to Captain. When Điện Biên Phủ fell, he was captured as a prisoner-of-war, and was only released in July 1955 back to the Army of the State of Việt Nam. He was successively promoted as follows: Major in 1960, Lieutenant-Colonel in 1964, Colonel in 1965, Brigadier-General in 1969, and Major-General in 1971. On November 5, 1974, he was appointed Commander of II Corps. Major-General Phạm Văn Phú was one of the 5 generals of the ARVN who committed suicide on April 30, 1975.

6. Ngô Quang Trưởng. ***The Easter Offensive of 1972***. Washington, D.C.: US Army Center of Military History, 1980, p. 54.

7. Ngô Quang Trưởng, op. cit., p. 65.

8. Trần Ngọc Thống, Hồ Đắc Huân, Lê Đình Thụy, op. cit., p. 235.

9. Hòa Khánh. ***Sư Đoàn 3 Bộ Binh trở lại chiến trường*** (The 3rd Infantry Division's return to the battlefield), online document, accessible in full-text at this URL: https://dongsongcu.wordpress.com/2016/03/10/su-doan-3-bo-binh-tro-lai-chien-truong/ The fact that the 3rd Infantry Division was able to recover really fast and return to the battlefield, and, after just one year, its evaluation by the General Staff as completely combat-competent, were owed firstly to its new Commander, Brigadier-General Nguyễn Duy Hinh, who was later promoted to Major-General on July 1, 1973.

10. Trần Ngọc Thống, Hồ Đắc Huân, Lê Đình Thụy, op. cit., p. 400.

11. Ngô Quang Trưởng, op. cit., p. 56.

12. Hành Quân Lam Sơn 72, tái chiếm Quảng Trị (Operation Lam Sơn 72, re-capture of Quảng Trị), online document, accessible in full-text at this URL: https://bienxua.wordpress.com/2017/08/09/hanh-quan-lam-son-72-tai-chiem-quang-tri/

13. Cổ Thành Quảng Trị và Đại Lộ Kinh Hoàng, (Quảng Trị Old Citadel and the Highway of Terror), online document, accessible in full-text at this URL: https://vi-vn.facebook.com/quanlucvnch/photos09888044351.59269.275596229205717/605102579588412/

14. Trương Đăng Sỹ. ***Nhảy Dù và Cổ Thành Đinh Công Tráng*** (The Airborne and the Đinh Công Tráng Old Citadel), online document, accessible in full-text at this URL: https://dongsongcu.wordpress.com/2016/09/21/nhay-du-va-co-thanh-dinh-cong-trang-2/

15. Trương Đăng Sỹ, ibid..

16. Melson, Charles D. và Curtis G. Arnold. ***U.S. Marines in Vietnam: the war that would not end, 1971-1973***. Washington, D.C.: U.S. Marines Corps Headquarters, History and Museums Division, 1991, p. 110. Online document, accessible in full-text at this URL: http://www.marines.mil/Portals/59/Publications/U.S.%20Marines%20in%20Vietnam%20The%20war%20that%20would%20not%20end%201971-1973%20PCN%2019000311200_1.pdf

17. Nguyễn Đăng Hòa. "*Trận đổ bộ Triệu Phong, 11/7/1972,*" (The Landing in Triệu Phong, July 11, 1972) in ***Tuyển tập 2: Hai mươi mốt năm chiến trận của binh chủng Thủy Quân Lục Chiến Việt Nam (1954-1975)*** (Selected Works 2: Twenty-one years of battles of the Vietnamese Marine Corps (1954-1975)). Santa Ana, Calif.: Tổng Hội TQLC/VN Tại Hoa Kỳ (General Association of the Vietnamese Marine Corps in the U.S.), 2005, pp. 404-414.

18. Andradé, Dale. ***America's last Vietnam battle: halting Hanoi's 1972 Easter Offensive***. Lawrence, Kansas: University Press of Kansas, 2001, p. 189-190.

19. Ngô Văn Định. ***Trận Quảng Trị năm 1972 của Lữ Đoàn 258 TQLC*** (The Battle of Quảng Trị in 1972 by the 258th Marine Brigade), online document, accessible in full-text at this URL: http://tqlcvn.org/hoiky/hk-tranQT72-ld258-tqlc.htm

20. Phạm Văn Chung. ***Cờ bay trên Cổ Thành Quảng Trị*** (Our flag flying on the Quảng Trị Old Citadel), online document, accessible in full-text at this URL: https://www.nguoi-viet.com/cuu-chien-binh/ccb-co-bay-tren-co-thanh-quang-tri/

21. Lê Quang Liễn. *"Đại đội 4/TĐ2/TQLC và trận tái chiếm tòa hành chánh Quảng Trị (14/9/72),"* (The 4th Company of the 2nd Marine Battalion and the battle to re-capture the Administrative Main Office of Quảng Trị Province (September 14, 1972)) in ***Tuyển tập 2: Hai mươi mốt năm chiến trận của binh chủng Thủy Quân Lục Chiến Việt Nam (1954-1975)*** (Selected Works 2: Twenty-one of battles of the Vietnamese Marine Corps (1954-1975)), op. cit., pp. 416-423.

22. Giang Văn Nhân. *"Tiểu đoàn 3/TQLC dựng cờ trên Cổ Thành Quảng Trị 15/9/1972,"* (The 3rd Marine Battalion raised the flag on the top of Quảng

Trị Old Citadel, September 15, 1972)) in ***Tuyển tập 2: Hai mươi mốt năm chiến trận của binh chủng Thủy Quân Lục Chiến Việt Nam (1954-1975)*** (Selected Works 2: Twenty-one years of battles of the Vietnamese Marine Corps, (1954-1975)), op. cit., pp. 438-450.

23. Ích Duệ. ***Vài nét về chiến trường Quảng Trị 1972*** (A few details of the 1972 Quảng Trị battlefield), online document, accessible in full-text at this URL: https://hieuminh.org/2012/07/26/vai-net-ve-chien-truong-quang-tri-1972/

24. Xuân Hải. Đại đội 120 người, hết trận đánh chỉ còn 17 (A Company with 120 men, reduced to 17 at the end of the battle), online document, accessible in full-text at this URL: http://infonet.vn/dai-doi-120-nguoi-het-tran-danh-chi-con-17-post128750.info

25. Cất bốc 12 hài cốt liệt sĩ ở thị xã Quảng Trị (Discovery of 12 additional remains of fallen soldiers in the City of Quảng Trị), online document, accessible in full-text at this URL: http://m.laodongxahoi.net/cat-boc-12-hai-cot-liet-si-o-thi-xa-quang-tri-1309305.html

Chapter Five

1. Moyar, Mark, "Vietnam: historians at war," ***Academic questions***, vol. 21, no. 1 (Spring 2008), e-journal article, accessible in full-text at this URL: https://www.nas.org/academic-questions/21/1/vietnam_historians_at_war

2. Halberstam, David. ***The Making of a quagmire: America and Vietnam during the Kennedy era.*** Rev. ed., with an introduction by Daniel J. Singal. Lanham, Md.: Rowman & Littlefield, 2008, pp. 77-92.

3. Sheehan, Neil. ***A Bright shining lie: John Paul Vann and America in Vietnam***. New York: Random House,1988, pp. 201-265.

4. Karnow, Stanley. ***Vietnam, a history: the first complete account of Vietnam at war***. New York: Penguin Books, 1984, pp. 259-262.

5. Sheehan, op. cit., p. 233.

6. Karnow, op. cit., pp. 259-260.

7. Halberstam, op. cit., p. 85.

8. Đoàn Thêm. ***Hai mươi năm qua: việc từng ngày (1945-1964)*** (The Past twenty years: daily events (1945-1964)***;*** tựa của Lãng Nhân (preface by Lãng Nhân). Los Alamitos, Calif.: Xuân Thu, [1989], p. 328.

9. ***Battle of Ap Bac***, online document, accessible in full-text at this URL: https://en.wikipedia.org/wiki/Battle_of_Ap_Bac#Aftermath

10. Lý Tòng Bá. ***25 năm khói lửa: hồi ký của một tướng lãnh cầm quân tại mặt trận*** (25 Years of battles: memoir of a general commanding troops at the battlefield). Las Vegas: The Author, 1995, pp. 65 and 68.

11. Moyar, Mark. ***Triumph forsaken: The Vietnam War, 1954-1965***. Cambridge, UK: Cambridge University Press, 2006, p. xvi.

12. Andradé, Dale. ***America's last Vietnam battle: halting Hanoi's 1972 Easter Offensive***. Lawrence: University Press of Kansas, 2001, p. 196.

13. Willbanks, James H. ***The Battle of An Loc***. Bloomington: Indiana University Press, 2005, pp. 146-147.

14. Caputo, Phillip, "S. Viets take skeleton of city." ***Chicago tribune***, issue of April 14, 1975, p. 3.

15. Veith, George J. và Merle L. Pribbenow, "Fighting is an art: the Army of the Republic of Vietnam's defense of Xuan Loc, 9-21 April 1975," ***Journal of military history***, vol. 68, no. 1 (Jan. 2004), pp. 163-213. The quotation is on p. 193. (The quotation is the English translation of the original Vietnamese Note no. 9, Chapter 20, Part 2, of General Hoàng Cầm's Memoir entitled ***Chặng đường 10.000 ngày: hồi ký của Thượng Tướng Hoàng Cầm*** (The 10,000-day journey: memoir of Senior-General Hoàng Cầm), online document, accessible in full-text at this URL: https://lichsuhuyenbivietnam.blogspot.com/2012/11/chang-uong-10000-ngay-hoi-ky-cua-thuong_15.html

16. Veith and Priibbenow, ibid., p. 213

Chapter Six

1. ***Memorandum for the President from George Ball, "A Compromise Solution in South Vietnam," 1 July 1965***, online document, accessible in full-text at this URL: https://www.mtholyoke.edu/acad/intrel/pentagon4/doc260.htm

2. Barrett, David M. "The mythology surrounding Lyndon Johnson, his advisers, and the 1965 decision to escalate the Vietnam War," ***Political science quarterly***, vol. 103, issue 4 (winter 1988/1989), p. 641.

3. Lâm Vĩnh-Thế. ***Tìm hiểu thêm về việc Thủy Quân Lục Chiến Hoa Kỳ đổ bộ vào Đà Nẵng ngày 8 tháng 3 năm 1965*** (Further research study on U.S. Marines' landing in Đà Nẵng on March 8, 1965), online document, accessible in full-text at this URL: https://tuyen-tap-vinh-nhon-lam-vinh-the.blogspot.com/2016/06/tim-hieu-them-ve-viec-thuy-quan-luc.html In this article, the author has referred to the Memoir by General William C. Westmoreland, Commander of MACV (Military Assistance Command, Vietnam), entitled ***A soldier reports***, new edition, published by De Capo Press in 1989. On page 122, General Westmoreland wrote: ***"I expressed concern "that we***

are headed toward a VC takeover," probably within a year."

4. ***In country: remembering the Vietnam War*** / edited by John Prados. Lanham, Md.: Ivan R. Dee Publisher, 2011. On p. 8, the editor stated: ***"... President Johnson considered General Westmoreland's large-scale reinforcement and approved it. The deployment of the First Cavalry Division (Airmobile), along with the Third Marine Division, followed by the First Infantry Division and the First Brigade/101st Airborne Division, was the first wave of the new MACV force. ... the fact is that in the twelve months ending in December 1965 the American force level in country increased from twenty-three thousand to 183,000 personnel."***

5. McNamara, Robert S. and Brian VanDeMark. ***In retrospect: the tragedy and lessons of Vietnam.*** New York: Random House, 1995, pp. 243-244.

6. McNamara, op. cit., p. 244.

7. ***Joint Chiefs of Staff***, online document, accessible in full-text at this URL: https://en.wikipedia.org/wiki/Joint_Chiefs_of_Staff. JCS was the inter-service General Staff of the U.S. Armed Forces, including all Generals (4-star), Chiefs of Staff of all four main services, i.e., Army, Navy, Air Force, and Marine Corps, headed by a Chairman, alternatively chosen from the four services, and nominated by the President. At this point in time, the Chairman of the JCS was Army General Earl (Bus) Wheeler.

8. McNamara, op. cit., p. 266.

9. McNamara, op. cil., p. 275.

10. McNamara, ibid.

11. McNamara, op. cit., p. 276.

12. McNamara, op. cit., p. 280.

13. McNamara, op. cit., p. 315.

14. ***Council on Foreign Relations,*** online document, accessible in full-text at this URL: *https://en.wikipedia.org/wiki/Council_on_Foreign_Relation*

15. ***Argument without end: in search of answers to the Vietnam tragedy*** / Robert S. McNamara, et al. New York: Public Affairs, 1999.

16. ***Argument without end***, op. cit., p. 368.

17. ***Argument without end***, op. cit., p. 319.

18. Lâm Vĩnh-Thế. ***Critical Review of the Vietnam War: the PBS documentary film directed by Ken Burns and Lynn Novick***, online document, accessible in full-text at this URL: https://tuyen-tap-vinh-nhon-lam-vinh-the.blogspot.com/2021/08/critical-review-of-vietnam-war-pbs.html

19. Trần Ngươn Phiêu. ***Gió mùa Đông Bắc (Chương 6)*** (The Northeast monsoon (Chapter 6)), online document, accessible in full-text at this URL: https://www.diendantheky.net/2011/04/gio-mua-ong-bac-chuong-6.html

20. Nguyễn Kỳ Nam. ***Hồi-ký "1925-1964." Tập II: 1945-1954*** (Memoir "1925-1964": Volume II: 1945-1954). Sài Gòn: Nhựt-báo Dân Chủ Mới (New Democracy Daily Newspaper), 1964, p. 231.

21. Trần Ngươn Phiêu, op. cit., Chapter 7.

22. Hoàng Hưng. ***Cái chết của Khái Hưng*** (The Death of Khái Hưng), online document, accessible in full-text at this URL: https://baotiengdan.com/2019/07/29/cai-chet-cua-khai-hung/

23. Lâm Lễ Trinh. ***Mạn đàm với BS Nguyễn Lưu Viên: từ Hà Nội, La Celle Saint-Cloud đến những ngày VNCH hấp hối*** (Conversation with Dr. Nguyễn Lưu Viên: from Hà Nội, La Cell Saint-Cloud to the agonizing days of the RVN), online document, accessible in full-text at this URL: http://aihuuluatkhoa.com/yahoo_site_admin/assets/docs/MAN_DAM_VOI_BSI_NLV.5092817.pdf

24. Nguyễn Minh Cần. ***Xin đừng quên! Nửa thế kỷ trước... Mở hồ sơ tội ác Hồ Chí Minh: vấy máu Cải Cách Ruộng Đất*** (Please do not forget! Half a century ago... Reopening the criminal file of Hồ Chí Minh: the bloody Land Reform), online document, accessible in full-text at this URL: http://www.geocities.ws/xoathantuong/nmc_xdq.htm

25. H.V.N. "Cộng sản Việt Nam mới thật là Ngụy," (The Vietnamese Communists are the Real Usurpers), ***Tạp chí Dân Quyền*** (Journal of Civil Rights) ***(Montreal, Canada)***, no. 51 (May/1982), pp. 20-21.

26. Đoàn Thêm, op. cit., p. 37.

27. Bảo Đại. ***Con rồng Việt Nam: hồi ký chính trị (1913-1987)*** (The Dragon of Vietnam: political memoir (1913-1987)). [No place of publication: Nguyễn Royal Family, 1990, p. 284.

28. Đoàn Thêm, op. cit., p. 56.

29. ***Hiệp định Genève, 1954*** (The 1954 Geneva Accords), online document, accessible in full-text at this URL: https://vi.wikipedia.org/wiki/Hi%E1%BB%87p_%C4%91%E1%BB%8Bnh_Gen%C3%A8ve,_1954

30. ***Fourth Interim Report of the International Commission for Supervision and Control in Vietnam***. London, U.K.: HMSO, 1955, p. 30.

31. Nguyễn Quốc Tấn Trung. ***30/4 – Xâm lược hay giải phóng: từ góc nhìn công pháp quốc tế*** (April 30 – Invasion or liberation: from the international public law point of view), online document, accessible in full-text at this URL: https://www.luatkhoa.org/2017/04/30-4-xam-luoc-hay-giai-phong-tu-goc-nhin-cong-phap-quoc-te/

32. Palmer, Bruce. ***The 25-year war: America's military role in Vietnam***. Lexington: University Press of Kentucky, 1984, p. 125.

33. ***The Real lessons of the Vietnam War: reflections twenty-five years after the fall of Saigon*** / edited by John Norton Moore & Robert F. Turner. Durham, N.C.: Carolina Academic Press, 2002, p. 391.

34. Lâm Vĩnh Thế. ***Tài liệu SNIE 14.3-67: một bài học đắt giá của việc chính-trị-hóa tình báo*** (Document SNIE 14.3-67: a dear price paid for the politicization of intelligence), online document, accessible in full-text at this URL: https://tuyen-tap-vinh-nhon-lam-vinh-the.blogspot.com/2017/10/tai-lieu-snie-143-67-mot-bai-hoc-at-gia_5.html

35. Lindsay, James. M. ***TWE remembers: General Westmoreland says the "End begins to come into view" in Vietnam***, online document, accessible in full-text at this URL: https://www.cfr.org/blog/twe-remembers-general-westmoreland-says-end-begins-come-view-vietnam

36. ***Tết Mậu Thân 1968 qua những số liệu*** (Tết of the Year of the Monkey 1968, through the statistics), online document, accessible in full-text at this URL: https://www.nhandan.com.vn/chinhtri/item/7976502-.html This is the Web page of the online daily newspaper ***Nhân Dân điện tử*** (electronic ***People***), the official journal of the VCP, voice of the Party, Government and People of Vietnam; this article was published online on Friday, September 17, 2010, at 13:25 pm.

37. Sorley, Lewis. ***A Better war: the unexamined victories and final tragedy of America's last years in Vietnam***. New York: Harcourt Brace, 1999, p. 66.

38. ***Phoenix Program***, online document, accessible in full-text at this URL: https://en.wikipedia.org/wiki/Phoenix_Program

39. Sorley, op. cit., pp. 204-205. The information provided by the author was extracted from p. 7 of the monograph entitled ***Lam Sơn 719*** authored by Major-General Nguyễn Duy Hinh, and published by U.S. Army Center for Military History in Washington, D.C. in 1979.

40. Gerson, Michael S., et al. ***The Sino-Soviet border conflict: deterrence, escalation, and the threat of nuclear war in 1969***, online document, accessible in full-text at this URL: https://www.cna.org/CNA_files/PDF/D0022974.A2.pdf

41. Lind, Michael. ***Vietnam: the necessary war: a reinterpretation of America's most disastrous military conflict***. New York: Simon & Schuster, 1999, p. xvii.

Chapter Seven

1. Asselin, Pierre. ***A Bitter peace: Washington, Hanoi and the making of the Paris Agreement***. Chapell Hill, N.C.: University of North Carolina Press, 2002, pp 7-8.

2. Bùi Diễm with David Chanoff. ***In the jaws of history***; foreword by Jane Hamilton-Merritt. Bloomington: Indiana University Press, 1999, pp. 240-241.

3. Johnson, Lyndon Baines. ***The Vantage point: perspectives of the presidency, 1963-1969***. New York: Holt, Rinehart and Winston, 1971, pp. 517-518.

4. Bùi Diễm, op. cit., p. 244. At the bottom of the page, the author also gave the following note: *"In **The Man Who Kept the Secrets**, Thomas Powers wrote, "During the week which ended Saturday, October 17, the National Security Agency intercepted a radio message from the South Vietnamese Embassy to Saigon explicitly urging Thieu to stand fast against an agreement until after the election. As soon as Johnson learned of the cable, he ordered the FBI to place Madame Chennault under surveillance and to install a phone tap on the South Vietnamese Embassy."* Beverly Deepe, mentioned by Ambassador Bùi Diễm in the quotation from his book, was the correspondent in Saigon of the ***Christian Science Monitor***. Ms. Deepe sent a lengthy teletype back to Washington about the Chennault affair, confirming that the South Vietnamese had made a deal with Nixon. The ***Christian Science Monitor*** never printed this story.

5. Đoàn Thêm. ***Việc từng ngày: 1968*** (Daily events: 1968); tựa của Lãng Nhân (preface by Lãng Nhân). [Sài Gòn]: Cơ Sở xuất bản Phạm Quang Khai (Phạm Quang Khai Publishing House), 1969; Los Alamitos, Calif.: Xuân Thu re-published, 1989, p. 399.

6. Kissinger, Henry. ***White House years.*** Boston: Little, Brown & Co., 1979, pp. 1324-1325.

7. Nguyễn Phú Đức. ***The Vietnam's peace negotiations: Saigon's side of the story***. Christiansburg, Va.: Dalley Book Service, 2005, pp. 10-13.

8. The American troop levels in the RVN during 1968-1973 were as follows: 536.100 (1968), 475.200 (1969), 334.600 (1970), 156.800 (1971), và 24.200 (1972). Source: U.S. Department of Defense Manpower Data Center, accessible at this URL: http://www.americanwarlibrary.com/vietnam/vwatl.htm

9. Kissinger, op. cit., p. 1318.

10. Nixon, Richard. ***The Memoirs of Richard Nixon***. New York: Grosset & Dunlap, 1978, p. 700.

11.Nguyễn Phú Đức, op. cit., p. 310.

12. Nguyễn Phú Đức, op. cit., pp. 310-311.

13. Kissinger, op. cit., p. 1326.

14. Nguyễn Phú Đức, op. cit., pp. 315-316.

15. Nixon, op. cit., p. 600.

16. Nixon, op. cit., p. 693.

17. Nixon, op. cit., p. 696.

18. Kissinger, op. cit., p. 1385.

19. Nixon, op. cit., pp. 698-699.

20. Nguyễn Phú Đức, op. cit., pp. 332-333.

21. ***United States presidential election, 1972***, online document, accessible in full-text at this URL: https://en.wikipedia.org/wiki/United_States_presidential_election,_1972

22. Nguyễn Tiến Hưng. ***Khi đồng minh tháo chạy*** (When the ally ran away). San Jose, Calif.: Hứa Chấn Minh Publishing House, 2005, pp. 529-532.

23. Nguyễn Phú Đức, op. cit., p. 341.

24. Kissinger, op. cit., p. 1410.

25. Nguyễn Phú Đức, op. cit., p. 353.

26. Nguyễn Phú Đức, op. cit., pp. 354-355. The author wrote as follows: ***"I asked him whether he had come up with something new on the withdrawal of the NVA, as President Nixon, the day before, did not foreclose the issue, Kissinger said that it would be impossible to have the NVA withdrawal in the agreement."***

27. Nguyễn Phú Đức, op. cit., p. 356.

28. Nguyễn Phú Đức, op. cit., p. 361.

29. Nixon, op. cit., p. 737.

30. Nguyễn Phú Đức, op. cit., p. 365.

31. Nguyễn Phú Đức, op. cit., p. 367.

32. ***Operation Linrbacker II: The Christmas bombing***, online document, accessible in full-text at this URL: http://thevietnamwar.info/operation-linebacker-ii-christmas-bombing/, p. 2.

33. Nguyễn Tiến Hưng, op. cit., pp. 547-548.

34. Kissinger, op. cit., p. 1469.

35. Nguyễn Phú Đức, op. cit., p. 373.

36. Nixon, op. cit., p. 737.

Chapter Eight

1. ***Tiểu sử Đại Tướng Cao Văn Viên*** (Biography of General Cao Văn Viên), online document, accessible in full-text at this URL: http://nhaydu.com/index_83hg_files/main_files/Tuong/TS-TuongCaoVanVien.htm.

2. Hughes, Ken. ***The Myth that Congress cut off funding for South Vietnam***, online document, accessible in fulltext at this URL: https://historynewsnetwork.org/article/126150

3. Nguyễn Đức Phương, ***Chiến tranh Việt Nam toàn tập: từ trận đầu (Ấp Bắc – 1963) đến trận cuối (Sài Gòn – 1975)*** (Complete work of the Vietnam War: from the first battle (Ấp Bắc – 1963) to the last battle (Sài Gòn – 1975)). Toronto: Làng Văn (Literature Village), 2001, p. 732.

4. Nguyễn Tiến Hưng, ***Tâm tư Tổng Thống Thiệu*** (President Thiệu's inner thoughts). San Jose, Calif.: Cơ sở xuất bản Hứa Chấn Minh (Hứa Chấn Minh Publishing House), 2010, p. 52.

5. Nguyễn Tiến Hưng, op. cit., p. 57.

6. Phạm Bá Hoa, Đôi dòng ghi nhớ: hồi ký chính trị, 1963-1975 (A few lines of memories: political memoir, 1963-1975). Ấn bản lần 4 (4th ed.). Houston, Texas: Ngày Nay (Today), 2007, p. 271.

7. Phạm Bá Hoa, op. cit., pp. 273-274.

8. Đỗ Sơn, ***Chuẩn Tướng Phạm Duy Tất và sự thật cuộc triệt thoái Quân Đoàn II*** (Brigadier-General Phạm Duy Tất and the truth of the retreat from II Corps). Burke, Va.: Nhà xuất bản THAO UYEN PHAM (THAO UYEN PHAM Publishing House), 2013, p. 111.

9. Phạm Bá Hoa, op. cit., p. 275.

10. Đỗ Sơn, op. cit., pp. 98 and 122.

11. The issue of who was given by General Phú the general command of the whole retreat of II Corps is still debatable up to today, because there was absolutely no operation order on paper. However, except for the case of the book authored by Đỗ Sơn, all documents, in particular the two books in English published by the U.S. Army Center of Military History, ***The Final collapse*** by General Cao Văn Viên (1983), and ***Vietnam: from cease-fire to capitulation*** by U.S. Army Colonel William E. Le Gro (1981), recorded that Genertal Phú designated General Tất to command all forces in this retreat. These two books both have a fairly high level of reliability.

12. Nguyễn Đức Phương, op. cit., p. 735.

13. Đỗ Sơn, op. cit., p. 132.

14. Hoàng Khởi Phong, ***Ngày N+....*** (Day D+...), online e-book, accessible in full-text at this URL: http://www.talawas.org/talaDB/showFile.php?res=1663&rb=08, Phần 1 (Part 1), Pleiku-Tuy Hòa, Đoạn Ngày N+2, 12 giờ trưa (Section Day D+2, 12 pm).

15. Cao Văn Viên, ***The Final collapse***. Washington, D.C.: U.S. Army Center of Military History, 1985, p. 92.

16. Nguyễn Đức Phương, op. cit., p. 738.

17. Cao Văn Viên, op. cit., p. 95.

18. Nguyễn Tiến Hưng, ***Tâm tư Tổng Thống Thiệu,*** op. cit., p. 526.

Chapter Nine

1. ***1972 United States presidential election***, online document, accessible in full-text at this URL: https://en.wikipedia.org/wiki/1972_United_States_presidential_election

2. ***93rd United Stated Congress***, online document, accessible in full-text at this URL: https://en.wikipedia.org/wiki/93rd_United_States_Congress

3. Nixon, op. cit., p. 715.

4. Nguyễn Tiến Hưng. ***Khi Đồng Minh tháo chạy,*** op. cit., p. 548.

5. Isaacson, Walter. ***Kissinger: a biography***. New York: Simon & Schuster, 1992, p. 487.

6. ***Operations Enhance and Enhance Plus***, online document, accessible in full-text at this URL: https://en.wikipedia.org/wiki/Operations_Enhance_and_Enhance_Plus

7. ***War Powers Resolution***, online document, accessible in full-text at this URL: https://en.wikipedia.org/wiki/War_Powers_Resolution

8. Nguyễn Phú Đức. ***The Viet-Nam peace negotiations: Saigon's side of the story*** / edited by Arthur J. Dommen. Christianburg, Va.: Dalley Book Service, 2005, p. 373.

9. ***1968 United States presidential election***, online document, accessible in full-text at this URL: https://en.wikipedia.org/wiki/1968_United_States_presidential_election

10. Kadura, Johannes. ***The War after the War: the struggle for credibility during America's exit from Vietnam***. Ithaca, N.Y.: Cornell University Press, 2016, pp. 16-17.

11. ***Text of Declaration by Paris Conference on Vietnam, March 3, 1973***, online document, accessible in full-text at this URL: https://www.nytimes.com/1973/03/03/archives/text-of-declaration-by-paris-conference-on-vietnam.html

12. ***USSAC/7AF in Thailand (1973-1975): policy changes and the military role***, online document, accessible in full-text at this URL: https://apps.dtic.mil/dtic/tr/fulltext/u2/a586318.pdf, p. 28.

13. Hartsook, E.H. ***The Air Force in South East Asia: the end of the U.S. involvement in Vietnam, 1973-1975***. Washington, D.C.: Office of Air Force History, Headquarters, USAF, 1980, online document, accessible in full-text at this URL: https://media.defense.gov/2011/Mar/23/2001330102/-1/-1/0/AFD-110323-032.pdf, p. 16.

14. Hartsook, ibid.

15. ***The Paris Agreement on Vietnam: twenty-five years later; Conference transcript, The Nixon Center, Washington, DC, April 1998***, online document, accessible in full-text at this URL: https://www.mtholyoke.edu/acad/intrel/paris.htm

16. Watergate was the political crisis that led to President Nixon's resignation on August 8, 1974. Everything started on June 17, 1972 when police arrested a group of five men, who illegally broke into the office of the Democratic Party Election Campaign in Watergate Hotel in downtown Washington, D.C. with the intention to wiretap phone conversations of the Campaign. President Nixon and his close associates tried to cover it up and made it become gradually more and more serious. Finally, facing with the risk of being impeached by Congress, President Nixon had to resign. Vice-President Gerald Ford became President and pardoned Mr. Nixon. The whole Watergate affair was presented in details in this online document, ***Watergate*** scandal, accessible in full-text at this URL: https://en.wikipedia.org/wiki/Watergate_scandal

17. Berman, Larry. ***No peace, no honor: Nixon, Kissinger, and betrayal in Vietnam***. New York: Free Press, 2001, pp. 261-262. Author Berman gave the date of the article as April 27, 175; this detail was incorrect and could be a mistake made by the publisher because ***The Wall Street Journal*** was not issued on April 27, 1975.

18. ***Text of Joint Communique issued after Nixon-Thieu talks***, online document, accessible in full-text at this URL: https://www.nytimes.com/1973/04/04/archives/text-of-joint-communique-issued-after-nixonthieu-talks-full.html

19. ***The Paris Agreement on Vietnam ...***, op. cit.

20. Kadura, op. cit., p. 60.

21. Kohut, Andrew. ***From the archives: how the Watergate crisis eroded***

public support for Richard Nixon, online document, accessible in full-text at this URL: https://www.pewresearch.org/fact-tank/2019/09/25/how-the-watergate-crisis-eroded-public-support-for-richard-nixon/

22. Kadura, op. cit., p. 65.

23. Mr John Wesley Dean, III, was the White House Counsel in Nixon administration from 1970. He had played some part in the cover-up of the Watergate affair. He was relieved by President Nixon of his position at the end of April 1973, at the same time of the two close associates of Nixon, John D. Ehrlichman, Assistant to the President for Domestic Affairs and Harry Robbins "Bob" Halderman, White House Chief of Staff. Mr. Richard G. Kleindienst, Attorney Genera, also resigned on the same day. At the end of June 1973, when testifying before the Senate Investigation Committee, he revealed clearly the obstruction of justice, aimed at covering up their involvement in the Watergate affair of high-ranking officials of the White House, including himself and President Nixon. Mr. Dean read a 245-page self-incriminating report in almost 7 hours. He received a 4-month sentence for obstruction of justice. Later he authored two books about his activities in the Watergate affair, ***Blind ambition: The White House years*** (published by Simon & Schuster in 1976) and ***Lost honor*** (published by Stratford Press in 1982). Both John Ehrlichman và Bob Halderman received 18-month sentences.

24. The Senate investigation committee on the Watergate was officially called ***Select Committee on Presidential Campaign Activities***, created by the U.S. Senate on February 7, 1973, chaired by Senator Sam Ervin (Democrat, North Carolina). This committee was dissolved on June 27, 1974 after having submitted its report to the Senate.

25. Kadura, op. cit., p. 77.

26. Kadura, op. cit., p. 78.

27. Kudura, ibid.

28. Kissinger, Henry. ***Ending the Vietnam War: a history of America's involvement in and extrication from the Vietnam War***. New York: Simon & Schuster, 2003, p. 493.

29. Kadura, op. cit., p. 3-4.

30. Kadura, op. cit., p. 90.

31. Willbanks, James H. ***Abandoning Vietnam: how America left and South Vietnam lost its war***. Lawrence: University Press of Kansas, 2004, p. 196

32. Willbanks, op., cit., pp. 215-216.

33. Willbanks, op. cit., p. 215.

34. Cao Văn Viên. ***The Final collapse***. Washington, D.C.: U.S. Army Center for Military History, 1985. (Indochina Monographs). Chapter 4, pp. [42]-57.

35. DAO was the acronym for the Defense Attache Office of the U.S. Embassy in Saigon, and was established to co-ordinate all military support activities for the RVN after the Paris Accords was signed. It was almost like a replacement for MACV (Military Assistance Command, Vietnam). The main office of DAO was located at Tân Sơn Nhứt Airbase with numerous branch offices scattered all over the 4 Military Regions of the RVN. It was the largest U.S. defense attache office in the world, with a staff of many thousand men. Its last Commander was Major-General Homer D. Smith, a U.S. Army General specialized in Logistics.

36. Cao Văn Viên, op. cit., p. 48

37. Nguyễn Hữu Thiện. ***Ngành khu trục trong Không Lực Việt Nam Cộng Hòa*** (The Fighter branch in the Air Force of the Republic of Vietnam), online document, accessible in full-text at this URL: https://hoiquanphidung.com/showthread.php?23742-Ng%C3%A0nh-Khu-Tr%E1%BB%A5c-trong-Kh%C3%B4ng-L%E1%BB%B1c-Vi%E1%BB%87t-Nam-C%E1%BB%99ng-H%C3%B2a Trong tài liệu này, tác giả đã viết rõ như sau (In this document, the author stated clearly as follows): ***"Về phi cơ, do tình trạng thiếu bom đạn, thiếu nhiên liệu, thiếu phụ tùng thay thế, vào tháng 9/1974, KQVN đã phải cho đình động (đình chỉ hoạt động) 224 phi cơ, trong số này có toàn bộ lực lượng khu trục cánh quạt, gồm 61 chiếc A-1 Skyraider của PĐ-514, PĐ-518 ở Biên Hòa, và PĐ-530 ở Pleiku."*** (Translation: *"In terms of aircraft, because of shortage of bombs and ammunitions, of fuels, of replacement accessories, in September 1974, the VNAF ordered the suspension of 224 aircraft, including all 61 A-1 Skyraider propeller fighters of Squadrons 514th and 518th in Biên Hòa, and Squadron 530th in Pleiku.")*

38. Cao Văn Viên, op. cit., p. 51.

39. Cao Văn Viên, op. cit., p. 53

40. Willbanks, op. cit., p. 218.

41. Willbanks, op. cit., p. 260.

42. Willbanks, op. cit., p. 267.

43. Willbanks, op. cit., pp. 260-261.

BIBLIOGRAPHY

Books

Ahern, Thomas L., Jr. *CIA and the generals: covert support to military government in South Vietnam.* Langley, VA.: Central Intelligence Agency, 2009.

Airpower and the 1972 spring invasion / edited by A.J.C. Lavalle. Washington, D.C.: United States Air Force, Office of Air Force History, 1985 (U.S.A.F. Southeast Asia monograph series, v.2, monograph 3).

Andradé, Dale. *America's last Vietnam battle: halting Hanoi's Easter Offensive.* Lawrence: University Press of Kansas, 2001.

Argument without end: in search of answers to the Vietnam tragedy / Robert S. McNamara, et.al. New York: Public Affairs, 1999.

Asselin, Pierre. A *Bitter peace: Washington, Hanoi and the making of the Paris Agreement.* Chapel Hill, N.C.: University of North Carolina Press, 2002.

Bảo Đại. *Con rồng Việt Nam: hồi ký chính trị (1913-1987)* (The Dragon of Vietnam: political memoir (1913-1987)). [No place of publication]: Nguyễn Phước Tộc xuất bản (Nguyễn Phước Royal Family published), 1990.

Berman, Larry. *No peace, no honor: Nixon, Kissinger, and betrayal in Vietnam.* New York: Free Press, 2001.

Brand, Matthew C. *Airpower and the 1972 Easter Offensive.* Fort Leavenworth, Kansas: U.S. Army Command and General Staff College, 2007.

Bùi Diễm. *Gọng kìm lịch sử* (In the jaws of history). Paris: Phạm Quang Khai, 2000.

Bùi Tá Khánh. "Chuyến bay tử thần vào Đồi 31 Hạ Lào" (The Deadly flight into Hill 31 in Lower Laos), in Quân sử Không Quân Việt Nam Cộng Hòa (History of the Air Force of the Republic of Vietnam), op. cit., pp. 281-284.

Cao Văn Viên. *The Final collapse.* Washington, D.C.: U.S. Army Center for Military History, 1985. (*Indochina monographs*).

Clarke, Jeffrey J. *United States Army in Vietnam: advice and support: the final years, 1965-1973.* Washington, D.C.: U.S. Army Center for Military History, 1988.

Đoàn Thêm. *Hai mươi năm qua: việc từng ngày (1945-1964)* (The Past twenty years: daily events (1945-1964); tựa của Lãng Nhân (preface by Lãng Nhân). Los Alamitos, Calif.: Xuân Thu, 1989.

----------------. *Việc từng ngày: 1968* (Daily events: 1968); tựa của Lãng Nhân (preface by Lãng Nhân). [Sài Gòn]: Cơ Sở xuất bản Phạm Quang Khai (Phạm

Quang Khai Publishing House), 1969; Los Alamitos, Calif.: Xuân Thu, 1989.

Đỗ Sơn. *Chuẩn Tướng Phạm Duy Tất và sự thật cuộc triệt thoái Quân Đoàn II (Brigadier-General Phạm Duy Tất and the truth of the retreat from II Corps).* Burke, Va.: Nhà xuất bản THAO UYEN PHAM (THAO UYEN PHAM Publishing House), 2013

Fourth Interim Report of the International Commission for Supervision and Control in Vietnam. London, UK: HMSO, 1955.

Frankum, Ronald B. *Historical dictionary of the War in Vietnam.* Lanham, Md.: Scarecrow Press, 2011.

Giang Văn Nhân. "Tiểu đoàn 3/TQLC dựng cờ trên Cổ Thành Quảng Trị 15/9/1972," (The 3rd Marines Battalion raised the flag on the Quảng Trị Citadel on Septemeber 15, 1972) in *Tuyển tập 2: hai mươi mốt năm chiến trận của binh chủng Thủy Quân Lục Chiến Việt Nam (1954-1975)*, pp. 438-450.

Halberstam, David. *The Making of a quagmire: America and Vietnam during the Kennedy era.* Rev. ed. with an introduction by Daniel J. Singal. Lanham, Md.: Rowman & Littlefield, 2008.

Hartsook, E. H. *The Air Force in South East Asia: the end of the U.S. involvement in Vietnam, 1973-1975.* Washington, D.C.: Office of the Air Force History, Headquarters, USAF, 1980.

Hoàng Khởi Phong. *Ngày N+.... (Day D+...)*, online e-book, accessible in full-text at this URL: http://www.talawas.org/talaDB/showFile.php?res=1663&rb=08

In country: remembering the Vietnam War / edited by John Prados. Landham, Md.: Ivan R. Dee Publisher, 2011.

Isaacson, Walter. *Kissinger: a biography.* New York: Simon & Schuster, 1992.

Johnson, Lyndon B. *The Vantage point: perspectives of the presidency, 1963-1969.* New York: Holt, Rinehart and Winston, 1971.

Kadura, Johannes. *The War after the War: the struggle for credibility during America's exit from Vietnam.* Ithaca, N.Y.: Cornell University Press, 2016.

Karnow, Stanley. *Vietnam, a history: the first complete account of Vietnam at war.* New York: Penguin Books, 1984.

Kissinger, Henry. *Ending the Vietnam War: a history of America's involvement in and extrication from the Vietnam War.* New York: Simon & Schuster, 2003.

----------------------. White House years. Boston: Little, Brown & Co., 1979.

Lâm Vĩnh-Thế. *Republic of Vietnam, 1963-1967: Years of Political Chaos.*

Hamilton, Ont.: Hoài Việt, 2010.

Lê Quang Liễn. "Đại đội 4/TĐ2/TQLC và trận tái chiếm tòa hành chánh Quảng Trị (14/9/72)," (The 4th Company of the 2nd Marine Battalion and the battle to re-capture the Administrative Main Office of Quảng Trị Province (September 14, 1972)) in *Tuyển tập 2: Hai mươi mốt năm chiến trận của binh chủng Thủy Quân Lục Chiến Việt Nam (1954-1975)*, pp. 416-423.

Lê Xuân Nhuận. *Biến-loạn Miền Trung: hồi ký* (Revolt in Central Vietnam: memoir). Alameda, Calif.: Xây Dựng, 2012.

Lind, Michael. *Vietnam: the necessary war: a reinterpretation of America's most disastrous military conflict. New York: Simon & Schuster, 1999.*

Lý Tòng Bá. *25 năm khói lửa: hồi ký của một tướng lãnh cầm quân tại mặt trận* (25 Years of battles: memoir of a general commanding troops at the battlefield). Las Vegas: Tác giả xuất bản (The Author published), 1995.

McNamara, Robert S. và Brian VanDemark. *In retrospect: the tragedy and lessons of Vietnam.* New York: Random House, 1995.

Melson, Charles D. và Curtis G. Arnold. *U.S. Marines in Vietnam: the war that would not end, 1971-1973.* Washington, D.C.: U.S. Marines Corps Headquarters, History and Museums Division, 1991.

Moyar, Mark. *Triumph forsaken: the Vietnam War, 1954-1965.* Cambridge, UK: Cambridge University Press, 2006.

Ngô Quang Trưởng. *The Easter Offensive of 1972.* Washington, D.C.: U.S. Army Center for Military History, 1980. (*Indochina monographs*).

Nguyễn Đăng Hòa. "Trận đổ bộ Triệu Phong, 11/7/1972," (The Landing in Triệu Phong, July 11, 1972) in *Tuyển tập 2: Hai mươi mốt năm chiến trận của binh chủng Thủy Quân Lục Chiến Việt Nam (1954-1975)*, pp. 404-414.

Nguyễn Đức Phương. *Chiến Tranh Việt Nam toàn tập: từ trận đầu (Ấp Bắc – 1963) đến trận cuối (Sài Gòn – 1975)* (Complete work of the Vietnam War: from the first battle (Ấp Bắc – 1963) to the last battle (Sài Gòn – 1975)). Toronto: Làng Văn (Literature Village), 2001.

Nguyễn Hữu Thiện. "Phiên hiệu của các Phi Đoàn Trong KQVN" (Registration numbers of the squadrons in the AFVN), in Quân sử Không Quân Việt Nam Cộng Hòa (History of the Air Force of the Republic of Vietnam), pp.352-353.

Nguyễn Kỳ Nam. Hồi-ký "1925-1964." Tập II: 1945-1954 (Memoir "1925-1964": Volume II: 1945-1954). Sài Gòn: Nhựt báo Dân Chủ Mới xuất bản (New Democracy Daily Newspaper), 1964.

Nguyễn Kỳ Phong. *Từ điển Chiến Tranh Việt Nam, 1954-1975* (Dictionary of the Vietnam War, 1954-1975). Garden Grove, Calif.: Tự Lực, 2009.

Nguyễn Phú Đức. *The Vietnam's peace negotiations: Saigon's side of the story.* Christiansburg, Va.: Dalley Book Service, 2005.

Nguyễn Tiến Hưng. *Khi đồng minh tháo chạy* (When the ally ran away). San Jose, Calif.: Cơ sở xuất bản Hứa Chấn Minh (Hứa Chấn Minh Publishing house), 2005.

--------------------------. *Tâm tư Tổng Thống Thiệu* (President Thiệu's inner thoughts). San Jose, Calif.: Cơ sở xuất bản Hứa Chấn Minh (Hứa Chấn Minh Publishing house), 2010.

Nguyễn Văn Dưỡng. *Inside An Loc: the battle to save Saigon, April – May 1972.* Jefferson, N.C.: McFarland, 2016.

Nixon, Richard. *The Memoirs of Richard Nixon.* New York: Grosset & Dunlap, 1978.

Palmer, Bruce. *The 25-year war: America's military role in Vietnam.* Lexington: University Press of Kentucky, 1984.

Phạm Bá Hoa. *Đôi dòng ghi nhớ: hồi ký chính trị, 1963-1975* (A few lines of memories: political memoir, 1963-1975). Ấn bản lần 4. Houston: Ngày Nay (Today), 2007.

Phạm Ngọc Sang. "Trận Phan Rang: hồi ức của Chuẩn Tướng Phạm Ngọc Sang," (The Battle of Phan Rang: memoir of Brigadier-General Phạm Ngọc Sang), in *Quân sử Không Quân Viêt Nam Cộng Hòa* (History of the Air Force of the Republic of Vietnam).

Quân sử Không Quân Việt Nam Cộng Hòa (Military history of the Air Force of the Republic of Vietnam). Melbourne: Lý Tưởng Úc Châu (Ideals, Australia), 2005.

Real lessons of the Vietnam War: reflections twenty-five years after the fall of Saigon / edited by John Norton Moore & Robert F. Turner. Durham, N.C.: Carolina Academic Press, 2002.

Sheehan, Neil. *A Bright shining lie: John Paul Vann and America in Vietnam.* New York: Random House, 1988.

Sorley, Lewis. *A Better war: the unexamined victories and final tragedy of America's last years in Vietnam.* New York: Harcourt Brace, 1999.

Trần Ngọc Thống, Hồ Đắc Huân, Lê Đình Thụy. *Lược sử Quân Lực Việt Nam Cộng Hòa* (Brief history of the Armed Forces of the Republic of Vietnam). San Jose, Calif.: Hương Quê, 2011.

Tuyển tập 2: hai mươi mốt năm chiến trận của binh chủng Thủy Quân Lục Chiến Việt Nam (1954-1975) (Selected Works no. 2: twenty-one years of fighting of the Vietnamese Marines Corps (1954-1975)). Santa Ana, Calif.: Tổng hội TQLC/VN tại Hoa Kỳ (General Association of the Vietnamese Marines Corps, 2005.

Willbanks, James H. *Abandoning Vietnam: how America left and South Vietnam lost its war.* Lawrence: University Press of Kansas, 2004.

-------------------------. *The Battle of An Loc.* Bloomington: Indiana University Press, 2005.

Internet Documents

1968 United States presidential election, online document, accessible in full-text at this URL: https://en.wikipedia.org/wiki/1968_United_States_presidential_election

1972 United States presidential election, online document, accessible in full-text at this URL: https://en.wikipedia.org/wiki/1972_United_States_presidential_election

93rd United Stated Congress, online document, accessible in full-text at this URL: https://en.wikipedia.org/wiki/93rd_United_States_Congress

American troop levels in the RVN during 1968-1973 were as follows: 536.100 (1968), 475.200 (1969), 334.600 (1970), 156.800 (1971), và 24.200 (1972). Source: U.S. Department of Defense Manpower Data Center, accessible at this URL: http://www.americanwarlibrary.com/vietnam/vwatl.htm

Battle of Ap Bac, online document, accessible in full-text at this URL: https://en.wikipedia.org/wiki/Battle_of_Ap_Bac#Aftermath

Bell UH-1 Iroquois, online document, accessible in full-text at this URL: https://en.wikipedia.org/wiki/Bell_UH-1_Iroquois

Boeing CH-47 Chinook, online document, accessible in full-text at this URL: http://vietnamwar.wikia.com/wiki/Boeing_CH-47_Chinook

Cất bốc 12 hài cốt liệt sĩ ở thị xã Quảng Trị (Discovery of 12 additional remains of fallen soldiers in the City of Quảng Trị), online document, accessible in full-text at this URL: http://m.laodongxahoi.net/cat-boc-12-hai-cot-liet-si-o-thi-xa-quang-tri-1309305.html

Cessna A-37 Dragonfly, online document, accessible in full-text at this URL: https://en.wikipedia.org/wiki/Cessna_A-37_Dragonfly

Cessna O-1 Bird Dog, online document, accessible in full-text at this URL: https://en.wikipedia.org/wiki/Cessna_O-1_Bird_Dog

Cessna 185 Skywagon, online document, accessible in full-text at this URL:

https://www.skybrary.aero/index.php/C185

Council on Foreign Relation, online document, accessible in full-text at this URL: https://en.wikipedia.org/wiki/Council_on_Foreign_Relation

Cố Trung Tá Phạm Văn Trung PĐT PĐ 249 (Late Lieutenant-Colonel Pham Văn Trung, Commander of Squadron 249), online document, accessible in full-text at this URL: https://hoiquanphidung.com/showthread.php?2061

Cổ Thành Quảng Trị và Đại Lộ Kinh Hoàng (Quảng Trị Old Citadel and the Highway of Terror), online document, accessible in full- text at this URL: https://vi-vn.facebook.com/quanlucvnch/photos /a.287209888044351.59269.275596229205717/605102579588412/

Đại Tá Phan Văn Huấn / Liên Đoàn 81 Biệt Cách Nhảy Dù (Colonel Phan Văn Huấn / 81st Commando Airborne Brigade), online document, accessible in full-text at this URL: http://conhungnguoianh.blogspot.ca/2012/03/ai-ta-phan-van-huan-lien-oan-81-biet.html

De Havilland Canada DHC-4 / C-7 Caribou, online document, accessible in full-text at this URL: http://nhungdoicanh.blogspot.ca/2008/08/de-havilland-canada-dhc-4-c-7-caribou.html

Douglas A-1 Skyraider, online document, accessible in full-text at this URL: https://en.wikipedia.org/wiki/Douglas_A-1_Skyraider#Specifications_.28A-1H_Skyraider.29

Douglas AC-47 Spooky, online document, accessible in full-text at this URL: https://en.wikipedia.org/wiki/Douglas_AC-47_Spooky#Specifications_.28AC-47.29

Douglas EC-47D Dakota, online document, accessible in full-text at this URL: http://dc3dakotahistory.org/c-47dakota-military/ec-47/

Đỗ Văn Hiếu. *Ngành trực thăng trong Không Lực Việt Nam Cộng Hòa* (The Helicopter branch in the Air Force of the Republic of Vietnam), online document, accessible in full-text at this URL: http://hoiquanphidung.com/showthread.php?9287-Ng%C3%A0nh-Tr%E1%BB%B1c-Th%C4%83ng-Trong-Kh%C3%B4ng-L%E1%BB%B1c-Vi%E1%BB%87t-Nam-C%E1%BB%99ng-H%C3%B2a

Fairchild AC-119, online document, accessible in full-text at this URL: https://aerocorner.com/aircraft/fairchild-ac-119/#aircraft-specifications

Fairchild C-119 Flying Boxcar, online document, accessible in full-text at this URL: https://en.wikipedia.org/wiki/Fairchild_C-119_Flying_Boxcar#Specifications_.28C-119C.29

Fairchild C-123 Provider, online document, accessible in full-text at this URL: https://en.wikipedia.org/wiki/Fairchild_C-123_Provider

Gerson, Michael S., et al. *The Sino-Soviet border conflict: deterrence, escalation, and the threat of nuclear war in 1969*, online document, accessible in full-text at this URL: https://www.cna.org/CNA_files/PDF/D0022974.A2.pdf

Hà Giang. *Cố Trung Tướng VNCH Ngô Quang Trưởng đã về nhà* (The Late Lieutenant-General Ngô Quang Trưởng of the RVN has come home), online document, accessible in full-text at this URL: http://aihuubienhoa.com/a1532/co-trung-tuong-vnch-ngo-quang-truong-da-ve-nha-ha-giang

Hành Quân Lam Sơn 72, tái chiếm Quảng Trị (Operation Lam Sơn 72, re-capture of Quảng Trị), online document, accessible in full-text at this URL: https://bienxua.wordpress.com/2017/08/09/hanh-quan-lam-son-72-tai-chiem-quang-tri/

Hiệp định Genève, 1954 (The 1954 Geneva Accords), online document, accessible in full-text at this URL: https://vi.wikipedia.org/wiki/Hi%E1%BB%87p_%C4%91%E1%BB%8Bnh_Gen%C3%A8ve,_1954

Hòa Khánh. *Sư Đoàn 3 Bộ Binh trở lại chiến trường* (The 3rd Infantry Division's return to the battlefield), online document, accessible in full-text at this URL: https://dongsongcu.wordpress.com/2016/03/10/su-doan-3-bo-binh-tro-lai-chien-truong/

Hoàng Hưng. *Cái chết của Khái Hưng* (The Death of Khái Hưng), online document, accessible in full-text at this URL: https://baotiengdan.com/2019/07/29/cai-chet-cua-khai-hung/

Hồ Ngọc Cẩn (đại tá) (Hồ Ngọc Cẩn (Colonel)), online document, accessible in full-text at this URL: https://vi.wikipedia.org/wiki/H%E1%BB%93_Ng%E1%BB%8Dc_C%E1%BA%A9n_(%C4%91%E1%BA%A1i_t%C3%A1)#Qu%C3%A2n_l%E1%BB%B1c_Vi%E1%BB%87t_Nam_C%E1%BB%99ng_h%C3%B2a

Hughes, Ken. *The Myth that Congress cut off funding for South Vietnam*, online document, accessible in fulltext at this URL: https://historynewsnetwork.org/article/126150

Ích Duệ. *Vài nét về chiến trường Quảng Trị 1972* (A few details of the 1972 Quảng Trị battlefield), online document, accessible in full-text at this URL: https://hieuminh.org/2012/07/26/vai-net-ve-chien-truong-quang-tri-1972/

Joint Chiefs of Staff, online document, accessible in full-text at this URL: https://en.wikipedia.org/wiki/Joint_Chiefs_of_Staff

Kohut, Andrew. *From the archives: how the Watergate crisis eroded public support for Richard Nixon*, online document, accessible in full-text at this URL: https://www.pewresearch.org/fact-tank/2019/09/25/how-the-watergate-crisis-eroded-public-support-for-richard-nixon/

Kỷ niệm 40 năm chiến thắng "Hà Nội – Điện Biên Phủ trên không": những điều chưa biết về "pháo đài chiến lược" B-52 của Không Quân Mỹ (40th Anniversary of the Victory "Hà Nội – Điện Biên Phủ in the air": unknown stories about the "stratofortress" B-52 of the American air force), online document, accessible in full-text at this URL: https://thethaovanhoa.vn/the-gioi/nhung-dieu-chua-biet-ve-phao-dai-chien-luoc-b52-cua-khong-quan-my-n20121218112605556.htm

Lâm Lễ Trinh. *Mạn đàm với BS Nguyễn Lưu Viên: từ Hà Nội, La Celle Saint-Cloud đến những ngày VNCH hấp hối* (Conversation with Dr. Nguyễn Lưu Viên: from Hà Nội, La Cell Saint-Cloud to the agonizing days of the RVN), online document, accessible in full-text at this URL: http://aihuuluatkhoa.com/yahoo_site_admin/assets/docs/MAN_DAM_VOI_BSI_NLV.5092817.pdf

Lâm Vĩnh-Thế. *Critical Review of the Vietnam War: the PBS documentary film directed by Ken Burns and Lynn Novick*, online document, accessible in full-text at this URL: https://tuyen-tap-vinh-nhon-lam-vinh-the.blogspot.com/2021/08/critical-review-of-vietnam-war-pbs.html

-------------------. *Tài liệu SNIE 14.3-67: một bài học đắt giá của việc chính-trị-hóa tình báo* (Document SNIE 14.3-67: a dear price paid for the politicization of intelligence), online document, accessible in full-text at this URL: https://tuyen-tap-vinh-nhon-lam-vinh-the.blogspot.com/2017/10/tai-lieu-snie-143-67-mot-bai-hoc-at-gia_5.html

-------------------. *Tìm hiểu thêm về việc Thủy Quân Lục Chiến Hoa Kỳ đổ bộ vào Đà Nẵng ngày 8 tháng 3 năm 1965* (Further research study on U.S. Marines' landing in Đà Nẵng on March 8, 1965), online document, accessible in full-text at this URL: https://tuyen-tap-vinh-nhon-lam-vinh-the.blogspot.com/2016/06/tim-hieu-them-ve-viec-thuy-quan-luc.html

-------------------. *Tình báo trong Chiến Tranh Việt Nam* (Intelligence in the Vietnam War), online document, accessible in full-text at this URL: https://tuyen-tap-vinh-nhon-lam-vinh-the.blogspot.com/2016/11/tinh-bao-trong-chien-tranh-viet-nam.html

Lê Đắc Lực. *An Lộc Địa (The Land of An Lộc)*, online document, accessible in full-text at this URL: https://dongsongcu.wordpress.com/2016/08/12/an-loc-dia/

Lindsay, James. M. *TWE remembers: General Westmoreland says the "End begins to come into view" in Vietnam*, online document, accessible in full-text at this URL: https://www.cfr.org/blog/twe-remembers-general-westmoreland-says-end-begins-come-view-vietnam

Lockheed C-130 Hercules, online document, accessible in full-text at this URL: https://en.wikipedia.org/wiki/Lockheed_C-130_Hercules#Specifications_.28C-130H.29

Mạch Văn Trường. *Trung Đoàn 8 Bộ Binh và trận chiến An Lộc (Mùa Hè 1972): hồi ký của Chuẩn Tướng Mạch Văn Trường* (The 8 th Infanty Regiment and the Battle of An Lộc: memoir of Brigadier-General Mạch Văn Trường), online document, accessible in full-text at this URL: https://dongsongcu.wordpress.com/2021/07/04/trung-doan-8-bo-binh-va-tran-chien-an-loc-mua-he-1972-hoi-ky-cua-chuan-tuong-mach-van-truong/

Melson, Charles D. and Curtis G. Arnold. *U.S. Marines in Vietnam: the war that would not end, 1971-1973.* Washington, D.C.: U.S. Marines Corps Headquarters, History and Museums Division, 1991, p. 110. Online document, accessible in full-text at this URL: http://www.marines.mil/Portals/59/Publications/U.S.%20Marines%20in%20Vietnam%20The%20war%20that%20would%20not%20end%201971-1973%20PCN%2019000311200_1.pdf

Memorandum for the President from George Ball, "A Compromise Solution in South Vietnam," 1 July 1965, online document, accessible in full-text at this URL: https://www.mtholyoke.edu/acad/intrel/pentagon4/doc260.htm

Minh Dũng. *Trung Tướng Ngô Quang Trưởng: Tư Lệnh Quân Đoàn I và Vùng I Chiến Thuật* (Lieutenant-General Ngô Quang Trưởng: Commander of I Corps and Miltary Region I), online document, accessible in full-text at this URL: http://www.luanhoan.net/danang/htm/danang10_12.htm

Ngô Văn Định. *Trận Quảng Trị năm 1972 của Lữ Đoàn 258 TQLC* (The Battle of Quảng Trị in 1972 by the 258th Marine Brigade), online document, accessible in full-text at this URL: http://tqlcvn.org/hoiky/hk-tranQT72-ld258-tqlc.htm

Nguyễn Đức Thắng, Phan Trọng Chinh, Lê Minh Dảo, Lý Tòng Bá, online document, accessible in full-text at this URL: http://vanghe.blogspot.ca/2011/09/nguyen-uc-thang-phan-trong-chinh-le.html

Nguyễn Hữu Thiện. *Ngành khu trục trong Không Lực Việt Nam Cộng Hòa* (The Fighter branch in the Air Force of the Republic of Vietnam), online document, accessible in full-text at this URL: http://hoiquanphidung.com/content.php?4149-Ng%C3%A0nh-Khu-Tr%E1%BB%A5c-trong-Kh%C3%B4ng-L%E1%BB%B1c-Vi%E1%BB%87t-Nam-C%E1%BB%99ng-H%C3%B2a

Nguyễn Minh Cần. *Xin đừng quên! Nửa thế kỷ trước... Mở hồ sơ tội ác Hồ Chí Minh: vấy máu Cải Cách Ruộng Đất* (Please do not forget! Half a century ago... Reopening the criminal file of Hồ Chí Minh: the bloody Land Reform), online document, accessible in full-text at this URL: http://www.geocities.ws/xoathantuong/nmc_xdq.htm

Nguyễn Mậu Quý. *Trung Tướng Nguyễn Viết Thanh* (Lieutenant-General Nguyễn Viết Thanh), online document, accessible in full-text at this URL: http://www.generalhieu.com/nvthanh-u.htm

Nguyễn Quốc Khuê. *Liên Đoàn 3 Biệt Động Quân với trận chiến An Lộc –*

Bình Long (The 3rd Rangers Brigade with the Battle of An Lộc – Bình Long), online document, accessible in full-text at this URL: https://www.nguoi-viet.com/cuu-chien-binh/ccb-t4-lien-doan-3-biet-dong-quan-voi-tran-chien-loc-binh-long/

Nguyễn Quốc Tấn Trung. *30/4 – Xâm lược hay giải phóng: từ góc nhìn công pháp quốc tế* (April 30 – Invasion or liberation: from the international public law point of view), online document, accessible in full-text at this URL: https://www.luatkhoa.org/2017/04/30-4-xam-luoc-hay-giai-phong-tu-goc-nhin-cong-phap-quoc-te/

Nguyễn Văn Dưỡng. *Tướng Lê Văn Hưng tuyên bố "tử thủ An Lộc,"* (General Lê Văn Hưng announced: "fight to the death to keep An Lộc"), online document, accessible in full-text at this URL: https://dongsongcu.wordpress.com/2017/09/06/tuong-le-van-hung-tuyen-bo-tử-thủ-an-loc/

Nguyễn Văn Ức. *Phi Đoàn 221 trực thăng* (The Helicopter Squadron 221), online document, accessible in full-text at this URL: https://hung-viet.org/a21141/phi-doan-221-truc-thang

Những Giai Thoại Sạch của Tướng Thắng (Anecdotes of General Thắng's incorruptibility), online document, accessible in full-text at this URL: http://www.generalhieu.com/ndthang-u.htm

Northrop F-5A Freedom Fighter, online document, accessible in full-text at this URL: http://www.wmof.com/f5a.htm

Operation Linrbacker II: The Christmas bombing, online document, accessible in full-text at this URL: http://thevietnamwar.info/operation-linebacker-ii-christmas-bombing/

Operations Enhance and Enhance Plus, online document, accessible in full-text at this URL: https://en.wikipedia.org/wiki/Operations_Enhance_and_Enhance_Plus

Paris Agreement on Vietnam: twenty-five years later; Conference transcript, The Nixon Center, Washington, DC, April 1998, online document, accessible in full-text at this URL: https://www.mtholyoke.edu/acad/intrel/paris.htm

Phạm Văn Cần. *Phi Đoàn 427 – C-7A- Caribou: không vận chiến thuật* (Squadron 427 – C-7A – Caribou: tactical air transport), online document, accessible in full-text at this URL: http://hoiquanphidung.com/showthread.php?9466-Phi-%C4%91o%C3%A0n-427-c-7a-caribou

Phạm Văn Chung. *Cờ bay trên Cổ Thành Quảng Trị* (Our flag flying on the Quảng Trị Old Citadel), online document, accessible in full-text at this URL: https://www.nguoi-viet.com/cuu-chien-binh/ccb-co-bay-tren-co-thanh-quang-tri/

Phi Đoàn 716 Hoàng Long và Phi Đoàn 718 Thiên Long (Squadron 716 Hoàng Long (Royal Dragon) and Squadron 718 Thiên Long (Divine Dragon)), online document, accessible in full-text at this URL: http://phong7bttm.blogspot.ca/2016/02/phi-oan-thien-long-718.html

Phi hành đoàn cuối cùng của Không Quân VNCH hy sinh cho Tổ Quốc (Sacrifice for the Fatherland of the last aircrew of the Air Force of the Republic of Vietnam), online document, accessible in full-text at this URL: https://thntsaigon.forumvi.com/t175-topic

Phoenix Program, online document, accessible in full-text at this URL: https://en.wikipedia.org/wiki/Phoenix_Program

Sikorsky H-34, online document, accessible in full-text at this URL: https://en.wikipedia.org/wiki/Sikorsky_H-34#Specifications_.28H-34_Choctaw.29

Text of Declaration by Paris Conference on Vietnam, March 3, 1973, online document, accessible in full-text at this URL: https://www.nytimes.com/1973/03/03/archives/text-of-declaration-by-paris-conference-on-vietnam.html

Text of Joint Communique issued after Nixon-Thieu talks, online document, accessible in full-text at this URL: https://www.nytimes.com/1973/04/04/archives/text-of-joint-communique-issued-after-nixonthieu-talks-full.html

Tết Mậu Thân 1968 qua những số liệu (Tết of the Year of the Monkey 1968, through the statistics), online document, accessible in full-text at this URL: https://www.nhandan.com.vn/chinhtri/item/7976502-.html

Thành-Giang. *Hoa không gian 1: những chị Hằng của Phi Đoàn 314* (Space flowers 1: the pretty ladies of Squadron 314), online document, accessible in full-text at this URL: https://hoiquanphidung.com/showthread.php?21896-Hoa-Kh%C3%B4ng-Gian-1-Nh%E1%BB%AFng-ch%E1%BB%8B-H%E1%BA%B1ng-c%E1%BB%A7a-Phi-%C4%90o%C3%A0n-314

Thành-Giang. *Phi Đoàn 431 Phượng Long* (Squadron 431 Phoenix Dragon), online document, accessible in full-text at this URL: http://lhccshtd.org/LHCCSHTD_SH/kq/thanhgiang/2015/pd431/LSCCSHTD_SH_kq_thanhgiang_2015_pd431_hashPD431PhuongLong_2015AUG09.htm

Tiểu Đoàn 6 Nhảy Dù (The 6th Airborne Battalion), online document, accessible in full-text at this URL: http://nhaydu.com/index_83hg_files/main_files/TieuSu-TDND/TS-TD6ND.pdf

Tiểu sử Đại Tướng Cao Văn Viên (Biography of General Cao Văn Viên), online document, accessible in full-text at this URL: http://nhaydu.com/index_83hg_files/main_files/Tuong/TS-TuongCaoVanVien.htm.

Trần Lý. *Những phi vụ hành quân cuối cùng của Không Quân VNCH trên không phận Sàigòn* (The Last sorties of the AFVN above Saigon area), online document, accessible in full-text at this URL: http://www.luanhoan.net/Bai%20Moi%20Trong%20Ngay/html/bm%2015-6-24.htm

Trần Mạnh Khôi. *Sơ lược về sự thành lập các đơn vị Không Quân* (A Summary of the creation of the Vietnamese air force units), online document, accessible in full-text at this URL: http://hoiquanphidung.com/showthread.php?9293-S%C6%A1-l%C6%B0%E1%BB%A3c-v%E1%BB%81-s%E1%BB%B1-th%C3%A0nh-l%E1%BA%ADp-c%C3%A1c-%C4%91%C6%A1n-v%E1%BB%8B-Kh%C3%B4ng-Qu%C3%A2n

Trần Ngươn Phiêu. *Gió mùa Đông Bắc (Chương 6)* (The Northeast monsoon (Chapter 6)), online document, accessible in full-text at this URL: https://www.diendantheky.net/2011/04/gio-mua-ong-bac-chuong-6.html

Trần Phước Hội. *Thành lập Phi Đoàn 217: giai đoạn H-34* (Creation of Squadron 217: H-34 phase), online document, accessible in full-text at this URL: http://hoiquanphidung.com/showthread.php?9448-Th%C3%A0nh-l%E1%BA%ADp-Phi-%C4%90o%C3%A0n-217

Trận Hắc Dịch: ngày 9 & 10/2/1965 (The Battle of Hắc Dịch: 9 & 10 February 1965), online document, accessible in full-text at this URL: http://nhaydu.com/index_83hg_files/left_files/T-Chien/1965-TranHacDich.pdf

Trương Đăng Sỹ. *Nhảy Dù và Cổ Thành Đinh Công Tráng* (The Airborne and the Đinh Công Tráng Old Citadel), online document, accessible in full-text at this URL: https://dongsongcu.wordpress.com/2016/09/21/nhay-du-va-co-thanh-dinh-cong-trang-2/

Tưởng nhớ Trung Tướng Phan Trọng Chinh (In remembrance of Lieutenant-General Phan Trọng Chinh), online document, accessible in full-text at this URL: http://vietnamcuongthinh.blogspot.ca/2015/03/tuong-nho-trung-tuong-phan-trong-chinh.html

United States presidential election, 1972, online document, accessible in full-text at this URL: https://en.wikipedia.org/wiki/United_States_presidential_election,_1972

USSAC/7AF in Thailand (1973-1975): policy changes and the military role, online document, accessible in full-text at this URL: https://apps.dtic.mil/dtic/tr/fulltext/u2/a586318.pdf

Võ Ý. *Ngành quan sát không lực VNCH* (The Observation branch of the Air Force of the Republic of Vietnam), online document, accessible in full-text at this URL: https://hoiquanphidung.com/showthread.php?9282-Ng%C3%A0nh-Quan-S%C3%A1t-Kh%C3%B4ng-L%E1%BB%B1c-VNCH&s=cfaed16e0f4ddef9f7e5c62fb3a85ee2

Vũ Văn Bảo. *QLVNCH: Phi Đoàn 237 CH-47A Chinook* (ARVN: Squadron

237 CH-47A Chinook), online document, accessible in full-text at this URL: http://chauxuannguyen.org/2016/03/18/qlvnch-phi-doan-237-ch-47a-chinook-vu-van-bao/

Vương Hồng Anh. *Lữ Đoàn 1 Nhảy Dù ở Bình Long 1972* (The 1st Airborne Brigade in Bình Long 1972), online document, accessible in full-text at this URL: https://ongvove.wordpress.com/2012/03/05/l%E1%BB%AF-doan-1-nh%E1%BA%A3y-du-%E1%BB%9F-binh-long-1972/

War Powers Resolution, online document, accessible in full-text at this URL: https://en.wikipedia.org/wiki/War_Powers_Resolution

Willbanks, James H. *The most brilliant commander: Ngo Quang Truong*, online document, accessible in full-text at this URL: http://www.historynet.com/the-most-brilliant-commander-ngo-quang-truong.htm

Xuân Hải. *Đại đội 120 người, hết trận đánh chỉ còn 17* (A Company with 120 men, reduced to 17 at the end of the battle), online document, accessible in full-text at this URL: *http://infonet.vn/dai-doi-120-nguoi-het-tran-danh-chi-con-17-post128750.info*

Journal Articles

Barrett, David M. "The mythology surrounding Lyndon Johnson, his advisers, and the 1965 decision to escalate the Vietnam War," *Political science quarterly*, vol. 103, issue 4 (winter 1988/1989).

Caputo, Phillip, "S. Viets take skeleton of city." *Chicago tribune*, issue of April 14, 1975.

H.V.N. "Cộng sản Việt Nam mới thật là Ngụy," (The Vietnamese Communists are the Real Usurpers), *Tạp chí Dân Quyền* (Journal of Civil Rights) (Montreal, Canada), no. 51 (May/1982).

Moyar, Mark, "Vietnam: historians at war," *Academic questions*, vol. 21, no. 1 (Spring 2008), e-journal article, accessible in full-text at this URL: https://www.nas.org/academic-questions/21/1/vietnam_historians_at_war

Veith, George J. and Merle L. Pribbenow, "Fighting is an art: the Army of the Republic of Vietnam's defense of Xuan Loc, 9-21 April 1975," *Journal of military history*, vol. 68, no. 1 (Jan. 2004).

Online Database Documents

"CIA report on the Situation in South Vietnam as of 10/24/66," CIA classified document, dated 24-Oct-1966, declassified 4-Mar-1994, 15 pages, accessible in full-text in the database called *Declassified Documents Reference*

System (DDRS), pp. II-1 và II-2

"CIA report on the Siituation in South Vietnam covering period 10/31-11/6/66," CIA classified document, dated 7-Nov-1966, declassified 16-Dec-1993, 24 pages, accessible in full-text in *DDRS*, pp. II-1 và II-2.

"Intelligence report on the situation in South Vietnam," CIA classified document, dated 19-12-1966, declassified 16-6-1998, 24 pages, accessible in full-text in *DDRS*, p. II-4.

INDEX

Contacting the Author
Lâm Vĩnh-Thế
Hoaivietnhan1981@gmail.com

Contacting the Publisher
Nhân Ảnh
han.le3359@gmail.com
(408) 722-5626

www.ingramcontent.com/pod-product-compliance
Lightning Source LLC
Chambersburg PA
CBHW070757120726
47910CB00001B/203
9781088015803